Research and
Development
Project
Selection

WILEY SERIES IN ENGINEERING & TECHNOLOGY MANAGEMENT

Series Editor: Dundar F. Kocaoglu, Portland State University

Research and Development Project Selection

JOSEPH P. MARTINO

A WILEY – INTERSCIENCE PUBLICATION

JOHN WILEY & SONS, INC.

NEW YORK   CHICHESTER   BRISBANE   TORONTO   SINGAPORE

Copyright©1995 by John Wiley & Sons, Inc.

This publication is designed to provide accurate and
authoritative information in regard to the subject
matter covered. It is sold with the understanding that
the publisher is not engaged in rendering legal, accounting,
or other professional services. If legal advice or other
expert assistance is required, the services of a competent
professional person should be sought.

Library of Congress Cataloging in Publication Data:
Martino, Joseph Paul, 1931–

R & D project selection / Joseph P. Martino
    p.   cm.—(Wiley series in engineering management)
Includes index.
    ISBN 0-471-59537-3 (alk. paper)
    1. Research—Methodology. 2. Research—Decision making.
I. Title. II. Title: R and D project selection. III. Series
Q180.55.M4C66 1994
658.5′7—dc20   94-30753

Printed in the United States of America

10 9 8 7 6 5 4 3 2 1

In loving memory of Mary, for all her support and encouragement when I needed it most

PREFACE

Since at least the 1960s, the selection of R&D projects has been a matter of concern to academic researchers, to R&D managers, and to scientists and engineers. The problem of choosing the "best" projects out of a menu of project proposals continues to draw the attention of everyone concerned. The Institute of Electrical and Electronics Engineers (IEEE) *Transactions on Engineering Management*, under both its founding editor, Albert Rubenstein, and its current editor, Dundar Kocaoglu, is effectively the "journal of record" for research on R&D project selection. Over the years it has carried literally dozens of papers on the subject.

With U.S. industry facing an ever-more-competitive world, a world in which the United States no longer has the technological dominance it enjoyed in the 1950s and 1960s, R&D project selection becomes even more important. Choosing the right projects can mean the difference between remaining competitive and falling behind. Interest in project selection methods, among both academic scholars and industrial R&D managers, is no longer a matter of minor importance. It has become literally a matter of survival for industry.

This book is intended to summarize current knowledge about methods for selecting R&D projects, and to present that knowledge in a form useful to both R&D managers and researchers. As such, it should meet the needs of several audiences. First, it is directly responsive to the needs of practicing R&D managers. The methods described are presented in forms that are directly usable in practice. Moreover, the data requirements and special features of each method are also described. Second, it can serve to help scientists and engineers tailor their projects and their proposals to enhance the likelihood of support, by helping them focus on the true needs of those who provide the support, whether government agencies or industrial R&D laboratories. Third, it can help introduce graduate and undergraduate students to the issue of R&D project selection. The methods presented can be used immediately by them in a work setting, to enhance their ability to choose worthwhile projects to propose to their superiors. As a textbook, it contains problems that can help reinforce the student's knowledge of the methods. Finally, it presents a summary of the relevant literature, in the form of an annotated bibliography. This literature can not only serve to direct the reader to sources of additional information, but can help the academic researcher determine what lines of research have been fruitful, and the direction of current trends in scholarly research on R&D project selection methods.

J. P. MARTINO

Sidney, OH
January, 1995

CONTENTS

___1
INTRODUCTION

All research and development (R & D) managers face a common problem: They have more potential projects to be carried out than they have resources (money, staff, equipment) to carry them out. In some way, they must select those projects that will be attempted, from among the larger number proposed.

The projects on the managers' menus may be proposed by their own technical staffs, they may be requested by other groups in the firm (marketing, production, customer service, etc.), they may be intended to fix problems uncovered by field service technicians, they may be a direct response to product improvement requests by customers, or they may be a reaction to the activities of a competitor. Regardless of the source of the projects, the selection process must in some way select from the entire menu the subset that maximize the payoff to the parent organization funding the R & D.

Failure to select the "best" projects has two costs. First is the resources spent on poor projects. This amounts to expending valuable resources with little or no gain resulting. An even greater cost, however, may be the opportunity costs on marginal or apparently healthy projects that might have succeeded with additional resources, and the new starts that were deferred or not undertaken because of lack of resources. Thus expending resources on poor projects not only loses those resources, it loses the benefits that might have been achieved had the resources been put on good projects. Hence, selecting the "best" projects is a critical decision for the R & D manager.

Thus the key issue addressed in this book is How to select R & D projects so that they maximize some measure of utility or benefit to the parent organization.

This problem is not a new one. Since the 1960s, the R & D management literature, and the operations research literature, have been filled with articles describing project selection methods. These literatures have also been filled with survey articles, which report that little use is made of the various project selection techniques, and with editorials decrying the failure of R & D managers to utilize these techniques.

In reality, the failure of R & D managers to utilize the published project selection techniques is not unexpected. In some cases, the techniques described in the literature were developed to meet the specific requirements of some firm or some industry, and they cannot readily be applied in other firms or industries. In other cases the techniques were developed in academic settings, and they do not adequately reflect the realities faced by R & D managers in industrial or government laboratories. In such cases, it is not surprising that the methods are not used widely.

The shortcomings of the project selection methods described in the literature can be summarized as follows:

1. They often have inadequate treatment of interactions, both benefit contribution and resource utilization.
2. They fail to deal with uncertainty of both benefit contribution and parameter estimation.
3. They involve multiple, interrelated decision criteria that have no common, natural underlying measure.
4. They may fail to recognize the time variant property of parameters and criteria, and the associated problem of continuity in research program and staff.
5. They often treat the project selection problem as a once-a-year decision event rather than an ongoing process.
6. They often do not include considerations, such as the timing of the decision.
7. They often cannot deal with a diversity of projects ranging from basic research to engineering.
8. They may fail to recognize the importance of individual R & D personnel.
9. They may not deal with the need to establish and maintain balance in the program: basic versus applied; offensive versus defensive; breakthrough versus improvement; product versus process; high risk/high payoff versus low risk/moderate payoff.

The purpose of this book is to present the range of techniques available from the literature in usable form, to the R & D manager. The techniques presented here are all intended, in one way or another, to convert estimates of the anticipated outputs from R & D projects into forms commensurate with the criteria utilized by the parent organization to evaluate other investments and expenditures. In each case, this means computing some kind of utility measure for a project or set of projects. This utility measure is chosen to be compatible with the utility measures used by the parent organization for its other investment decisions. The R & D manager can then effectively use one or more of the project selection techniques presented here to justify the choice of a project or set of projects in competition with alternative uses of funds by other elements of the parent organization.

By presenting the methods in this way, the barriers that have prevented extensive use of formal project selection techniques in the past may be overcome. The R & D managers will find that the various project selection techniques are actually helpful in choosing projects from among the many proposed to them, and are helpful in defending those choices to others in the larger organization.

The remainder of the book is organized in three parts. The first part, consisting of Chapters 2–9, presents the various methods that might be used by the R & D manager to select individual projects or a portfolio of projects. The second part, consisting of Chapters 10–13, presents the factors that should be taken into account in making project selections, and that were presented without explanation in Part 1. The third part, consisting of Chapters 14–20, describes data requirements for the various factors that might be taken into account in a project selection decision. Chapter 21 provides a summary of the book.

Appendix 1 is an annotated bibliography of relevant articles from the R & D management literature. Appendix 2 provides several hypothetical menus of possible projects. These are used to illustrate the methods, and as input for the problems at the end of each chapter. Appendix 3 contains numerical tables of historical and statistical data.

1.1 FURTHER READINGS

Baker, N. and J. Freeland (1975). Recent Advances in R & D Benefit Measurement and Project Selection Methods. *Management Science*. **21**(10), June, 1164–1175.

Clarke, T. E. (1974). Decision-Making in Technologically Based Organizations: A Literature Survey of Present Practice. *IEEE Transactions on Engineering Management*. **21**(1), February, 9–23.

Liberatore, M. J. and J. Titus (1983). The Practice of Management Science in R & D Project Management. *Management Science*. **29**(8), August, 962–974.

PART I
METHODS

The methods used for R & D project selection can be categorized as follows: ranking, economic decision theory (single and multi-stage), portfolio optimization, cognitive modeling, and ad hoc decision methods. Each of these general categories includes several methods. However, the methods in each category are similar in approach, and share the same strengths and weaknesses.

Each of these categories of methods will be presented in the chapters of Part I. These chapters will describe the methods, present examples, and discuss strengths and weaknesses of the methods.

____2
RANKING

Ranking methods are used to rank-order a set of proposed projects. In principle, once the projects have been rank-ordered, the manager proceeds from the top of the list toward the bottom, funding projects in order until the budget is exhausted. Ranking methods are easy to use and simple to understand. However, they answer the question, "Which is the best project in the list?" They do not address the question, "Are any of the projects in the list really good projects?" That is, ranking methods may simply pick the best of a bad lot, without giving the decision maker any warning that none of the projects are very good. The question of "goodness" of projects requires more than simply ranking, and this issue will be taken up in the subsequent chapters in Part I.

This chapter will describe the more common ranking methods: pairwise comparisons, scoring models, and the analytic hierarchy procedure (AHP).

2.1 PAIRWISE COMPARISONS

The starting point of pairwise comparisons is for each project to be compared with every other project. If there are N projects, this requires $N*(N - 1)/2$ comparisons. In the simplest form, the comparison made is a global one: Which of the two projects being compared is "better." A more sophisticated version of pairwise comparisons would ask, "how much better?" That is, one project might be rated twice as good as the other, three times as good, and so on. A yet more sophisticated version might involve two or more criteria (e.g., technical feasibility or cost). All pairs of projects are compared on each criterion. If there are M criteria and N projects, this requires $M*N*$

$(N - 1)/2$ comparisons. Once the comparisons are available, the two most common methods for converting them into rankings are the dominance count method and the anchored scale method (this latter method is derived from a technique originally developed by Russell Ackoff).

Dominance Count

Assume five projects have been given the comparisons shown in the matrix in Table 2.1, where a 1 in the cell indicates the row project is equal to or better than the column project, that is, Project A is better than Projects D and E, but is inferior to Projects B and C, and is equal to itself. Note that the matrix is reciprocal; if A is better than D, then D must be inferior to A. Thus once the above-diagonal cells are filled, the below-diagonal cells are also known. Scores are obtained by counting the 1's in each row. This value is the number of projects the row project dominates. Here Project C dominates every project and is ranked first, B is second, A first, D fourth, and E fifth. This method works best with small numbers of projects. It readily identifies the best and the worst projects. If there are many projects, however, this method usually leads to many ties among projects in the "middle." Thus some additional tie-breaking method may be required.

For large numbers of projects, making the comparisons can be a time-consuming task. However, once the values are entered into a spreadsheet, the @COUNT function, available on many spreadsheets, can be used to carry out the counting process.

Anchored Scale Method

The anchored scale method can be used for small numbers of projects, but is particularly appropriate when the number of projects is too large for $N*$ $(N - 1)/2$ comparisons to be made conveniently. It is carried out as follows. The best and the worst projects in the list are selected, and arbitrarily assigned scores of 100 and 1, respectively. Each other project is then compared with one or both of these "anchor point" projects. If a project is evaluated as being one-half as good as the best project (or half-way between

TABLE 2.1   Matrix of Projects Showing Dominance Count

Projects	A	B	C	D	E	Count
A	1	0	0	1	1	3
B	1	1	0	1	1	4
C	1	1	1	1	1	5
D	0	0	0	1	1	2
E	0	0	0	0	1	1

the best and worst), it is given a score of 50; if one-third as good, a score of 33, and so on. This method assumes that the best and worst projects can be identified readily. Its primary value is in ranking the other projects between the best and worst. As with the dominance count method, this method often leads to ties or to "bunching up" of projects in the middle, especially if there are many projects to be ranked.

Note that both the above pairwise comparison methods require global comparisons. That is, two projects are compared on an overall basis, with all factors taken into account simultaneously. It is often easier and more effective to make comparisons between projects if the judgments can be made on the basis of one criterion at a time. That is, the comparison task is decomposed into several comparisons, each one on a single factor. The remaining methods described in this chapter do allow the user to decompose comparisons in this fashion.

2.2 SCORING MODELS

A scoring model involves a mathematical formula or algebraic expression that produces a score for each project under consideration. The formula incorporates those factors believed to be important. Each factor is weighted to reflect its importance relative to the other factors. Each project is scored on each factor. The scores are substituted in the formula, and an overall score computed for each project. Projects are then ranked in order of their scores. Thus, if comparisons among projects are necessary, those comparisons can be made on the basis of one factor or criterion at a time (e.g., comparisons on relative likelihood of success or on estimated market share).

Scoring models can incorporate both objective and judgmental data. Objective data, such as costs, can be included among the factors in the model. Likewise, judgments, such as likelihood of success, can be incorporated. Scoring models can thus take into account all the kinds of data that may be available regarding candidate projects.

Typically, a scoring model will be expressed as a fraction or ratio, with desirable variables (benefits) in the numerator and undesirable variables (costs) in the denominator. The higher the score, the more desirable is the entity. Either or both of benefits and costs may have probabilities associated with them. Thus each may need to be multiplied by a factor related to the probability that the benefit or cost will actually be realized. Unfortunately, in practice, costs are usually certain to occur, while benefits are usually problematical, having probabilities less than 1.0. Nevertheless, scoring models can accommodate probabilities associated with either benefits or costs.

To illustrate the nature of a scoring model, a non-R & D example will be used. Let us assume that the problem is one of selecting a breakfast cereal.

The various factors that might have a bearing on the choice are

Vitamins
Minerals
Protein
Calories
Fiber
Taste
moNetary cost
pReparation time
cLeanup time
desirability of the priZe in the box

(The capitalized letters will be used in the model as the symbols for the different variables.)

The variables can be divided into three categories: overriding variables, tradeable variables, and optional variables.

Overriding variables are those such that if they are absent, the entity being scored is worthless. That is, if their value is zero, the entire score should be zero. Algebraically, this means they must multiply the entire expression.

Tradeable variables are those that can be traded one for another, in the sense that we are willing to sacrifice some of one in order to get more of another. We may even be willing to let one go to zero if we thereby get sufficiently more of another. Tradeable variables must be added together. They must be multiplied by coefficients (weights) that represent the trade-off rates.* For instance, suppose there are two variables X and Y, which can be traded off one against the other. In the scoring model, they would be grouped as:

$$(aX + bY)$$

where a and b are the weights associated with X and Y, respectively. Thus if X increases by one unit, Y must decrease by a/b units in order to keep the total value constant. Therefore an increment of X can be traded for an increment of Y in the ratio a/b.[†] There may be several such groups of variables. Ordinarily, each group must be nonzero if the score is to be nonzero. Thus the groups multiply the remainder of the expression.

---

*This is an important point. The range of values should be the same for each variable. Relative importance of the variables should be reflected in their weights, not in the range of values or "maximum number of points" allowed.

†Note this assumes the trade-off is linear, and thus independent of the values of X and Y. This is really a very heroic assumption, and in practical cases will probably be valid only for limited ranges of X and Y.

An optional variable is one such that if present, it should alter the score, but if absent it should not affect the score. If W is an optional variable, it would appear in the expression in the form $(1 + dW)$. If it is absent in a particular case, it has a value of zero, and the term reduces to simply 1, which multiplies the rest of the expression. If its value is not zero, however, it is included in the computation of the score. The coefficient d represents the ratio by which the score should be changed for each unit change in W. That is, it represents the sensitivity of the total score to changes in W.

Let us now apply this to the breakfast cereal case. The results will of course be subjective, but the point is that the model can be tailored to individual cases.

Taste will be an overriding variable: If it does not taste good we will reject it completely. Thus Taste must multiply the remainder of the expression.

Vitamins, Minerals, Protein, and Fiber are desirable properties of the cereal. We want as much of these as possible. However, since we will eat other things at other meals, we are willing to trade these factors one for another. Thus they should be grouped and added, with weights representing our willingness to make trade-offs among them.

The variables moNetary cost and cLeanup time are undesirable. These variables should go in the denominator.

The factor Calories involves some ambiguity. For those persons on the verge of starvation, Calories would be a benefit. For those persons striving to keep their weight down, Calories would be a cost. Thus whether we put Calories in the denominator or the numerator will depend on whether we look upon that factor as a cost or a benefit, respectively. For the purposes of our model, let us assume it is a cost.

We still have two optional variables, pReparation time and priZe in the box. For ready-to-eat cereals, preparation time is zero—we simply pour the cereal out of the box. Cooked cereals, however, require some preparation, and the time for this should be reflected in the model as an undesirable factor. If there is a prize in the box, this should increase the score for a particular cereal. However, if there is no prize, the score should not go to zero. Thus we treat this as an optional variable in the numerator.

Our final model will be as follows:

$$\frac{T^a(bV + cM + dP + eF)(1 + jZ)}{N^f(1 + gR)L^h C^i}$$

Note the exponents on T, N, L, and C. These exponents represent the weights of these variables, to reflect their relative importance. Simply multiplying them by a coefficient would not have the desired effect of weighting their importance, since the coefficients could be factored out as constant multipliers of the entire expression. In effect, the exponents can be considered as linear weights on the logarithms of those variables that are not part of a group. Note also that the group of variables could be raised to a power if it were to be weighted at something other than 1.0 by comparison with Taste.

It is customary to normalize the coefficients within a group of tradeable variables so that they sum to one. That is, the constraint

$$b + c + d + e = 1$$

would be applied to the above expression. This occurs because the sum of the coefficients can be factored out as a multiplier of the entire expression, and simply changes the scale without altering relative scores. If there is only one group of tradeable factors, normalization is not necessary, since the only effect is to change the scale of the results. If there are two or more groups, however, normalization can be important, since without it, a group with many factors may outweigh a group with few factors simply because of the difference in number of factors. This is not appropriate. In such a case, all groups should have their coefficients normalized. If the groups as such are to have different weights, the group expression should be raised to a power, as in the example above, where individual factors were raised to powers.

Now let us apply this procedure to an example of selection of R & D projects. Assume we have decided that total market size M, potential market share S, probability of technical success T, and project cost C are the relevant factors we wish to take into account in evaluating projects (in this case, C and M are likely to be objective factors while S and T are judgmental factors). Assume further that we are willing to trade market share for market size, that is, accept a smaller market share if the total market is sufficiently large. However, market share is assumed to be twice as important as market size. The firm would prefer not even to be in a market, regardless of size, if its market share was very small. Thus the scoring model might be

$$\text{Score} = T*(M + 2*S)/C$$

Note that normalizing the coefficients of the tradeable variables is not really necessary here. The only effect of normalizing the coefficients would be to divide all scores by three. Relative standing would be unchanged.

Scoring models allow both subjective factors (e.g., probability of success) and objective factors (e.g., project cost) to be included. However, it is necessary to scale all variables to have the same range of magnitudes. If the variables are not scaled properly, small percentage changes in a variable with large numerical magnitude will affect the score more than large percentage changes in a variable with a small numerical magnitude. This change would be an undesirable effect. As noted above, importance of a factor should be reflected in its weight (coefficient or power), not in its range of allowable magnitudes.

A recommended rescaling method is as follows. For each project in the set to be scored, obtain values for the judgmental factors on a suitable scale, such as 1–10. For all the projects in the set to be scored, compute the mean and standard deviation (s. d.) for each objective factor (e.g., mean and s. d. of cost or of expected market size). For each factor, subtract its mean, then divide by its standard deviation. The result should be that the scores for each factor will range from about −3 to about +3. For each factor, multiply all scores by a number that will extend the range to about −5 to +5. This multiplier will in general be different for each factor. Finally, add to each score a constant that increases the smallest value to between 0 and 1. This additive constant in general will be different for each factor. If necessary, truncate the upper end so that all scores above 10 are replaced by 10. This transformation results in rescaling all objectively measurable factors to a 1–10 scale, while retaining the relative size of each score. (Note that truncating is necessary only if subjective factors, rated on a 1–10 scale, are included. This results in all factors having the same scale range. If all factors are objective, each factor is standardized as above and truncation is not necessary.)

Project Menu 1 from Appendix 2 will be used for this example. There are 16 projects available for selection. However, the R & D budget for this decision period is only $500K. Thus we must select a menu of projects that does not exceed that budget. We want the best projects possible within that budget limitation.

We will take into account only those factors selected for the scoring model, ignoring the remainder of the factors defined for this set of projects.

Table 2.2 portrays a portion of the spreadsheet used to compute the scores. The raw data for each factor have been standardized as described above. The right-most column shows the formulas for computing the scores,

TABLE 2.2 Scoring Model Showing Formulas

B	A	B	C	D	E	F	G	H	I	J	K
1					Prob.						
2			Market	Market	Tech.						
3		Cost	Share	Size	Success	Score					
4	(Weight	1	2	1	1						
5	Project										
6	1	3.31	1.99	2.96	1.25	+$E$4*E6*($D$4*D6+$C$4*C6)/($B$4*B6)					
7	2	2.15	2.48	2.25	1.80	+$E$4*E7*($D$4*D7+$C$4*C7)/($B$4*B7)					
8	3	2.38	1.50	0.99	7.70	+$E$4*E8*($D$4*D8+$C$4*C8)/($B$4*B8)					
9	4	2.73	2.97	1.86	5.09	+$E$4*E9*($D$4*D9+$C$4*C9)/($B$4*B9)					
10	5	1.80	10.32	9.17	3.45	+$E$4*E10*($D$4*D10+$C$4*C10)/($B$4*B10)					
11	6	0.64	10.32	10.11	0.57	+$E$4*E11*($D$4*D11+$C$4*C11)/($B$4*B11)					
12	7	0.75	6.40	4.37	7.70	+$E$4*E12*($D$4*D12+$C$4*C12)/($B$4*B12)					
13	8	2.50	3.95	7.52	9.62	+$E$4*E13*($D$4*D13+$C$4*C13)/($B$4*B13)					
14	9	3.89	1.50	5.94	2.35	+$E$4*E14*($D$4*D14+$C$4*C14)/($B$4*B14)					
15	10	7.14	2.48	3.98	1.11	+$E$4*E15*($D$4*D15+$C$4*C15)/($B$4*B15)					
16	11	9.00	1.50	5.16	10.03	+$E$4*E16*($D$4*D16+$C$4*C16)/($B$4*B16)					
17	12	3.66	2.97	8.85	5.50	+$E$4*E17*($D$4*D17+$C$4*C17)/($B$4*B17)					
18	13	8.07	4.44	3.19	2.76	+$E$4*E18*($D$4*D18+$C$4*C18)/($B$4*B18)					
19	14	6.79	4.44	0.99	3.03	+$E$4*E19*($D$4*D19+$C$4*C19)/($B$4*B19)					
20	15	9.00	7.87	1.70	5.37	+$E$4*E20*($D$4*D20+$C$4*C20)/($B$4*B20)					
21	16	8.19	6.89	2.96	4.68	+$E$4*E21*($D$4*D21+$C$4*C21)/($B$4*B21)					

TABLE 2.3   Scoring Model Showing Scores

C	A	B	C	D	E	F	G
1					Prob.		Cumulative
2			Market	Market	Tech.		Cost
3		Cost	Share	Size	Success	Score	
4	(Weight	1	2	1	1		
5	Project						
6	7	0.75	6.40	4.37	7.70	175.15	26
7	8	2.50	3.95	7.52	9.62	59.37	67
8	5	1.80	10.32	9.17	3.45	57.07	102
9	6	0.64	10.32	10.11	0.57	27.27	127
10	12	3.66	2.97	8.85	5.50	22.24	178
11	4	2.73	2.97	1.86	5.09	14.54	221
12	3	2.38	1.50	0.99	7.70	12.89	261
13	15	9.00	7.87	1.70	5.37	10.40	358
14	16	8.19	6.89	2.96	4.68	9.57	448
15	11	9.00	1.50	5.16	10.03	9.08	545
16	2	2.15	2.48	2.25	1.80	6.04	583
17	9	3.89	1.50	5.94	2.35	5.40	636
18	14	6.79	4.44	0.99	3.03	4.41	714
19	13	8.07	4.44	3.19	2.76	4.13	803
20	1	3.31	1.99	2.96	1.25	2.62	851
21	10	7.14	2.48	3.98	1.11	1.39	932

rather than the scores themselves. The $ signs in the cell addresses in the formulas are "absolute" references, in this case the addresses of the cells containing the weights.* The remainder of the cell addresses are "relative," that is, columns in the *same row*. By entering the formula in the cell for the first project (F6), using absolute addresses for the weights and relative addresses for the factor scores, the formula can then be "copied," using the spreadsheet COPY command, down the rest of the column, and the relative addresses will be adjusted to the correct row for each project. This simplifies setting up the spreadsheet. By placing the weights in their own cells instead of incorporating them into the formulas, it is easy for the analyst to change one or more weights, without rewriting all the formulas. This makes sensitivity analysis easier.

Table 2.3 shows the final results for the 16 projects. The table has been sorted on final score, and cumulative dollar cost computed, starting with the project at the top of the list and working down. Given the budget limit of $500K, the allocation process must stop at a cumulative total of $448K. Projects funded are 7, 8, 6, 12, 4, 3, 15, and 16. The remaining $52K could be used to fund Project 2, which has a cost of $38K, even though it is inferior to Project 11. Note also that the scores of most of the projects funded are well below the score of the top-most project. This finding might lead the manager to wonder whether they were in fact worth funding. However, as pointed out above, ranking methods do not determine the absolute merits of projects, only their relative merits.

---

*Note that different spreadsheets may use different means for designating absolute references.

Note that since all factors were standardized, it is not necessary to truncate their range to 1–10, since there are no judgmentally scaled values with which compatibility is required. Had one of the factors been rated on a 1–10 scale and not standardized, truncation of the standardized values would have been necessary to retain compatibility.

Computing a scoring model is readily accomplished on a spreadsheet once the data are entered. Typically, the projects would be entered as rows, with the data for each factor in the appropriate columns. The final column would contain the formula for the scoring model, and the computation of the scores. The projects can then be sorted readily on the final column, giving a ranking of the projects according to their scores. Use of a spreadsheet also allows easy sensitivity testing of the rankings, by allowing the analyst to make changes in the factor values to determine what effect this has on project rankings.

The scoring model provides a method for ranking R & D projects relative to one another. Instead of requiring a global judgment on each project, it decomposes the ranking problem through use of a formula that incorporates the factors considered to be important. Both objective and subjective factors can be incorporated into a scoring model. Standardization provides a means for adjusting the magnitudes of the factors so they are compatible. The relative importance of the different factors should be reflected in the weights assigned to them, not in the factor values themselves.

2.3 ANALYTIC HIERARCHY PROCEDURE

The analytical hierarchy procedure was developed by Saaty [1980] as a tool to assist in making sound decisions. It produces ranks for projects when the criteria can be decomposed hierarchically. The process always starts at the top, develops the hierarchy downward as a tree, then works back up. A generic example is shown in Figure 2.1. There is some overall goal to be achieved. In meeting this goal, several criteria must be satisfied. Several first-level criteria are shown as C1.1, C1.2, and C1.3. Some of these criteria can be decomposed into lower level subcriteria. One set of these is shown as C2.1.1 and C2.1.2. Finally, at the bottom of the hierarchy is a list of entities whose relative merits are to be determined. This list is of course the same for all branches of the tree.

At each level, the analyst produces a matrix of pairwise comparisons reflecting how the items at the *next lower level* rate with respect to the item at that level. For instance, the analyst would start by producing a matrix of comparisons among the three first-level criteria relative to the overall goal. That is, a matrix would be prepared showing the relative importance (preference, desirability, value, etc.) of C1.1, C1.2, and C1.3 in meeting the overall goal. The analyst would then prepare a matrix of comparisons showing how those second-level criteria subordinate to a first-level criterion relate to that

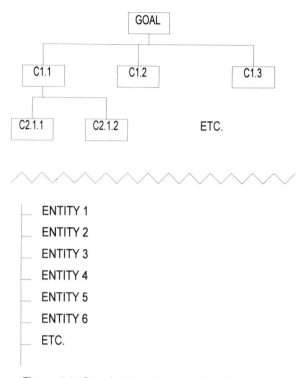

Figure 2.1. Generic hierarchy of criteria and entities.

first-level criterion. In the figure, this would mean a matrix showing the relative importance of C2.1.1, C2.1.2, and so on, with respect to C1.1. This process would continue downward, until matrices are prepared showing the relative standing of the entities with respect to the lowest level criterion in each branch. Note that there need not be the same number of levels in each branch.

By convention, the matrix entries show the degree to which the *row* item is preferred (or important, valuable, desirable, etc.) to the *column* item. Saaty developed a verbal scale that allows judgments (e.g., "slightly more important" or "much more important") to be converted to a 1–10 scale. Filling out the matrix requires $N*(N-1)/2$ comparisons. The diagonal values are of course 1, and the values in the lower triangular matrix are simply the reciprocals of those in the upper triangular matrix.

In project selection, the top of the tree is total project merit. This result may be affected by several factors. In turn, some of these may be further decomposed. Ultimately, each project is listed, to be compared with respect to the criterion immediately above the list.

To illustrate this, we will utilize the same project menu as for the scoring model, and the same factors: probability of technical success T, total market size M, expected market share S, and project cost C. These factors might be

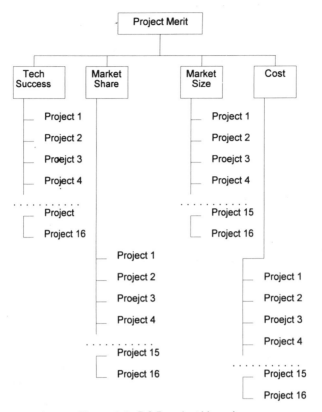

Figure 2.2. R & D project hierarchy.

further decomposed. Cost, for instance, might be decomposed into R & D, capital, and manufacturing cost. For this example, however, this further decomposition will not be made. At the bottom of the tree there will be the several projects that are to be ranked. At each level in the tree, the factors are compared pairwise. Figure 2.2 illustrates the hierarchy.

We begin with the matrix showing relative preferences of the four first-level criteria with regard to the goal. In the scoring model, all criteria were weighted at 1 except market share, which was assigned a weight of 2. We will use these same weights in this example.

Table 2.4 shows the matrix of relative preferences, given the weights. These are shown inside the double line, cells C5–F8. The weights are shown in cells C3–F3 and also cells A5–A8. The entry in each cell in the relative preference matrix is the *row* weight divided by the *column* weight. There is a simple way to do this. The formula $A5/$C3 is entered in cell C5. This means that the value in the *current row* in Column A is divided by the value in the *current column* in row 3. This cell entry can then be copied down the rest of Column C, and the block C5–C8 then copied in Columns D, E, and F. The end result of this is to produce the desired preferences, the ratio of row

TABLE 2.4   Pairwise Comparison of Criteria Relative sto Project Merit

Preferences	A	B	C	D	E	F
1			T	S	M	C
2						
3	Weights		1	2	1	1
4						
5	1		1	0.5	1	1
6	2		2	1	2	2
7	1		1	0.5	1	1
8	1		1	0.5	1	1
9						
10			5	2.5	5	5

TABLE 2.5   Normalized Preferences and Priorities to Project Merit

NormPref	A	B	C	D	E	F	G	H	I
1		T	S	M	C				
2							Row Sums		Priorities
3	T	0.2	0.2	0.2	0.2		0.8		0.2
4	S	0.4	0.4	0.4	0.4		1.6		0.4
5	M	0.2	0.2	0.2	0.2		0.8		0.2
6	C	0.2	0.2	0.2	0.2		0.8		0.2

preference to column preference. Note that all the diagonal entries are 1, as they should be.

The next step is to obtain a set of criteria weights from this matrix of relative preferences. Saaty does this by computing the eigenvalue of the matrix, then taking the eigenvector associated with the largest eigenvalue. He presents theoretical reasons for using the eigenvector as the set of relative priorities derived from the matrix. However, the computation of an eigenvector is somewhat difficult. He presents an approximation method that can be carried out comparatively easily, and that gives results fairly close to the theoretical ideal. We will use the approximation method in what follows.

First calculate the column sums of the pairwise comparison matrix. These sums are shown in cells C10–F10 in Table 2.4. The matrix is then normalized by dividing each column by its sum (i.e., normalized to have column sums equal to 1). Table 2.5 shows the matrix with normalized columns.

Next calculate the row sums of the normalized matrix. The row sums are shown in Table 2.5, Column G. These row sums are then divided by the number of columns (i.e., compute the mean value of each row). The mean values are shown in Column I of Table 2.5. These mean values of course sum to 1, since they are averages of columns that sum to 1. These become the relative priorities of the criteria for which the matrix was generated. Criterion 2, Market share, is twice as important as each of the other criteria.* A

---

*This may seem like a great deal of work to get a result that we already knew. However, the simplicity of the result follows directly from the simplicity of the pairwise comparison matrix, which had only one criterion differing in preference from the rest. Had the matrix contained a range of values, the proper priority weightings would not have been obvious, and the procedure would have generated information not otherwise readily obtainable.

spreadsheet makes these computations fairly simple, once the data have been entered.

The next step is to make pairwise comparisons of the projects with respect to *each* of the criteria. We must generate four matrices, containing, respectively, the pairwise comparisons of the projects with respect to probability of technical success, market share, market size, and cost. Since there are 16 projects, each matrix will contain $16 \times 15/2 = 120$ individual comparisons. The remainder of each matrix is determined either as a 1 (on the diagonal) or as the reciprocal of one of the comparisons. Thus a total of $4 \times 120 = 480$ comparisons would be required to fill out all four matrices.

In some applications, these comparisons would be made judgmentally (e.g., relative probability of technical success might have to be obtained judgmentally). However, we have values for each of the factors for each project (although presumably the probabilities were obtained judgmentally). Thus we can compute the relative preferences directly as the ratios of the values for the factors. For the four 16×16 matrices, this can be done simply, as was done for the preference matrix, by entering the project values in a row and a column, then entering in the upper left corner of the matrix a formula containing the appropriate relative and absolute references. This formula is then copied to the remaining cells of the matrix.

For T, M, and S, this means the cell entry is the ratio of the value for the *row* entity divided by the value for the *column* entity. For instance, market share for Project 1 is 11, and market share for Project 2 is 12. Thus the entry in the cell in the first row and second column of the matrix is $11/12$, and the entry in the cell in the second row, first column, is $12/11$. For cost C, the situation is reversed, since a lower cost project is preferred to a higher cost project. Thus for Project 1, cost is \$48K, and for Project 2, cost is \$38K. Thus the entry in the cell in the first row and second column is $38/48$, and in the cell in the second row and first column $48/38$. Once each matrix is filled out, the same computations are carried out as for the criteria matrix: normalize the columns to sum to 1, then average the rows.

Table 2.6 shows the matrix for relative project preferences with respect to costs. Three other matrices would be computed in the same way for probability of technical success, market share, and market size, respectively.

Computing overall project priorities is then done by multiplying each project's priority score with respect to a criterion by the weight of that criterion, then summing across all criteria. This computation is shown in Table 2.7 for this example. The criteria weights are repeated in row 23, Columns B–E. These are then multiplied by the project priorities above them to obtain the scores in Column G. This computation can be simplified by using the @SUMPRODUCT function, if it is available in the spreadsheet being used. Final project priorities are shown in Column G.

If there are several levels of criteria, then the multiplications are chained through the levels: project score multiplied by the weights of the criteria above that project in its branch. Since there may be different numbers of criteria levels in different branches, it is important that the scores sum to one

TABLE 2.6 Relative Cost Preferences among Projects

Projects	A	B	C	D	E	F	G	H	I	J	K	L	M	N	O	P	Q
		P1	P2	P3	P4	P5	P6	P7	P8	P9	P10	P11	P12	P13	P14	P15	P16
	Cost ($1000)	48	38	40	43	35	25	26	41	53	81	97	51	89	78	97	90
5	48	1.000	0.792	0.833	0.896	0.729	0.521	0.542	0.854	1.104	1.688	2.021	1.063	1.854	1.625	2.021	1.875
6	38	1.263	1.000	1.053	1.132	0.921	0.658	0.684	1.079	1.395	2.132	2.553	1.342	2.342	2.053	2.553	2.368
7	40	1.200	0.950	1.000	1.075	0.875	0.625	0.650	1.025	1.325	2.025	2.425	1.275	2.225	1.950	2.425	2.250
8	43	1.116	0.884	0.930	1.000	0.814	0.581	0.605	0.953	1.233	1.884	2.256	1.186	2.070	1.814	2.256	2.093
9	35	1.371	1.086	1.143	1.229	1.000	0.714	0.743	1.171	1.514	2.314	2.771	1.457	2.543	2.229	2.771	2.571
10	25	1.920	1.520	1.600	1.720	1.400	1.000	1.040	1.640	2.120	3.240	3.880	2.040	3.560	3.120	3.880	3.600
11	26	1.846	1.462	1.538	1.654	1.346	0.962	1.000	1.577	2.038	3.115	3.731	1.962	3.423	3.000	3.731	3.462
12	41	1.171	0.927	0.976	1.049	0.854	0.610	0.634	1.000	1.293	1.976	2.366	1.244	2.171	1.902	2.366	2.195
13	53	0.906	0.717	0.755	0.811	0.660	0.472	0.491	0.774	1.000	1.528	1.830	0.962	1.679	1.472	1.830	1.698
14	81	0.593	0.469	0.494	0.531	0.432	0.309	0.321	0.506	0.654	1.000	1.198	0.630	1.099	0.963	1.198	1.111
15	97	0.495	0.392	0.412	0.443	0.361	0.258	0.268	0.423	0.546	0.835	1.000	0.526	0.918	0.804	1.000	0.928

TABLE 2.7   Computation of Project Priority Scores

Scores	A	B	C	D	E	F	G
1					Prob.		
2			Market	Market	Tech.		Project
3	Project	Cost	Share	Size	Success		Score
4							
5	1	0.062	0.043	0.043	0.036		0.045
6	2	0.079	0.047	0.047	0.040		0.052
7	3	0.075	0.039	0.039	0.089		0.056
8	4	0.070	0.050	0.050	0.067		0.058
9	5	0.086	0.109	0.109	0.054		0.093
10	6	0.120	0.109	0.109	0.030		0.095
11	7	0.115	0.078	0.078	0.089		0.087
12	8	0.073	0.058	0.058	0.104		0.070
13	9	0.057	0.039	0.039	0.045		0.044
14	10	0.037	0.047	0.047	0.035		0.042
15	11	0.031	0.039	0.039	0.108		0.051
16	12	0.059	0.050	0.050	0.071		0.056
17	13	0.034	0.062	0.062	0.048		0.054
18	14	0.038	0.062	0.062	0.051		0.055
19	15	0.031	0.089	0.089	0.070		0.074
20	16	0.033	0.081	0.081	0.064		0.068
21							
22	Criteria						
23	Weights	0.2	0.4	0.2	0.2		

at each level. Thus a project score will not be influenced by the length of a branch.

The final rankings are shown in Table 2.8. The projects have been ranked in descending order of score, and cumulative costs calculated. Projects 6, 5, 7, 15, 8, 16, 4, and 12 are funded within the budget. Project 2 could also be funded within the budget, even though it ranks below two other more expensive projects.

TABLE 2.8   Project Scores and Rankings

Selection	A	B	C	D
1				
2		Project	Cost	Cumulative
3	Project	Score	($1000)	Cost
4				
5	6	0.095	25	25
6	5	0.093	35	60
7	7	0.087	26	86
8	15	0.074	97	183
9	8	0.070	41	224
10	16	0.068	90	314
11	4	0.058	43	357
12	12	0.056	51	408
13	3	0.056	40	448
14	14	0.055	78	526
15	13	0.054	89	615
16	2	0.052	38	653
17	11	0.051	97	750
18	1	0.045	48	798
19	9	0.044	53	851
20	10	0.042	81	932

Note that the AHP method and the scoring model funded the same list of projects. This will not always be the case. Since the two methods approach the problem differently, it is to be expected that they will not always agree entirely.

The computations necessary for AHP can readily be carried out using a spreadsheet, as was done in the example above.* However, computer programs for carrying out the rankings are available commercially. While these commercial programs may tend to constrain the form of the model somewhat, they are usually very easy to use. They allow the analyst to respond to a set of questions, while relegating the actual computations to the background. They are thus suited for use by managers who do not wish to become involved in the detailed calculations.

2.4 SUMMARY

Ranking methods provide a means for ordering a list of candidate projects in relative value or worthiness of support. All ranking methods depend in some way on pairwise comparisons between projects. These comparisons may be global, or they may be decomposed in such a way as to allow comparisons on each of several factors. While decomposing the comparisons allows for more precision in judgment, it also requires many more comparisons.

Those ranking methods allowing the comparisons to be decomposed into comparisons on each of several factors allow incorporation of both objective and judgmental data, whereas global comparisons allow judgmental data only. Both scoring models and the AHP require that actual values be scaled to have the same range. Standard procedures are available for this scaling in each method.

2.5 QUESTIONS FOR CLASS DISCUSSION

1. By using the same four factors from Project Menu 1 of Appendix 2 as were used in the scoring models and AHP examples, prepare a matrix similar to that of Table 2.1, basing your preferences on a global judgment of the relative merits of each project. Do you find that the global judgments are easy to make? Do you find that you tend to focus on a single factor (e.g., cost or market share) and base your "global" judgments on that? Do you find that you try to combine the factors in some way and "solve the model in your head?" What are the merits of using a method that decomposes comparisons into comparisons on individual factors?

2. Devise a scoring model that would be suited for an industry such as pharmaceuticals, where market size and market share are both important, and successful

---

*Analysts who are more mathematically inclined will find that the AHP computations can be even simpler if more powerful programs, such as MathCad (C), Derive (C), or Mathematica (C), are used.

projects can usually recover their costs. Using Project Menu 2 from Appendix 2, score the projects using your model.

3. By using the same four factors as were used in the AHP example in this chapter, utilize AHP to rank the projects in Project Menu 2 of Appendix 2.

2.6 FURTHER READINGS

Bard, J. F., R. Balachandra, and P.E. Kaufmann (1988). An Interactive Approach to R & D Project Selection and Termination. *IEEE Transactions on Engineering Management*. **35**(3), August, 139–146.

Cooper, M. J. (1978). An Evaluation System for Project Selection. *Research Management*. **21**, July, 29–33.

Fiksel, J., L.A. Cox, D.L. Richardson, and A.G. Adamantiades (1983). Selection of Nuclear Safety Research and Development Projects Through Value-Impact Analysis. *Nuclear Safety*. **24**(1), January–February, 12–25.

Gear, T. E., A.G. Lockett, and A.P. Muhlemann (1982). A Unified Approach to the Acquisition of Subjective Data in R & D. *IEEE Transactions on Engineering Management*. **29**(1), February, 11–19.

Islei, G., G. Lockett, B. Cox, and M. Stratford (1991). A Decision Support System Using Judgmental Modeling: A Case of R & D in the Pharmaceutical Industry. *IEEE Transactions on Engineering Management*. **38**(3), August, 202–209.

Liberatore, M. J. (1987). An Extension of the Analytic Hierarchy Process for Industrial R & D Project Selection and Resource Allocation. *IEEE Transactions on Engineering Management*. **34**(4), February, 12–18.

Liberatore, M. J. (1988). A Decision Support System Linking Research and Development Project Selection With Business Strategy. Project Management Journal. **19**(5), November, 14–21.

Lockett, G., B. Hetherington, and P. Yallup (1984). Modeling a Research Portfolio Using AHP: A Group Decision Process. *R & D Management*. **16**(2), April, 151–160.

Melachrinoudis, E. and K. Rice (1991). The Prioritization of Technologies in a Research Laboratory. in *IEEE Transactions on Engineering Management*. **38**(3), August, 269–278.

Miles, R. F., Jr. (1980). The SIMRAND Methodology: Simulation of Research and Development Projects. *Large Scale Systems*. **7**(1), August, 59–67.

Moore, J. R. Jr. and N.R. Baker (1969). An Analytical Approach to Scoring Model Design—Application to Research and Development Project Selection. *IEEE Transactions on Engineering Management*, **16**(3), August, 90–98.

Saaty, T. L. (1982). *Decision Making for Leaders*, Belmont, CA: Lifetime Learning Publications.

Saaty, T. L. (1983). Priority Setting in Complex Problems. *IEEE Transactions on Engineering Management*, **30**(2), August, 140–155.

Saaty, T. L. (1980). *The Analytic Hierarchy Process*, New York: McGraw-Hill.

____3
ECONOMIC

Economic methods for project selection attempt to evaluate projects on their contribution to the firm's profits. Economic methods must in some way take into account the cash flow involved with the project, from initiation, through development, to sales and either end-of-life cycle or some specified time horizon. Methods include net present value (NPV), internal rate of return (IRR), and cash flow payback. As usually used, these methods are deterministic. However, all can be extended to incorporate expected value considerations. Economic methods do address the question of whether a project has financial payoff for a firm. However, they often require information that cannot be obtained early in the life of a project.

3.1 NET PRESENT VALUE

Net present value is often used on capital budgeting. The basic idea is that a dollar now is worth more than a dollar at some time in the future, because the dollar now can earn money in the interim. This fact is illustrated in Figure 3.1, which shows the present value of a dollar at various future times, for discount rates (interest rates) of 5 and 10%. For instance, $0.61 invested today at 5% interest would be worth $1.00 in 10 years. Therefore the present value of a dollar to be received or spent 10 years from now is $0.61. As shown in Figure 3.1, the higher the discount rate, the lower the present value of a future payment or receipt.

Table 3.1 illustrates the point that the relative ranking of two revenue streams can change depending on the discount rate. Revenue stream one has higher total revenue than revenue stream two, but most of it is farther out in

24

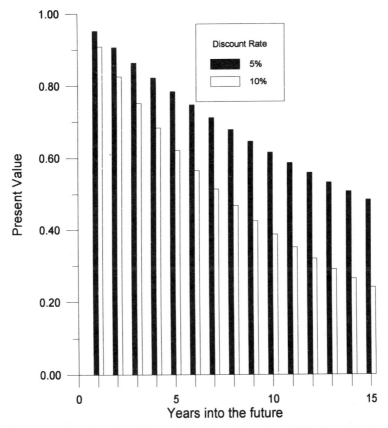

Figure 3.1. Present value of $1 at various future times, 5 and 10% discount rates.

the future. Thus at a high discount rate, this far future revenue is discounted relative to the lower but nearer revenue of stream two. At a discount rate of 15%, the two revenue streams have almost equal NPV values. At discount rates higher than 15%, however, revenue stream two, although smaller in total magnitude, has a higher NPV than does revenue stream one. Note also how low the NPV values are for high discount rates. A dollar of revenue to be received 16 years in the future has a very small present value at even fairly low discount rates.

Computation of NPV serves two purposes. First, it makes comparisons possible between early and late values in the same cash flow stream. For instance, how much is a profit worth 10 years from now, in comparison with an R & D expenditure now on the project, which will lead to that profit? Second, it makes comparisons possible between cash flow streams that have different profiles of income and expenditures. By computing the NPV of each cash flow stream, it is possible to convert them to a single value and compare them.

TABLE 3.1 Relative Ranking of Income Streams versus Discount Rate

txtxmpl	A	B	C	D	E	F	G
1	Revenue Stream 1				Revenue Stream 2		
2		Discount				Discount	
3	Revenue	Rate	NPV		Revenue	Rate	NPV
4	1	0.01	92.45		2	0.01	78.90
5	1	0.05	58.96		2	0.05	52.30
6	1	0.10	35.20		2	0.10	33.07
7	1	0.15	22.09		2	0.15	22.18
8	1	0.20	14.55		2	0.20	15.71
9	1	0.30	7.23		2	0.30	9.08
10	1				2		
11	1				2		
12	12				9		
13	12				9		
14	12				9		
15	12				9		
16	12				9		
17	12				9		
18	12				9		
19	12				9		
20							
21	104				88		

Thus in comparing different income and expenditure streams, future dollar values must be discounted back to the present by the appropriate interest rate. Let a stream of expenditures and revenues be represented by $F(i)$, the cash flow in the ith period. Let the discount rate be r per period. Let the time horizon be the Nth period. Then the NPV of the cash flow is

$$\text{NPV} = \sum_{i=0}^{N} \frac{F(i)}{(1+r)^i}$$

To illustrate the use of NPV in ranking projects, consider Project Menu 3 in Appendix 2. There are 16 projects, each with a different time profile of costs (R & D cost, capital investment for the product, and advertising of the product) and net profit on sales (exclusive of advertising). Table 3.2 shows the NPV of each project, at 10% discount rate and 15-year time horizon (rankings might be different at different discount rates). The rankings of the projects reflect the NPV, and in principle would be used to compare the relative merits of the different projects, as well as the merits of each project against alternative investments, such as plant expansion for an existing product.

Net present value can be computed readily using a spreadsheet. Most spreadsheets include an NPV function that performs the NPV calculation directly. The user need not specify or perform the individual multiplications and summations. Use of a spreadsheet eliminates the arithmetic, but of

TABLE 3.2 Projects Ranked According to Net Present Value

Project	NPV
2	788
4	715
6	707
8	575
1	290
10	277
3	235
5	232
12	225
14	215
7	185
9	-76
11	-106
13	-150
15	-166
16	144

course does not eliminate the more difficult task of estimating future expenditures and revenues, or the proper discount rate.

Without using something like NPV, it would not be possible to compare projects with different streams of expenses and revenues, nor would it be possible to take into account the time value of money (a dollar received or not spent now is worth more than a dollar received or not spent at a future time).

The method of NPV can be used only when the stream of revenues and expenditures is known from the present out to some time horizon. It cannot be used if that stream is not known. When the method of NPV can be used, it provides a direct measure of the total economic value of a project to the firm, a value that can be compared with the value of alternative investments that may have different cash flow profiles. This method thus allows comparison of R & D projects with each other, and with alternative investments, such as capital equipment or advertising.

However, the method has several shortcomings. As already mentioned, it requires data about future costs and revenues that may not be possible to obtain early in the life cycle of the project. Thus it may not be possible to compute the NPV of a basic research project, at a time when it is not clear what kind of product or process it will result in.

Net present value also assumes the discount rate is constant over time, which may not be true. It assumes that the decision maker is indifferent between a dollar this year and $1 + r$ dollars next year. This may not be true if the decision maker anticipates a money crunch this year, but ample funds from some other source next year.

Moreover, NPV ignores possible discontinuities, such as bankruptcy. A bankruptcy cannot be offset by high potential income in years after the bankruptcy, since that income will never be realized. Some of these shortcomings are overcome by a modified version known as generalized present value.

Generalized Present Value

This value is an alternative to standard NPV, which eliminates the requirement that the discount rate be constant over time. It can best be described using an example. Suppose the decision maker is confronted with the following anticipated cash flow stream:

$$100, 110, 150, 170, 180$$

The decision maker then compares this with the following cash flow stream:

$$100, 110, 150, X, 0$$

That is, the anticipated cash flow is replaced by a cash flow that is zero in the final year, and whose value X in the next-to-final year is to be determined. The decision maker must then choose a value for X such that he/she is indifferent between the two cash flows. Clearly X must be at least 170 but not more than 350. That is, the cash received in the final year is worth something, hence X must be 170 or greater. However, while the decision maker may certainly *prefer* more sooner to less later, it makes no sense to assert he/she is *indifferent* between more sooner and less later. Hence, X must take on some value between the cash flow in the next-to-last year and the sum of the cash flows in the next-to-last year and the last year.

In selecting the value of X, which makes him/her indifferent between the two cash flows, the decision maker may take into account more than just the time value of money. Other factors to be considered may include demands for funds elsewhere in the firm, revenue from elsewhere in the firm, anticipated changes in tax laws, anticipated changes in interest rates, anticipated changes in accounting rules, possible market shifts, and actions of competitors. That is, while the choice of the value for X to make the two cash flows equivalent is highly subjective, the decision maker's subjectivity can be disciplined by explicitly taking into account factors that might affect the relative preferences for the two streams of income or expenditure.

Assume the decision maker selects the value 332 for X, that is, he/she is indifferent between 180 in the final year and an *additional* 162 in the next-to-final year. This implies a discount rate of 11%. However, it would be inappropriate to assert this is the decision maker's discount rate. The choice of the increment in the next-to-last year may have been influenced by many things other than the time value of money. The most that can be said is that *in this particular case*, the decision maker is indifferent between an additional 162 in the next-to-last year and 180 in the last year.

Once the cash flow profile has been shortened by one year, the process is repeated. A new cash flow is selected such that the decision maker is indifferent between the modified cash flow with zero in the last year, and one that has zero values for the last *two* years, and some value in the second-from-last year greater than that in the original revenue stream. This process is continued until the original revenue stream is replaced by one that has a nonzero value only in the first year, and zero values in all succeeding years out to the time horizon. This value becomes the *present value* of the original revenue stream.

Note that this method can be carried out only by the responsible decision maker, who must make the indifference choices. While an analyst may prepare the estimates of cash flow, the analyst should not try to substitute his/her judgment of the indifference values for that of the decision maker. However, the analyst may make use of some of the methods to be described in Part III to assist the decision maker in carrying out the necessary subjective judgments.

3.2 INTERNAL RATE OF RETURN

Internal rate of return is the discount rate that would reduce the NPV of a cash flow profile to zero. Put another way, it is the interest rate one would have to pay on borrowed money to make the NPV of the cash flow zero. There is no formula for computing IRR directly. The IRR must be computed iteratively, by assuming a discount rate, computing NPV, and adjusting the assumed discount rate until the computed NPV is zero. However, most spreadsheets include an IRR function that performs the calculation for the user. The user is thus relieved of the computational effort. However, the more difficult task of estimating future expenditures and revenues remains for the user.

In terms of project selection, the greater the IRR, the better the project, in the sense that it can pass a higher "hurdle rate" for discounting, and that it achieves payback sooner. The use of IRR will be illustrated from the same list of projects as was used for NPV. Table 3.3 shows the rankings. For this set of projects, the rankings are almost the same by both methods. Note that Project 10 has a higher NPV than Projects 3 and 5, but a lower IRR, resulting in differences in ranking for the two methods. Note also that those projects with negative NPV also have IRR less than the discount rate used in the NPV computation. This result is simply in accordance with the definition of IRR as the discount rate that makes NPV equal to zero.

**TABLE 3.3   Projects Ranked According
to Internal Rate of Return**

2	0.28
4	0.27
6	0.25
8	0.23
1	0.18
3	0.17
5	0.16
10	0.15
7	0.15
12	0.14
14	0.14
16	0.13
9	0.08
11	0.07
13	0.06
15	0.06

Internal rate of return is widely used for choosing among not only R & D projects but other types of capital investments. One significant advantage that it has is that the analyst need not estimate the future interest rate (discount rate), as is required with NPV. However, it has a significant shortcoming. A project with high IRR may have a small NPV, and actually may be of less value to the company than a project with greater NPV but lower IRR. This finding is shown in the reversed rankings of Projects 10 and 3 by the two methods. Thus IRR is not always an effective substitute for NPV. When comparing R & D projects with other capital projects, NPV may be a more useful method.

3.3   CASH FLOW PAYBACK

This measure is the time from start of the project until net cash flow becomes positive, that is, the project pays back all the funds invested in it to that point. As usually used, this method does not take into account the time value of money, nor any of the other reasons for preferring cash flow in one period to cash flow in another. It looks only at when the investment is recouped, without considering alternative uses for the same funds. (As such, it reflects humorist Will Rogers' comment: "I'm less worried about the return *on* my investment than about the return *of* my investment.") Payback time is a simple and easily understood method. However, it requires estimates of future income from the project. These may be difficult to obtain, especially for projects in the basic research stage.

**TABLE 3.4   Time Until Cash Flow
Becomes Positive (Time to Payback)**

Project	Year
2	9
6	9
4	9
3	10
5	10
7	10
8	10
12	12
1	12
10	12
14	12
16	12
11	13
13	13
15	13
9	13

To illustrate the use of cash flow payback, the time until the cumulative cash flow becomes positive is shown in Table 3.4 for projects from Project Menu 3. Payback times range from 9 to 13 years, with several ties. The ties could presumably be broken by applying some other criterion, such as total cost. Project rankings in years to payback differ significantly from those for either NPV or IRR. However, some projects are ranked highly by all three methods.

Time to payback fails to take into account either the time value of money or the rate of return on the investment. However, it is "robust" in the sense that it reduces the risks associated with estimates of future discount rates and market conditions. In principle, projects that reach payback sooner represent less risk than projects that reach payback later, even though the latter may have a higher NPV or IRR. Hence, despite its lack of sensitivity to overall project size and return, it is often used by risk-averse decision makers to reduce the risks inherent in basing decisions on estimates of future conditions.

3.4 EXPECTED VALUE

As usually employed, NPV, IRR, and cash flow payback assume a single cash flow profile from start to end of the project. In many cases there may be two or more alternative profiles. For instance, the possible revenue stream may differ depending on economic conditions. The cost stream may differ depending on the outcome of one phase of the R & D project. The usual computations of NPV, IRR, or payback time can be extended to take into account these alternative possibilities. Each possible cash flow profile is assigned a probability of occurrence, based on estimated probability of the R & D outcome, of economic conditions, or whatever. An expected cash flow profile is computed by multiplying each possible profile by its probability and summing the products. The NPV (or IRR, or payback) is computed for the expected cash flow profile. The result then is the expected NPV (or IRR or cash flow payback). While using the expected value requires more data than is required for the more usual ways of dealing with cash flow profiles, it presents a more realistic view of affairs, since it takes into account alternative possibilities.

To illustrate the use of expected value, consider Project Menu 5. There are 16 projects, each with anticipated R & D, capital and advertising expenditures, and three possible profit streams. Each profit stream is assigned a probability of occurrence. We can compute an expected profit stream by multiplying each profit stream by its probability of occurring, and summing the products. This expected profit stream is then used in the usual manner to calculate an expected cash flow profile. Expected NPV or IRR values are computed directly from this expected cash flow stream. By accumulating the expected cash flow stream, we can determine the expected year in which the initial expenditures are recovered. Table 3.5 compares the rankings by expected NPV and expected IRR values. There are some differences in the rankings of the projects under the two methods, again in cases where projects

TABLE 3.5 Project Rankings by Expected NPV and IRR

Project	Expected NPV		Project	Expected IRR
2	912		2	0.30
6	778		4	0.27
4	754		6	0.27
8	718		8	0.25
10	338		1	0.19
3	329		3	0.19
1	322		5	0.17
14	301		12	0.16
12	290		14	0.16
5	263		10	0.16
16	220		7	0.16
7	218		16	0.14
9	-21		9	0.10
13	-31		13	0.09
11	-123		11	0.07
15	-144		15	0.07

have small expected NPV but large expected IRR or vice versa. However, some projects rank high by both methods.

3.5 SUMMARY

Economic methods attempt to evaluate projects in terms of their economic return to the firm. Net present value is used to compare future returns with current expenditures, and cash flow streams with different profiles of expenditures and returns. Internal rate of return is used to compare alternative investments in terms of the return on investment that they represent. Internal rate of return can be used to compare an investment with the cost of borrowed money. Time to payback represents a conservative approach to evaluating investments, by reducing the risks associated with long-range forecasts of future discount rates and market conditions. Any of the three methods can be used to compare R & D projects with alternative investment opportunities open to the firm, including capital investments, advertising, and acquisitions. All three, however, require data that may not be possible to obtain early in the life of an R & D project.

3.6 QUESTIONS FOR CLASS DISCUSSION

1. Compute the NPV of projects in Project Menu 4 of Appendix 2. What is the rank order of the projects on this criterion?
2. Compute the IRR of projects in Project Menu 4 of Appendix 2. What is the rank order of the projects on this criterion?
3. Compute the time to payback for each of the projects in Project Menu 4 of Appendix 2. What is the rank order of the projects on this criterion?
4. Compute the expected NPV for projects in Project Menu 6 of Appendix 2. What is the rank order of the projects on this criterion?
5. Compute the expected IRR for projects in Project Menu 6 of Appendix 2. What is the rank order of the projects on this criterion?
6. Compute the expected time to payback for the projects in Project Menu 6 of Appendix 2. What is the rank order of the projects on this criterion?

3.7 FURTHER READINGS

Graves, S.B. and J.L. Ringguest (1991). Evaluating Competing R & D Investments. *Research-Technology Management*. July–August, 32–36.

Mehrez, A. (1988). Selecting R & D Projects: A Case Study of the Expected Utility Approach. *Technovation*. **8**, 299–311.

Thomas, H. (1985). Decision Analysis and Strategic Management of Research and Development. *R & D Management*. **15**(1), January, 3–22.

____4
DECISION THEORY

Decision theory is used in situations in which the decision maker faces a sequence of decisions (choices to be made), and between each two successive decisions, an outcome (chance event) of the previous decision intervenes. For instance, suppose an initial decision is made to start a project that has multiple stages. The first stage may have two or more alternative outcomes. Depending on the outcome of the first stage, another decision must be made, which initiates another stage, which in turn leads to another decision, and so on, until some final stopping point is reached, such as successful conclusion of the project.

The essential feature of this process, in decision theory, is that each stage in turn has chance outcomes. The possible outcomes, and the probability of each, must be specified at the time the initial decision is to be made.

The decisions and chance outcomes can be displayed as a "decision tree," the root of which is the initial decision, and the leaves being the ultimate outcomes. By convention, the choice nodes (decisions) are represented in the tree as squares, and the chance nodes (leading to alternative outcomes) are represented by circles.

Consider the following situation. A business manager has $30K available this year for investment, and expects to have $60K available next year. These funds could be invested in CDs at 5%. In two years these will be worth $96,075 ($30 for two years, $60K for one year). Alternatively, there is an R & D project that will cost $30K in the first year, and $60K in the second year.

At the end of the first year, the project can be reviewed. There is a 70% chance that the project outcome will be good at that point, and a 30% chance that the project outcome will be poor. A decision can then be made to cancel the project and invest the remaining $60K in CDs, which will be worth $63K at the end of the second year. Alternatively, the project can be completed at a cost of another $60K, in which case an additional $50K will be spent for marketing.

If the project is completed, the market may be high, or moderate, or else the product will be a failure. If the market is high, net profit will be $600K. If the market is moderate, net profit will be $200K. (Both net profits are exclusive of R & D and marketing costs.) If the product is a failure, there will be no net profit, and the firm will suffer a loss of not only the R & D investment but the marketing costs, or $140K. If the market is high, the net payoff at the end of year two is thus $600K − $140K or $460K. If the market is moderate, the payoff is $200K − $140K or $60K.

If the first year's R & D outcome is good, the probabilities for high, moderate, and fail markets are 0.6, 0.3, and 0.1, respectively. If the first year's R & D outcome is poor, the market probabilities are 0.2, 0.3, and 0.5 respectively.

The decision tree for this decision situation is illustrated in Figure 4.1.

The tree is solved by "folding it back," starting at the leaves. Each outcome's value is multiplied by its associated probability. The result is the expected value at each chance node. Thus the expected value at the chance node following the "complete" decision in the "good" branch is $280K. The "cancel" decision results in a value of $63K. Likewise, the expected value at the chance node in the "poor" branch is $40K, and again the "cancel" decision results in a value of $63K.

At this point, the tree must be "pruned." At the choice node in the "good" branch, the choice is between an outcome with expected value $280K

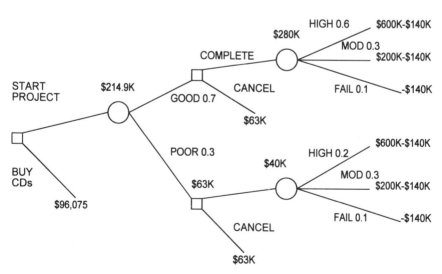

Figure 4.1. Decision tree.

and another outcome with value $63K. The "cancel" branch is "pruned away," and the choice is made to complete the project. Conversely, at the choice node in the "poor" branch," the value from completing the project is less than the value from canceling the project, hence the "complete" branch is pruned away. At the first chance node in the "start project" branch, the expected value is thus $214.9K. This is a better choice than the $96.075K available from buying CDs, so the "Buy CDs" branch is pruned away.

In general, then, the tree is folded back by computing the expected values at the final chance nodes. At the preceding choice nodes, all branches except the one with the greatest expected value are pruned away. This allows computation of the expected values at the next chance nodes back toward the root. This process of computing expected values at chance nodes, and pruning away all but the maximum expected value at the choice nodes, is continued until the root node is reached, with the expected value of the tree. Only the highest expected value paths through the tree are left, the others having been pruned away. The result is that the expected value of the project is known, and the best choices at each possible decision are known. Which choice nodes will actually be reached cannot be known in advance, of course, since each project stage still has chance outcomes.

Folding back the decision tree can be done conveniently using a spreadsheet. Table 4.1 shows how the decision tree of Figure 4.1 can be implemented in a spreadsheet. Note that in each cell, the formulas are shown, not the calculated values.

Note that the R & D and marketing costs are shown in cells at the top of the spreadsheet, as are the net profits from various levels of market success. These values are reused in several formulas in the spreadsheet. By placing them in their own cells, the need to repeat them in each formula is avoided. Instead, their cells can be referred to in the formulas. Also, by placing these values in their own cells, we keep formulas and data separate, which means that the data can be changed easily. This capability is useful in conducting sensitivity testing, as will be explained later.

Column K shows the final payoffs, as the net profit minus the cumulative expenditures for R & D and marketing. The cells with the dashes are used only to separate the outcomes associated with the various possible decisions. Column J shows the probabilities associated with each of the payoffs. As in Figure 4.1, these are different depending on the route by which the decision to complete the project was reached. Column I shows the names of the outcomes, and serves merely to label the outcomes. Column H shows the computation of expected values from the outcomes. Note that a special spreadsheet function, @SUMPRODUCT, is used. This takes the vector product of the two columns containing payoffs and probabilities. Use of this function avoids the need to write out the entire set of sums and products. The CANCEL decision results in a deterministic outcome from purchase of CDs, so no formula is needed. Column G contains the labels for the decisions made at the second choice nodes. Column F uses the @MAX function to

TABLE 4.1 Spreadsheet Showing Formulas in Decision Tree Example

formulas	A	B	C	D	E	F	G	H	I	J	K
1	R&D Costs			Marketing	50		Profits				
2	Year 1	30					High	600			
3	Year 2	60		Total	140		Moderate	200			
4							Fail	0			
5											
6	Root	Choice_1	Payoff	Outcome_1	Probability	Payoff	Choice_2	Payoff	Outcome_2	Probability	Payoff
7							Complete	@SUMPRODUCT(J7..J9,K7..K9)	High	0.6	+H2-$E$3
8									Moderate	0.3	+H3-$E$3
9									Fail	0.1	+H4-$E$3
10				Good	0.7	@MAX(H8,H11)					———
11							Cancel	63			
12											
13		Start	+E10*F10+E16*F16								
14		Project					Complete	@SUMPRODUCT(J13..J15,K13..K15)	High	0.2	+H2-$E$3
15									Moderate	0.3	+H3-$E$3
16	96.075			Poor	0.3	@MAX(H14,H17)			Fail	0.5	+H4-$E$3
17							Cancel	63			———
18											
19		Buy CDs	96.075								

select the largest of the payoffs from the possible choices at the second choice nodes. Column E contains the probabilities of the outcomes whose labels appear in Column D. These are, of course, the probabilities of arriving at the two second choice nodes. Column C contains the computation of expected value of all the outcomes to the right, as well as the deterministic value achieved by investing all the funds in CDs. Column B contains the labels for the choices possible at the outset. Column A contains the formula that expresses the expected value of the entire tree, once it is folded back.

Table 4.2 shows the computations rather than the formulas in the spreadsheet. It should be compared with Figure 4.1, to see that the formulas do in fact give the results portrayed in the more customary "tree" format.

A key point is that by use of a spreadsheet, the analyst can greatly simplify the solution of a decision tree. Moreover, the spreadsheet makes it easier to conduct sensitivity analyses. For instance, suppose the probabilities for market performance, given that the first stage of the project gave good results, were changed to High: 0.4; Moderate: 0.3; Fail: 0.3, respectively. What change, if any, would this make in the decision? The only thing that needs to be done is to change the entries in cells J7–J9. The folding back is then taken care of automatically by the spreadsheet formulas. The results are shown in Table 4.3. The project should still be started, but its expected value is now only $130.9K.

This example illustrates the point that for sensitivity analyses to be conducted easily, data and formulas should be kept separate. This is done in the tables by putting the investments and profits in separate cells, and referring to those cells when the values are needed. Thus a change in data needs to be made at only one place on the spreadsheet. This change will then be reflected in all formulas using that value.

This example of sensitivity testing does not fully exploit the capabilities of a spreadsheet. A further example will illustrate the power available, and also the benefits from keeping data and formulas separate.

As given, the probability of a "good" outcome for the first stage of the project is 0.7. At what probability for this outcome would the decision maker be indifferent between starting the project and investing the money in CDs? That is, at what value for probability of a "good" outcome would the expected value of the project, in cell C13, be equal to the return from the CDs in cell C19? We could experiment, trying various values in E10 (and their complementary values in E16), and observing the results in cell C13. However, the spreadsheet's SOLVE capability simplifies this. We replace the probability in E16 with $1 - E10$, so that whatever the value in cell E10, the value in E16 will be the complementary probability (i.e., the two sum to 1.0). Next we utilize the SOLVE command to allow the spreadsheet program to adjust cell E10 to achieve a value of 96.075 in cell C13. The results are shown in Table 4.4. In this decision tree, the (perhaps surprising) result is that for any probability of a "good" outcome at the first stage greater than about 0.16, starting the project is preferable to buying CDs.

TABLE 4.2 Spreadsheet Showing Values in Decision Tree Example

values	A	B	C	D	E	F	G	H	I	J	K
1	R&D Costs			Marketing	50		Profits				
2	Year 1	30					High	600			
3	Year 2	60		Total	140		Moderate	200			
4							Fail	0			
5											
6	Root Choice_1		Payoff	Outcome_1	Probability	Payoff	Choice_2	Payoff	Outcome_2	Probability	Payoff
7									High	0.6	460
8							Complete	280	Moderate	0.3	60
9									Fail	0.1	-140
10				Good	0.7	280					————
11							Cancel	63			
12											————
13	Start		214.9								
14	Project						Complete	40	High	0.2	460
15									Moderate	0.3	60
16	214.9			Poor	0.3	63			Fail	0.5	-140
17							Cancel	63			
18											

39

TABLE 4.3 Spreadsheet Showing Use for Sensitivity Testing

	A	B	C	D	E	F	G	H	I	J	K
1	R&D Costs			Marketing	50		Profits				
2	Year 1	30		Total	140		High	600			
3	Year 2	60					Moderate	200			
4							Fail	0			
5											
6	Root	Choice_1	Payoff	Outcome_1	Probability	Payoff	Choice_2	Payoff	Outcome_2	Probability	Payoff
7									High	0.4	460
8							Complete	160	Moderate	0.3	60
9									Fail	0.3	-140
10				Good	0.7	160					
11							Cancel	63			
12											
13	Start		130.9						High	0.2	460
14		Project					Complete	40	Moderate	0.3	60
15									Fail	0.5	-140
16	130.9			Poor	0.3	63					
17							Cancel	63			
18											
19		Buy CDs	96.075								

TABLE 4.4 Spreadsheet Showing Use of SOLVE for Sensitivity Analysis

	A	B	C	D	E	F	G	H	I	J	K
1	R&D Costs			Marketing	50		Profits				
2	Year 1	30					High	600			
3	Year 2	60		Total	140		Moderate	200			
4							Fail	0			
5											
6	Root	Choice_1	Payoff	Outcome_1	Probability	Payoff	Choice_2	Payoff	Outcome_2	Probability	Payoff
7									High	0.6	460
8							Complete	280	Moderate	0.3	60
9									Fail	0.1	-140
10				Good	0.15241935	280					
11							Cancel	63			------
12											------
13		Start	96.075								
14		Project					Complete	40	High	0.2	460
15									Moderate	0.3	60
16	96.075			Poor	0.84758065	63			Fail	0.5	-140
17							Cancel	63			------
18											
19		Buy CDs	96.075								

41

4.1 SUMMARY

Decision theory deals with situations in which the decision maker faces a series of choices, with chance outcomes following each choice. The probabilities of the possible outcomes are known. At the end of the sequence of choices and chance outcomes, some payoff will be achieved. The array of choices and chance outcomes can be displayed as a decision tree. Solving the tree involves computing expected values at chance nodes, and pruning away all but the best choice at the choice nodes. The process of solving a decision tree can readily be implemented in a spreadsheet.

Decision theory provides a means for dealing with R & D projects in which a succession of choices must be made, and each choice is followed by chance outcomes. Use of decision theory allows the analyst to plot the highest value branches through the tree, and prune away all other branches. Thus decision theory provides the decision maker with guidance as to what choice to make at each choice node, so as to achieve the highest expected value from the sequence of decisions.

4.2 QUESTIONS FOR CLASS DISCUSSION

1. By using the example in this chapter, at what value for the second year R & D cost will the decision maker be indifferent between starting the project and buying CDs?

2. Assume that the net profit (before deducting R & D and marketing costs) for the moderate market is always one-half the net profit for the high market, regardless of the outcome of the chance node for the first stage of the project. At what value of net profit for the high market will the decision maker be indifferent between starting the project and buying CDs?

3. Assume there is a third possible outcome from the first stage of the project, a "fair" result. Let the probabilities by good: 0.5; fair: 0.3; poor: 0.2. Let the market outcome probabilities following the "fair" outcome be high: 0.5; moderate: 0.4; fail: 0.1. Set up the spreadsheet for the expanded tree, and find the expected value in the root cell. Should the project be started, or should the decision maker buy CDs?

4.3 FURTHER READINGS

Hazelrigg, G. A., Jr., and F.L. Huband (1985). RADSIM—A Methodology for Large-Scale R & D Program Assessment. *IEEE Transactions on Engineering Management*. 32(3), August.

Thomas, H. (1985). Decision Analysis and Strategic Management of Research and Development. *R & D Management*, 15(1), January, 3–22.

____5
PORTFOLIO OPTIMIZATION

The project selection methods described in previous chapters rank, rate, or otherwise evaluate projects individually, without taking into account potential interactions among the projects, or alternative uses for the resources devoted to the projects. The object of the portfolio optimization methods is to select, from the list of candidate projects, the set that provides maximum payoff to the firm. Portfolio optimization methods can take into account resource dependencies, budget constraints, technical interactions, market interactions, and program considerations. Methods used are mathematical programming and sensitivity analysis.

5.1 PROJECT INTERACTIONS

Projects cannot always be considered in isolation. There are many possible interactions among projects, which require that the effects of one project on another be taken into account in choosing an optimum portfolio. These interactions are discussed below.

Resource Dependencies

Different projects may require the use of the same resources. This requirement may include specialized resources, such as unique test equipment, unique facilities, or people with unique skills. It may also include resources that can be saturated, such as computers or environmental test chambers. The object of taking resource dependencies into account is to assure that the

43

requirements of the set of programs included in the portfolio do not exceed the capacity of any specialized or unique resources.

Budget Constraints

The cost of projects included in the portfolio must stay within the period-by-period availability of funds. Since the profile of available funds may not be uniform, and since the cash demands of projects may not be uniform over their lives, assembly of the portfolio must take fund limitations into account.

Technical Interactions

Two or more projects may require the success of the same experiment or the same technical approach. Failure of the experiment or failure to develop the technology may delay or force cancellation of both projects. Alternatively, two projects may be related in such a way that failure of one increases the chances of success of the other. The portfolio should be designed to minimize chances of common failures of different projects.

Market Interactions

Two projects may interact in the ultimate marketplace. If they result in products that are partial or complete substitutes for one another, the success of one may cannibalize sales of the other. If, however, the projects result in products that are complementary, sales of one may enhance sales of the other. Evaluation of portfolio payoff should include any market interactions among projects included in the portfolio.*

Program Considerations

There may be company policies or political considerations that require the portfolio to include certain types of projects. For instance, there might be a policy that there be at least one project supporting a particular product in the current product line. These program considerations can be taken into account in assembling an "optimum" portfolio. Inclusion of such projects will of course reduce the total monetary payoff from the portfolio. However, their inclusion may be required to satisfy considerations that cannot be expressed in monetary terms.

Given these various types of project interactions and dependencies, we now look at methods for selecting optimum portfolios that take them into account.

---

*Note that refusal to undertake a project because the resulting product may cannibalize sales of an existing product means that the firm has abandoned the cannibalizing product to some other firm. Better to cannibalize your own sales than let someone else eat them up.

5.2   MATHEMATICAL PROGRAMMING

Mathematical programming refers to a class of techniques for selecting a set of entities out of some larger collection, such that the selected set maximizes some objective function, subject to a set of constraints. Suppose we have a collection X of projects $x(i)$. Suppose that a payoff $p(x(i))$ exists for each project. Suppose each project requires an amount of resources $r(i)$, and a total of R resources is available. Then a linear program would find the subset X' of X, which maximizes

$$\text{payoff}_{X' \text{ in } X} = \sum_{x(i) \text{ in } X'} p(x(i))$$

subject to

$$\sum_{x(i) \text{ in } X'} r(i) \le R$$

To illustrate this, we will use an example based on Project Menu 1 of Appendix 2. Suppose we wish to choose a set of projects from the 16 listed so that total revenue is maximized, where total revenue is computed as the product of market share and market size. However, we are faced with several constraints. First, the total R & D funds available in the next fiscal period is $500K. Second, only 1300 hours are available in the fabrication shop for construction of experimental apparatus, prototypes, and so on. Third, only 390 hours are available on the supercomputer. Thus the set of projects we select must satisfy all three constraints.

Table 5.1 shows a spreadsheet set up for a linear programming solution to the problem. The projects are listed in Column A, rows 5–20. Column B shows whether a project is selected (1) or not selected (0). The entries in the remaining columns are taken from Project Menu 1, except for Column F, which is the product of Columns D and E. As can be seen from the sums in row 22, the entire collection of projects exceeds all three constraints: cost, fabrication shop hours, and supercomputer hours.

The goal is to maximize total revenue, shown in cell B24 as the vector product of projects selected and project revenue. The constraints on costs, fabrication shop hours, and computer hours are shown, respectively, in cells F28, F29, and F30. In each case the resources required are computed as the vector product of the column of projects selected and the resource column.

The constraints in cells D25, D26, and D27 are out of the ordinary for linear programming, and deserve special attention. We wish to assure that the linear program does not try to "buy" resources by selecting a "negative" project. Hence, we constrain all the entries in Column B to be nonnegative. We do not want the "solution" to consist of replications of the most profitable project, hence we constrain all the entries in Column B to be not greater than 1. That is, a project can be selected at most one time for

TABLE 5.1 Spreadsheet Showing Constraints and Goal Formulas

FORMULAS	A	B	C	D	E	F	G	H	I
1							Fab.	Computer	
2	Project	Select	Cost	Market Share	Market Size	Revenue	Shop Hours	Hours	
3			($1000)	(Pct.)	($Mill.)	($Mill.)	Hours		
4	1	1	48	11	430	47	60	29	
5	2	1	38	12	340	41	189	48	
6	3	1	40	10	180	18	105	51	
7	4	1	43	13	290	38	174	23	
8	5	1	35	28	1220	342	191	20	
9	6	1	25	28	1340	375	55	51	
10	7	1	26	20	610	122	196	47	
11	8	1	41	15	1010	152	120	34	
12	9	1	53	10	810	81	208	51	
13	10	1	81	12	560	67	59	33	
14	11	1	97	10	710	71	224	28	
15	12	1	51	13	1180	153	82	40	
16	13	1	89	16	460	74	66	52	
17	14	1	78	16	180	29	176	24	
18	15	1	97	23	270	62	109	28	
19	16	1	90	21	430	90	235	50	
20									
21									
22	Total		932	258	10020	1761.5	2249	609	
23									
24	Total	@SUMPRODUCT(B5..B20,f5..f20)				Constraints			
25	Revenue			b5..b20	<=	1			
26				b5..b20	>=	0			
27				b5..b20	integer				
28				Total cost		@SUMPRODUCT(B5..B20,C5..C20)			<=500
29				Fab. Shop hours		@SUMPRODUCT(B5..B20,G5..G20)			<=1300
30				Computer hours		@SUMPRODUCT(B5..B20,H5..H20)			<=390

46

inclusion in the set. Finally, we cannot carry out one-half of a project. Hence, we constrain all the entires in Column B to be integers. The combination of these three constraints forces the entries in Column B to be either 0 or 1.

In this example we assume all projects are unique. However, there may be cases where the decision maker has a choice among several variations of the same project (i.e., on a "routine" or on a "crash" basis). We would not want the solution set to contain two versions of the same project. If there are several possible version of the same project, the set of constraints would be expanded to include constraints that assure that at most one version of a project is selected for inclusion. For instance, if X and Y are two versions of the same project (perhaps at different funding levels), a constraint, such as

$$X + Y \leq 1$$

would prevent both from appearing in the selected set.

There might be other types of constraints applied to cause the set to conform to policy decisions. For instance, suppose that company policy requires that the research laboratory always be working on at least one commercial development project. Assume that X, Y, and Z are such projects. Then a constraint of the form

$$X + Y + Z \geq 1 \qquad \text{(or equivalently, } X + Y + Z > 0\text{)}$$

might be applied, to force at least one such project into the solution set. As might be expected, making such a constraint active would be likely to reduce the total revenue, unless one such project would have appeared in the solution set even without the constraint. However, policy-based constraints such as this are usually intended to reflect considerations that cannot be converted into values commensurate with the goal values.

Most currently available spreadsheets have a built-in OPTIMIZE capability that can be used to solve the set of constraints. Table 5.2 shows the results of using the spreadsheet's OPTIMIZE capability, to maximize total revenue subject only to the constraint on cost. Total revenue is $1476.7 million. However, the constraints on both fabrication shop hours and supercomputer hours are violated. Total hours required in the fabrication shop are 1402, and total supercomputer hours required are 422. Hence, we must activate these constraints. (Note that because the solutions are required to be integers, it may be necessary to reduce the tolerance required of the spreadsheet's optimization routine below the default value, which is normally set to permit noninteger solutions.)

Table 5.3 shows the solution with both cost and fabrication shop constraints active. Total revenue is reduced to $1455.8 million. Total cost is reduced slightly, and supercomputer hours are actually within the allowable limit, even though this constraint was not active.

Table 5.4 shows the solution with both cost and supercomputer constraints active. Total revenue is $1467.2 million, up from that in Table 5.3. Supercom-

TABLE 5.2 Baseline Solution: Only Cost Constraint Active

	A	B	C	D	E	F	G	H	I	J
	Project	Select	Cost ($1000)	Market Share (Pct.)	Market Size ($Mill.)	Revenue ($Mill.)	Fab. Shop Hours	Computer Hours		
5	1	1	48	11	430	47	60	29		
6	2	1	38	12	340	41	189	48		
7	3	0	40	10	180	18	105	51		
8	4	0	43	13	290	38	174	23		
9	5	1	35	28	1220	342	191	20		
10	6	1	25	28	1340	375	55	51		
11	7	1	26	20	610	122	196	47		
12	8	1	41	15	1010	152	120	34		
13	9	1	53	10	810	81	208	51		
14	10	0	81	12	560	67	59	33		
15	11	0	97	10	710	71	224	28		
16	12	1	51	13	1180	153	82	40		
17	13	1	89	16	460	74	66	52		
18	14	0	78	16	180	29	176	24		
19	15	0	97	23	270	62	109	28		
20	16	1	90	21	430	90	235	50		
22	Total		932	258	10020	1761.5	2249	609		
24	Revenue	1476.7								

Constraints

b5..b20	<=	1			
b5..b20	>=	0			
b5..b20	integer				
Total Cost	496	<=	500		
Fab. Shop hours	1402	<=	1300	(not active)	
Computer hours	422	<=	390	(not active)	

48

TABLE 5.3 Solution with Cost and Fabrication Constraints Active

FABSHOP	A	B	C	D	E	F	G	H	I
1									
2				Market Share	Market Size	Revenue	Fab. Shop Hours	Computer Hours	
3	Project	Select	Cost ($1000)	(Pct.)	($Mill.)	($Mill.)			
4									
5	1	0	48	11	430	47	60	29	
6	2	0	38	12	340	41	189	48	
7	3	0	40	10	180	18	105	51	
8	4	0	43	13	290	38	174	23	
9	5	1	35	28	1220	342	191	20	
10	6	1	25	28	1340	375	55	51	
11	7	1	26	20	610	122	196	47	
12	8	1	41	15	1010	152	120	34	
13	9	1	53	10	810	81	208	51	
14	10	1	81	12	560	67	59	33	
15	11	0	97	10	710	71	224	28	
16	12	1	51	13	1180	153	82	40	
17	13	1	89	16	460	74	66	52	
18	14	0	78	16	180	29	176	24	
19	15	0	97	23	270	62	109	28	
20	16	1	90	21	430	90	235	50	
21									
22		9	932	258	10020	1761.5	2249	609	
23									
24	Total	1455.8		Constraints					
25	Revenue			b5..b20	<=	1	Total Cost	491	<=	500
26				b5..b20	>=	0	Fab. Shop hours	1212	<=	1300
27				b5..b20		integer	Computer hours	378	<=	390
			(not active)							

TABLE 5.4 Solution with Cost and Computer Constraints Active

COMPUTER	A	B	C	D	E	F	G	H	I
1									
2				Market	Market		Fab.		
3				Share	Size	Revenue	Shop	Computer	
4	Project	Select	Cost ($1000)	(Pct.)	($Mill.)	($Mill.)	Hours	Hours	
5	1	1	48	11	430	47	60	29	
6	2	0	38	12	340	41	189	48	
7	3	0	40	10	180	18	105	51	
8	4	1	43	13	290	38	174	23	
9	5	1	35	28	1220	342	191	20	
10	6	1	25	28	1340	375	55	51	
11	7	1	26	20	610	122	196	47	
12	8	1	41	15	1010	152	120	34	
13	9	1	53	10	810	81	208	51	
14	10	1	81	12	560	67	59	33	
15	11	0	97	10	710	71	224	28	
16	12	1	51	13	1180	153	82	40	
17	13	0	89	16	460	74	66	52	
18	14	0	78	16	180	29	176	24	
19	15	0	97	23	270	62	109	28	
20	16	1	90	21	430	90	235	50	
21									
22				258	10020	1761.5	2249	609	
23			932						
24	Total	1467.2		Constraints					
25	Revenue			b5..b20	<=				500
26				b5..b20	>=				1300
27			(not active)	b5..b20	integer				390
28				Total cost	<=	493			
29				Fab. Shop hours	<=	1380			
30				Computer hours	<=	378			

Constraints:
- b5..b20 <= 1
- b5..b20 >= 0
- b5..b20 integer
- Total cost: 493 <= 500
- Fab. Shop hours: 1380 <= 1300
- Computer hours: 378 <= 390

TABLE 5.5   Solution, with All Constraints Active

FAB_COMP	A Project	B Select	C Cost ($1000)	D Market Share (Pct.)	E Market Size ($Mill.)	F Revenue ($Mill.)	G Fab. Shop Hours	H Computer Hours	I
1									
2									
3									
4									
5	1	0	48	11	430	47	60	29	
6	2	0	38	12	340	41	189	48	
7	3	0	40	10	180	18	105	51	
8	4	0	43	13	290	38	174	23	
9	5	1	35	28	1220	342	191	20	
10	6	1	25	28	1340	375	55	51	
11	7	1	26	20	610	122	196	47	
12	8	1	41	15	1010	152	120	34	
13	9	1	53	10	810	81	208	51	
14	10	1	81	12	560	67	59	33	
15	11	0	97	10	710	71	224	28	
16	12	1	51	13	1180	153	82	40	
17	13	1	89	16	460	74	66	52	
18	14	0	78	16	180	29	176	24	
19	15	0	97	23	270	62	109	28	
20	16	1	90	21	430	90	235	50	
21									
22			932	258	10020	1761.5	2249	609	
23									
24	Total	1455.8		Constraints					
25	Revenue			b5..b20	<=	1			500
26				b5..b20	>=	0			1300
27				b5..b20	integer				390
28				Total cost	491	<=			500
29				Fab. Shop hours	1212	<=			1300
30				Computer hours	378	<=			390

51

puter hours required are actually the same as when the cost constraint and fabrication shop constraints are active, but a different set of projects is selected.

Table 5.5 shows the solution when all three constraints are active. Total revenue is reduced to $1455.8 million, although supercomputer hours are the same as when only cost and fabrication shop constraints are active. The same projects are selected as when cost and fabrication shop constraints only are active. Hence, it appears that the fabrication shop constraint is much more binding than the supercomputer constraint.

One conclusion that might be drawn from this example is that it would be worthwhile to increase the capacity of the fabrication shop, since a modest increase in capacity might allow greatly increased revenue (this issue will be taken up at greater length later in the section on sensitivity testing).

The example above utilized linear (actually integer) programming, which is suitable for most situations. However, if there are interactions among the projects such that the payoff of a set is not equal to the sum of the individual payoffs, then nonlinear programming would be required. Schmidt [1993] provides a model for dealing with these problems. However, it is too complex for consideration here.

As another possibility, if there are multiple objectives (e.g., revenue or market share), and a target value for each objective can be specified, then goal programming can be used. This may be linear or nonlinear. Whether linear or nonlinear, the constraint set is expanded to include constraints limiting the maximum deviation from each target value.

5.3 SENSITIVITY ANALYSIS

Any portfolio optimization scheme depends on the values supplied for payoffs, costs, probabilities, and so on. Changes in these will clearly change the optimum portfolio. Sensitivity analysis involves changing one or more of the values and rerunning the procedure for selecting the optimum portfolio. Sensitivity analysis has two purposes.

The first purpose is to determine how robust the optimum is. If minor changes in a few values alter the optimum portfolio significantly, then the solution is highly sensitive to these values. Conversely, if modest changes in the values do not change the portfolio significantly, then the portfolio is robust, and will not be made "wrong" by the inevitable errors contained in the estimates of the values.

The second purpose is to determine whether minor changes in one or more of the variables would make significant differences in the payoff. In the case of R & D projects, increases in the resources applied will usually result in greater payoff. However, the additional payoff may be small compared to the additional resources, or may be small compared to the payoff from using those resources in some other application. Hence, sensitivity analysis can, in effect, determine the "cost" of not increasing the resources applied to the available projects.

To illustrate this, the example worked in Section 5.2 will be subjected to sensitivity analysis. This will be accomplished by recomputing the optimum payoff for various values of R & D budget, available fabrication shop hours, and available supercomputer hours.

A key to carrying out this analysis is that recomputing the optimum after changing one or more constraints can be done simply and quickly. If recomputing the optimum were difficult or time consuming, conducting a sensitivity analysis would be out of the question. However, since a spreadsheet program can carry out the computation of the optimum combination within a few minutes at most, sensitivity analysis is quite feasible.

Table 5.6 shows the results of a sensitivity analysis on the set of projects used as an example in Section 5.2. The budget is increased from $500K to $700K in increments of $50K. For each budget level, fabrication shop hours are allowed to range from 1300 to 1450, and supercomputer hours from 390 to 440.

At the $500K level, we already know that the fabrication shop and computer constraints are just barely satisfied, and the major limitation is the budget. This is shown in the table for the $500K budget level. Increasing the other two resources available does not lead to any increase in payoff.

Increasing the budget to $550K immediately leads to an increase in payoff without any increase in the other two resources. Allowing increases in those resources results in increased payoff. At this budget level, the fabrication shop is the limiting constraint, since increases in supercomputer hours have no effect on payoff. This confirms what we already found in working the example at the $500K level.

Increasing the budget to $600K results, as expected, in greater payoff. However, at this level, the supercomputer starts to be the limiting constraint. Increases in available fabrication shop hours have no effect on payoff beyond 1325, unless available supercomputer hours are also increased.

Increasing the budget to $650K leads to further increases in payoff, and again we see that while the fabrication shop is the constraint that binds first, the supercomputer quickly becomes the binding constraint. There is no payoff increase unless available supercomputer hours are also increased.

Increasing the budget to $700K leads to no improvement at all. The fabrication shop and especially the supercomputer are the limiting constraints. Moreover, note that the spreadsheet "runs out of steam" and cannot complete the computations within its built-in limits for certain combinations of the variables.

This sensitivity analysis leads to the conclusion that a modest increase in fabrication shop hours would allow an increased payoff if additional funds were available to carry out projects. However, once that increase is made, the supercomputer becomes the limiting factor, and an increase in that resource will be necessary if additional projects are to be conducted. Moreover, the

TABLE 5.6   Sensitivity Analyses

Maximum cost = $500K

Fab Shop	Computer 390	400	410	420	430	440
1300	1455.8	1455.8				
1325	1455.8	1455.8				
1350						
1375						
1400						
1425						
1450						

Maximum cost = $550K

Fab Shop	Computer 390	400	410	420	430	440
1300	1483.8	1483.8				
1325	1491.6	1491.6				
1350	1491.6	1491.6				
1375						
1400						
1425						
1450						

Maximum cost = $600K

Fab Shop	Computer 390	400	410	420	430	440
1300	1493.1	1493.1	1503.1	1503.1	1503.1	1503.1
1325	1498.6	1498.6	1517.9	1517.9	1517.9	1517.9
1350	1498.6	1498.6	1517.9	1517.9	1517.9	1517.9
1375	1498.6	1498.6	1517.9			
1400	1498.6	1498.6	1517.9			
1425						
1450						

Maximum cost = $650K

Fab Shop	Computer 390	400	410	420	430	440
1300	1493.1	1493.1	1503.1	1503.1	1503.1	1503.1
1325	1498.6	1498.6	1517.9	1517.9	1517.9	1517.9
1350	1507.9	1507.9	1521.9	1517.9	1517.9	1517.9
1375	1507.9	1507.9	1521.9	1545.9	1545.9	1545.9
1400	1507.9	1507.9	1521.9	1545.9	1545.9	1565.2
1425	1507.9	1507.9	1521.9	1545.9	1545.9	1565.2
1450						

Maximum cost = $700K

Fab Shop	Computer 390	400	410	420	430	440
1300	1493.1	1493.1	1503.1	1503.1	1503.1	1503.1
1325	1498.6	1498.6	1517.9	1517.9	1517.9	1517.9
1350	1507.9	1507.9	1521.9	1521.9	1521.9	1521.9
1375	1507.9	1507.9	1521.9	1545.9	1545.9	1545.9
1400	1507.9	1507.9	1521.9	1555.2	1555.2	1565.2
1425	1507.9	N/A	1521.9	1555.2	1555.2	1565.2
1450	1507.9	N/A	N/A			

N/A = Solution not available within maximum iterations

maximum benefit that can be gained by increasing all three resources is $1565.2K − $1455.8K = $109.4K. To achieve this requires an increase in R & D funding of $150K, as well as investments in the fabrication shop and the supercomputer. One might conclude that these additional investments are not worthwhile, since the increased cost exceeds the increased payoff.

Another conclusion that needs to be drawn is that while a spreadsheet can be used to solve modest-sized problems, a more powerful program may be needed in many cases of practical interest. Thus the analyst or R & D manager should be prepared to utilize more capable programs if a spreadsheet proves inadequate. However, it is probably worthwhile to attempt a solution using a spreadsheet. If it works, nothing further is needed. Even if it fails, the analyst has laid out the problem and is ready to transfer the data to the more capable program.

5.4 SUMMARY

In many cases there are more candidate projects to be considered than can be accommodated within available resources. In such cases it is necessary to evaluate entire portfolios of projects, to determine which subset of the available projects provides the most benefit. If only a single resource is the limiting factor, methods such as those described in Chapter 2 are sufficient to obtain the optimum subset. However, if two or more resources impose constraints, then a programming approach is needed, to achieve an optimum within the constraints.

Integer programming is a suitable approach, and for modest-sized cases, can be carried out using a spreadsheet. For larger problems, a specialized computer program will be needed, but the layout of the problem remains the same as when using a spreadsheet. Regardless of the size of the problem, however, this approach provides a solution that maximizes the payoff without violating any of the constraints.

5.5 QUESTIONS FOR CLASS DISCUSSION

1. By using Menu 2 of Appendix 2, compute the optimal payoff for the projects subject to the constraint that funding available is $500 million, there are 1300 fabrication shop hours available, and there are 390 h available on the supercomputer. Carry out a sensitivity analysis to determine the effects of relaxing each of the three constraints.

2. By using Menu 2 of Appendix 2, compute the optimal payoff for the projects subject to the same constraint as in Question **1** and the additional constraints that the selected portfolio must include at least one basic research project and at least one commercial development project.

5.6 FURTHER READINGS

Aaker, D. A. and T. T. Tyerbjee (1978). A Model for the Selection of Interdependent R & D Projects. *IEEE Transactions on Engineering Management*. **25**, May, 30–36.

Cjaikowski, A. F. and S. Jones (1986). Selecting Interrelated R & D Projects in Space Technology Planning. *IEEE Transactions on Engineering Management*. **33**(1), February, 17–24.

Cochran, M. A., E. B. Pyle III, L. C. Greene, H. A. Clymer, and A. D. Bender (1971). Investment Model for R & D Project Evaluation and Selection. *IEEE Transactions on Engineering Management*. **18**(3), August, 89–100.

Fox, E. G. and N. R. Baker (1985). Project Selection Decision Making Linked to a Dynamic Environment. *Management Science*, **31**(10), October, 1272–1285.

Gear, A. E. (1974). Review of Some Recent Developments in Portfolio Modeling in Applied Research and Development. *IEEE Transactions on Engineering Management*. **21**(4), November, 119–125.

Khorramshagol, R., H. Azani, and Y. Gousty (1988). An Integrated Approach to Project Evaluation and Selection. *IEEE Transactions on Engineering Management*. **35**(4), November, 265–270.

Khorramshahgol, R. and Y. Gousty (1986). Delphic Goal Programming (DGP): A Multi-Objective Cost/Benefit Approach to R & D Portfolio Analysis. *IEEE Transactions on Engineering Management*. **33**(3), August, 172–175.

Lootsma, F. A., T. C. A. Mensch, and F. A. Vos (1990). Multi-criteria analysis and budget reallocation in long-term research planning. *European Journal of Operational Research*. **47**, 293–305.

Madey, G. R. and B. V. Dean (1985). Strategic Planning for Investment in R & D Using Decision Analysis and Mathematical Programming. *IEEE Transactions on Engineering Management*. **32**(2), May, 84–90.

Mehrez, A., S. Mossery, and Z. Sinuany-Stern (1982). Project Selection in a Small University R & D Laboratory. *R & D Management*. **12**(4), 169–174.

Morris, P. A., E. O. Teisberg, and A. L. Kolbe (1991). When Choosing R & D Projects, Go With Long Shots. *Research-Technology Management*. **34**(1), January–February, 35–40.

Ringuest, J. L. and S. B. Graves (1990). The Linear R & D Project Selection Problem: an Alternative to Net Present Value. *IEEE Transactions on Engineering Management*. **37**(2), May, 243–246.

Schmidt, R. L. (1993). A Model for R & D Project Selection with Combined Benefit, Outcome and Resource Interactions. *IEEE Transactions on Engineering Management*. **40**(4), November, 403–410.

Taylor, B. W., L. J. Moore, and E. R. Clayton (1982). R & D Project Selection and Manpower Allocation with Integer Nonlinear Goal Programming. *Management Science*. **28**(10), October, 1149–1158.

Vepsalainen, A. P. J. and G. L. Lauro (1988). Analysis of R & D Portfolio Strategies for Contract Competition. *IEEE Transactions on Engineering Management*. **35**(3), August, 181–186.

_____6
SIMULATION

Simulation is used when projects in a portfolio have alternative outcomes to which probabilities can be attached (e.g., success, partial success, or failure), when the projects have alternative paths to the end goal depending on the chance outcome, and when the projects have different payoffs for the different outcomes. The projects are simulated by drawing random numbers to determine outcomes and payoffs. This is done a sufficiently large number of times to assure statistically valid results. The result is an estimate of the probability of different outcomes.

Simulation can be applied to both single-stage projects of the type considered in Chapter 2 and multistage projects of the type considered in Chapter 4.

6.1 SINGLE-STAGE PROJECTS

To illustrate the simulation of single-stage projects, consider the projects of Menu 1 in Appendix 2. For each project, there is a potential revenue (product of market size and market share). However, to realize this revenue, the project must be both a technical and a market success. We can compute the expected revenue from each project as the product of market size, market share, probability of technical success, and probability of market success. The expected revenue from the entire portfolio is the sum of these individual values. When we carry out the computations, we find that the expected or mean value of revenue from the 16 projects is $413.5 million.

However, this computation tells us nothing about the spread of values about the mean. Simulation is intended to provide information about the spread of values.

Table 6.1 presents the listing of a BASIC program to carry out the simulation implicit in Menu 1. A program similar to this could be used for simulating the outcome of any list of projects. The listing is explained below, to aid in revising it for other cases.

Line 10, which defines the value of the number of iterations and the number of projects, allows these to be changed readily without the need to change the values at several points in the program.

Lines 200–280 read in potential revenue, probability of technical success, and probability of market success into the appropriate arrays. Lines 300–320 compute the total probability of success of each project as the product of technical and market success probabilities (these are assumed to be independent).

Line 400 starts the simulations, to be iterated a specified number of times. First, an array of random numbers is generated in lines 410–430. Next, the random numbers are compared with the total probabilities of the projects in lines 440–460, to determine whether the projects "succeed." Actual revenue is computed in lines 470–490, where the array of 1s and 0s representing success or failure is multiplied by the array of potential revenues. The actual revenues are summed in the appropriate cell of the array containing total revenues, and the process is repeated. Lines 600–630 print the results to a file. This raw data can then be subjected to further analysis. To carry out such analyses, it is useful to import the data file into a spreadsheet. The format in which the file is printed, namely, one data item per line, with the line terminated by a carriage return, makes it convenient to import the data into a spreadsheet.

One type of analysis to which the data can be subjected is a histogram. A histogram of the results of one set of 500 simulations is shown in Figure 6.1. To generate this histogram, the entire portfolio of projects was simulated 500 times, and the resulting actual revenues accumulated. As can be seen, the most common outcome is revenues of about $350 million. However, there were over 20 simulations in which the total revenues were less than $100 million, and a few cases in which the total revenues were over $1000 million. The mean revenue for these 500 simulations was $434.6 million, which should be compared with the computed mean of $413.5 million. The standard deviation of the simulated revenues was $199.7 million. These results are not likely to change much with additional simulations, although it would be expected that the mean of the simulations would converge to the computed mean.

This example of simulation involved only single-stage projects. Each project was initiated and then either succeeded or failed. However, simulation can also be used to evaluate portfolios in which there may be several stages to each project. The end result of this analysis is an estimate of the

TABLE 6.1   Listing of Project Simulation Program

```
10  NUMITERAT% = 500;NUMPROJ% = 16
20  OUTFILE$ = "EPROJSIM.DAT"
100  Dim POTREVENUE(16),PTECH(16),PMARKET(16),PT OTAL(16),
     PRANDOM(16),SELECT(16),ACTREVENUE(16),REVSUMS(NUMITERA T%)
200  For I% = 1 to NUMPROJ%
210  Read POTREVENUE(I%)
220  Next I%
230  For I% = 1 to NUMPROJ%
240  Read PTECH(I%)
250  Next I%
260  For I% = 1 to NUMPROJ%
270  Read PMARKET(I%)
280  Next
300  For I% = 1 to NUMPROJ%
310  PTOTAL(I%) = PTECH(I%)* PMARKET(I%)
320  Next I%
400  For I% = 1 to NUMITERAT%
410  For J% = 1 to NUMPROJ%
420  PRANDOM(J%) = rnd(0)
430  Next J%
440  For J% = 1 to NUMPROJ%
450  If PRANDOM(J%) < PTOTAL(J%) then SELECT(J%) = 1
     else SELECT(J%) = 0
460  Next J%
470  For J% = 1 to NUMPROJ%
480  ACTREVENUE(J%) = SELECT(J%)* PO TREVENUE(J%)
490  Next J%
500  For J% = 1 to NUMPROJ%
510  REVSUMS(I%) = REVSUMS(I%) + ACTREVENUE(J%)
520  Next J%
590  Next I%
600  Openc output #3, OUTFILE$
610  For I% = 1 to NUMITERAT%
620  Print #3,REVSUMS(I%)
630  Next I%
999  End
10100  Data 47,41,18,38,342,375,122,152,81,67,71,153,74,29,62,90
10110  Rem THIS IS REVENUE IN $MILLIONS
10200  Data .32,.36,.79,.60,.48,.27,.79,.93,.40,.31,.96,.63,
       .43,.45,.62,.57
10210  Rem THIS IS PROBABILITY OF TECHNICAL SUCCESS
10300  Data .42,.30,.72,.62,.21,.42,.50,.78,.71,.61,.30,
       .36,.78,.77,.49,.41
10310  Rem THIS IS PROBABILITY OF MARKET SUCCESS
```

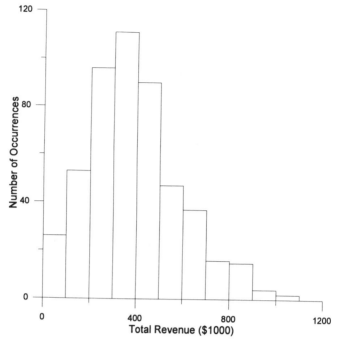

Figure 6.1. Distribution of simulation results.

probability of different outcomes for the entire portfolio. This issue will be taken up in Section 6.2, on multi-stage projects.

6.2 MULTI-STAGE PROJECTS

This technique is used for R & D projects in which multi-stage decisions will be required. For each possible project, a "project tree" is prepared. The project is divided into periods or phases, which need not be of the same length. At the end of each period, a chance outcome occurs, followed by a decision. Within each period, the project may be pursued at any of several resource levels, where multiple resources may be included (i.e., a vector of resources, such as personnel, funding, or specialized test equipment). Each such alternative level of effort is treated as a distinct alternative choice for a decision node. The project tree is extended to the desired time horizon, and the value of each path through the tree evaluated at the time horizon. Alternate branches in the tree may reflect uncertainty about resource levels needed or time to complete a particular phase.

Each project tree may be folded back as was shown in Chapter 4. Folding back the tree may eliminate some branches as being inferior to alternative branches. That is, the value at the end of the path is smaller than the value at the end of other paths that could be chosen instead. The reduced tree is then taken as a representation of the possible courses of the project.

TABLE 6.2   Set of Projects with Dependencies

Project	Phase 1	Phase 2	Phase 3	Payoff
P1	p = 0.8	p = 0.85	p = 0.9	p($500K) = 0.6 p($1000K) = 0.3 p($1500K) = 0.1
P2	p = 0.6	p = 0.5	p = 0.6	p($1000K) = 0.2 p($1500K) = 0.5 p($2000K) = 0.3
P3	p = 0.9	P2Phase1 Good: p = 0.8 Bad: p = 0.2	p = 0.7	p($700K) = 0.5 p($1100K) = 0.3 p($1800K) = 0.1
P4	p = 0.5	p = 0.6	P1Phase2 Good: p = 0.7 Bad: p = 0.2	p($500K) = 0.3 p($1000K) = 0.4 p($1500K) = 0.3
P5	p = 0.9	p = 0.8	P2Phase2 Good: p = 0.9 Bad: p = 0.1	p($500K) = 0.4 p($750K) = 0.5 p($1000K) = 0.1
P6	p = 0.5	p = 0.6	P5Phase2 Good p = 0.8 Bad p = 0.1	p($1000K) = 0.5 p($1500K) = 0.3 p($2000K) = 0.2
P7	p = 0.9	P8Phase1 Good: p = 0.7 Bad: p = 0.1	p = 0.8	p($750K) = 0.4 p($1000K) = 0.3 p($1250K) = 0.3
P8	p = 0.9	P5Phase1 Good: p = 0.9 Bad: p = 0.2	P6Phase2 Good: p = 0.8 Bad: p = 0.1	p($1000K) = 0.6 p($1250K) = 0.3 p($1500K) = 0.1

Each tree could be evaluated individually, as was shown in Chapter 4. However, if there are many trees, simulation may be a more appropriate approach, since it provides information about the range and relative frequency of occurrence of various possible outcomes. Simulation is even more appropriate if there are dependencies among projects, such that results in one affect probabilities of various results in another. This use of simulation will be illustrated with an example.

Table 6.2 shows a set of eight projects. Each project consists of three phases. Each phase has a probability of success associated with it. If all three phases of a given project are successful, there are three possible payoffs, each with its own probability. The range of payoffs can be taken as due to market conditions or external factors, independent of the technical success of the project. Note that the probabilities of payoffs for a given project must sum to 1.0.

Some of the projects are dependent on others, in the sense that if one phase of one project is unsuccessful, this lowers the probability of success of some phase of another project. This can be thought of as involving similar experiments or techniques. The probability associated with a dependent phase of a project is determined by the outcome of an earlier phase of another project, upon which it depends. For instance, Phase 2 of Project P3 depends on Phase 1 of Project P2. If that phase is successful, the probability of Phase 2 of Project P3 is 0.8; if unsuccessful, the probability of Phase 2 of Project P3 drops to 0.2 (note there is no requirement that these probabilities sum to 1.0, although they happen to do so in this case; they are alternatives rather than complements). Note that it is not necessary to construct the list such that projects are dependent only on those earlier in the list. Phase 2 of Project P7 is dependent on Phase 1 of Project P8, which comes after it in the list.

To simulate the outcome of this set of projects, it is necessary to draw random numbers to test each phase. If the random number is strictly less than the probability associated with the phase (including 0), the phase is successful. If the random number is equal to or greater than the probability of success, the phase fails, and the project is abandoned. If all three phases are successful, another random number is drawn to determine which of the payoffs is actually achieved. Note that if some projects have fewer phases than others, they can be "padded" at the end with dummy phases that have probability 1.0 of succeeding. By this means all projects can be made to have the same number of phases.

Table 6.3 is a listing of a BASIC program to carry out a simulation of the set of dependent projects. The data for the program is contained in lines after 1000. Lines 10,000–10,076 provide the payoff data and associated probabilities for each project. Lines 10,100–10,124 provide the probability of success for each phase of each project, *assuming that all previous phases of all other projects are successful.* Lines 10,200–10,224 provide the probability of success when certain phases of other projects are not successful. The data are entered as the number of the affecting project, phase of that project, number of the project affected, the phase affected, and the new (reduced) probability for the affected phase.

The simulation will be iterated 500 times (set by line 10). In lines 3000–3050, an array is filled with the probabilities of success for each phase of each project. The elements of this array may be changed as the simulation proceeds, hence they must be reset to their original values at the beginning of each simulation.*

---

*In effect this simulation is a simplified cross-impact model. However, it differs from the usual cross-impact model in that the outcome of each simulation run is stored separately for later analysis.

TABLE 6.3   Listing of Programs to Simulate Dependent Projects

```
  10 NUMITERAT% = 500
  12 NUMPROJ% = 8
  14 NUMPHASES% = 3
  16 MAXINTERACTS% = 20
 100 Dim TOTAL _PAYOFF(NUMITERAT%)
 102 Dim ONE _SIM_PAYOFF(NUMPROJ%)
 104 Dim PROJ_PAYOFF(NUMPROJ%,NUMPHASES%)
 106 Dim PROJ_PAYOFF_PROB(NUMPROJ%,NUMPHASES%)
 108 Dim PROJ_PHASE_OUTCOME(NUMPROJ%,NUMPHASES%)
 110 Dim PROJ_PHASE_PROB_REF(NUMPROJ%,NUMPHASES%)
 112 Dim PROJ_PHASE_PROB(NUMPROJ%,NUMPHASES%)
 114 Dim INTERACT(MAXINTERACTS%,6)
 200 OUTFILE$ ="PAYOFFS.DAT"
1000 For I% = 1 to NUMPROJ%
1010 For J% = 1 to NUMPHASES%
1020 Read PROJ_PAYOFF(I%,J%)
1030 Read PROJ_PAYOFF_PROB(I%,J%)
1040 Next J%
1050 Next I%
1060 For PROJECT% = 1 to NUMPROJ%
1070 For PHASE% = 1 to NUMPHASES%
1080 Read PROJ_PHASE_PROB_REF(PROJECT%,PHASE%)
1090 Next PHASE%
1100 Next PROJECT%
1110 NUMINTERACTS% = 1
1120 NEXT_INTERACT:
1130 Read FIRSTNUM
1140 If FIRSTNUM = 1 then Goto STARTSIM
1150 INTERACT(NUMINTERACTS%,1) = FIRSTNUM
1160 For J% = 2 to 5
1170 Read INTERACT(NUMINTERACTS%,J%)
1180 Next J%
1190 NUMINTERACTS% = NUMINTERACTS% + 1
1200 Goto NEXT_INTERACT

2000 Rem SIMULATION LOOP BEGINS HERE
2010 STARTSIM: For ITERATION% = 1 to NUMITERAT%

3000 Rem RESTORE PROJECT PHASE PROBABILITIES TO ORIGINAL
     VALUES
3010 For I% = 1 to NUMPROJ%
3020 For J% = 1 to NUMPHASES%
3030 PROJ_PHASE_PROB(I%,J%) = PROJ_PHASE_PROB_REF(I%,J%)
3040 Next J%
3050 Next I%

8000 Rem THIS SECTION DETERMINES SUCCESS OR FAILURE FOR
     PROJECT PHASES
8010 For PHASE% = 1 to NUMPHASES%
8020 For PROJECT% = 1 to NUMPROJ%
```

TABLE   6.3 (Continued)

```
8030  If PHASE% > 1 and PROJ_PHASE_OUTCOME(PROJECT%,PHASE%1) = 0 then
      [PROJ_PHASE_OUTCOME(PROJECT%,PHASE%) = 0;Goto UPDATE]
8040  TEST_NUM = rnd(0)
8050  If TEST_NUM < PROJ_PHASE_PROB(PROJECT%,PHASE%) then
      [PROJ_PHASE_OUTCOME(PROJECT%,PHASE%) = 1;Goto ENDLOOP1]
8060  UPDATE:
8070  For I% = 1 to NUMINTERACTS%
8080  If INTERACT(I%,1) = PROJECT% and INTERACT(I%,2) = PHASE% then
      PROJ_PHASE_PROB(INTERACT(I%,3)
      INTERACT(I%,4)) = INTERACT(I%,5)
8090  Next I%
8100  ENDLOOP1:Next PROJECT%
8110  Next PHASE%

9050  Rem THIS SECTION COMPUTES THE PAYOFFS
9060  For PROJECT% = 1 to NUMPROJ%
9070  If PROJ_PHASE_OUTCOME(PROJECT%,NUMPHASES%) = 0 then
      [ONE_SIM_PAYOFF(PROJECT%) = 0;Goto ENDLOOP2]
9080  TEST_NUM = rnd(0)
9090  If TEST_NUM < PROJ_PAYOFF_PROB(PROJECT%,1) then
      ONE_SIM_PAYOFF(PROJECT%) = PROJ_PAYOFF(PROJECT%,1)
9100  Else if TEST_NUM < PROJ_PAYOFF_PROB(PROJECT%,1)
      +PROJ_PAYOFF_PROB(PROJECT%,2)
      then ONE_SIM_PAYOFF(PROJECT%) = PROJ_PAYOFF(PROJECT%,2)
9110  Else ONE_SIM_PAYOFF(PROJECT%) = PROJ_PAYOFF(PROJECT%,3)
9120  ENDLOOP2:Next PROJECT%
9130  TOTAL = 0
9140  For PROJECT% = 1 to NUMPROJ%
9150  TOTAL = TOTAL + ONE_SIM_PAYOFF(PROJECT%)
9160  Next PROJECT%
9170  TOTAL_PAYOFF(ITERATION%) = TOTAL
9180  Next ITERATION%

9200  Rem THIS SECTION PRINTS PAYOFFS TO A FILE
9210  Openc output #3, OUTFILE$
9220  For ITERATION% = 1 to NUMITERAT%
9230  Print #3, TOTAL_PAYOFF(ITERATION%)
9240  Next ITERATION%
9250  Close #3
9999  End

10000  Rem PROJECT PAYOFFS AND PROBABILITIES
10002  Rem PROJECT P1
10004  Data 500,.6
10006  Data 1000,.3
10008  Data 1500,.1
10010  Rem PROJECT P2
10012  Data 1000,.2
10014  Data 1500,.5
10016  Data 2000,.3
```

TABLE   6.3 (Continued)

```
10020  Rem PROJECT P3
10022  Data 700,.5
10024  Data 1100,.3
10026  Data 1800,.1

10030  Rem PROJECT P4
10032  Data 500,.3
10034  Data 1000,.4
10036  Data 1500,.3

10040  Rem PROJECT P5
10042  Data 500,.4
10044  Data 750,.5
10046  Data 1000,.1

10050  Rem PROJECT P6
10052  Data 1000,.5
10054  Data 1500,.3
10056  Data 2000,.2

10060  Rem PROJECT P7
10062  Data 750,.4
10064  Data 1000,.3
10066  Data 1250,.3

10070  Rem PROJECT P8
10072  Data 1000,.6
10074  Data 1250,.3
10076  Data 1500,.1

10100  Rem PROBABILITIES IF INTERACTING PROJECTS SUCCESSFUL
10102  Rem BY PROJECT, BY PHASE
10110  Data .8,.85,.9
10112  Data .6,.5,.6
10114  Data .9,.8,.7
10116  Data .5,.6,.7
10118  Data .9,.8,.9
10120  Data .5,.6,.8
10122  Data .9,.7,.8
10124  Data .9,.9,.8

10200  Rem INTERACTIONS BETWEEN PROJECTS
10202  Rem AFFECTING PROJECT, PHASE, AFFECTED PROJECT, PHASE
       NEW PROBABILITY IF FAILURE
10210  Data 2,1,3,2,.2
10212  Data 1,2,4,3,.2
10214  Data 2,2,5,3,.1
10216  Data 5,2,6,3,.1
10218  Data 8,1,7,2,.1
10220  Data 5,1,8,2,.2
10222  Data 6,2,8,3,.1
10224  Data 1
```

Lines 8000–8110 represent the actual simulation. Note that the simulation loops through phases as the outer loop, then through projects as the inner loop. This is done for a reason. By doing the computations in this order, the outcomes of those phases affecting other projects are determined before the affected phases are tested, allowing the revised probabilities to be used. If the simulation looped through projects as the outer loop, it would be necessary to construct the list of projects so that any project could be affected only by projects that are prior to it in the list, and whose phases are therefore tested before the affected project is tested. Note that in line 8030, if an earlier phase of a project has been unsuccessful, it is assumed that the project is terminated. All later phases will be treated as having unsuccessful outcomes. Comparison with random numbers takes place in lines 8040 and 8050. Lines 8060–8100 update the probabilities in those cases where affecting phases have been unsuccessful.

Lines 9050–9170 compute the total payoff from those projects that successfully completed all three phases. Random numbers are drawn to determine which of the payoffs is realized.

Following all iterations of the simulation, lines 9200–9250 print the results of the simulations to a file. This raw data can then be subjected to further analysis, such as by importing into a spreadsheet.

Figure 6.2 is a histogram showing the results of 500 simulations of the set of projects in Table 6.2. The most frequent payoffs cluster around $8000K. However, there are a few above $10,000K, and one less than $1000K. Hence, the range of possible payoffs is quite large, even though almost all will fall between $6000K and $10,000K.

In this example we did not examine costs or other resource demands of the projects. However, the procedure could readily be modified to incorporate such factors. If each phase has a definite cost, which will be incurred if that phase is actually carried out, the simulation program can be modified to accumulate actual costs, thus providing (for instance) a histogram of the actual costs, which would be incurred by initiating all projects and terminating only those that involve a failed phase. If alternative costs of phases had probabilities associated with them, the simulation could deal with these just as the example above dealt with alternative payoffs.

If each phase involved multiple resources (e.g., cost, fabrication shop, and supercomputer, as in the examples of Chapter 5), the resource demands could be accumulated separately by the program. The results could be displayed as histograms of demands on each resource. In addition, the simulation results would provide estimates of the likelihood that the set of projects would exceed the available resources. For instance, if in 500 simulation runs there were 10 runs in which the total supercomputer hours demanded exceeded those available in a particular time period, the analyst could estimate that the likelihood of violating the supercomputer constraint would be about 2%.

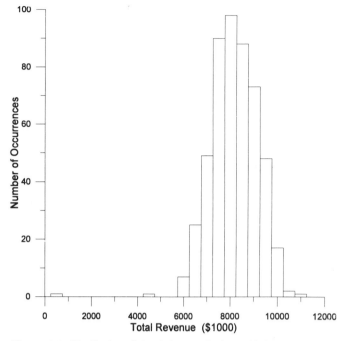

Figure 6.2. Distribution of simulation results for multiphase projects.

One thing a simulation of a set of multistage projects *cannot* readily do is permit interaction with the analyst. If decisions are to be made at the end of certain phases, they must be programmed into the simulation on the basis of results already obtained (e.g., terminate a project if a phase results in failure or always choose a specific alternative level of funding at a particular choice node in a tree). The reason for this is, of course, the vast number of interactions that would have to be made if they were permitted. Simulation of R & D projects in this fashion is intended to determine the range and frequency of outcomes given known probabilities at chance nodes and specified decision rules at choice nodes.

6.3 SUMMARY

Carrying out a simulation, especially for a large number of projects, provides a convenient way to estimate the range of possible outcomes, and the likelihood of specific outcomes. Simulation is an especially powerful tool for analyzing sets of projects that involve dependencies among the projects, since they are difficult to handle analytically. Simulation not only provides an estimate of the most likely outcome, but also provides information about the spread of possible outcomes.

6.4 QUESTIONS FOR CLASS DISCUSSION

1. Conduct a simulation of the projects in Menu 2 of Appendix 2. Carry out 500 simulations, and prepare a histogram of the results.

6.5 FURTHER READINGS

Lockett, A. G. and A. E. Gear (1973). Representation and Analysis of Multi-Stage Problems in R & D. *Management Science*. **19**(8), April, 947–960.

Mandakovic, T. and W. E. Souder (1985). An Interactive Decomposable Heuristic for Project Selection. *Management Science*. **31**(10), October, 1257–1271.

____7
COGNITIVE MODELING

In earlier chapters we examined methods by which analysts and decision makers can decompose global decisions into components that can be judged or analyzed separately. The analyses and judgments are then combined into a global evaluation of a project. Scoring models and the analytic hierarchy procedure (AHP) are particular examples of this approach to project selection.

In this chapter we present a method for reversing the process. We will examine a method for analyzing global decisions to determine the components that went into them. Cognitive modeling (also known as "policy capturing") attempts to understand, capture, or model the actual decision processes used by project managers. As a research tool, it is intended to lead to understanding of how decisions are made. As a project selection tool, it is intended to mimic the decisions that would be made by specific project managers.

In this latter application, it is intended to be used where large numbers of decisions would be made, in order to relieve the project managers of the task of making them. Clearly, in this application the use of cognitive modeling is of value only if it closely mimics the decisions that the project manager would have made. To the extent that it does capture the decision processes of project managers responsible for decisions about projects, it allows the expertise and knowledge of those managers to be applied without problems of fatigue or inconsistency.

We will consider two applications of policy capturing: the replication of decisions and the evaluation of decisions.

7.1 REPLICATION

Table 7.1 presents a list of projects from Project Menu 1 of Appendix 2. Assume that the president of the company has established a policy that selection of R & D projects must consider project cost, market share of the resulting product, probability of technical success, and the extent to which the project will improve the company's manufacturing processes (a judgmental rating on a 1–10 scale).

The director of R & D has selected for funding those projects indicated by a 1 in the final column. Those with a 0 were not selected for funding. For the moment, we assume that the director of R & D has properly interpreted the company president's policy. Now suppose there is a large list of candidate projects, some of which are to be selected for funding. We wish to replicate the R & D director's decision processes on this more extensive set of projects. The question then becomes, how did the R & D director weight the different factors that went into the decision? Put another way, what scoring model did he/she use?

Cognitive modeling proceeds by carrying out a linear regression analysis of the sample set of decisions. Currently available spreadsheets usually include the capability to perform linear regressions, and hence provide a ready means of conducting the cognitive modeling.

TABLE 7.1   Projects Selected by R & D Director

Project	Cost ($1000)	Market Share (Pct.)	Prob. Tech. Success (Pct.)	Mfg. Improv. Rating	Projects Selected
1	48	11	32	3	0
2	38	12	36	10	1
3	40	10	79	3	0
4	43	13	60	9	1
5	35	28	48	4	1
6	25	28	27	9	1
7	26	20	79	2	1
8	41	15	93	10	1
9	53	10	40	3	0
10	81	12	31	7	0
11	97	10	96	3	0
12	51	13	63	9	1
13	89	16	43	1	0
14	78	16	45	7	0
15	97	23	62	5	0
16	90	21	57	6	0

Table 7.2, rows 1–31, shows a spreadsheet that performs a linear regression on the data of Table 7.1 (the rows below 31 will be discussed in Section 7.2). Column F is the selections of the R & D director: 1 for a selected project, 0 for a nonselected project. Columns B–E are the data for each project. Column F is treated as the *dependent* variable, to be explained by the *independent* variables in Columns B–E. The spreadsheet computes the coefficients by which Columns B–E must be multiplied to obtain the values in Column F.

The regression results are shown in rows 24–31. The constant of the regression equation is in D24. The coefficients of Columns B, C, D, and E are, respectively, in C30, D30, E30, and F30. As might reasonably be expected, the coefficient of project cost is negative, indicating that the R & D director tended to prefer low-cost projects. The remainder of the coefficients are positive, indicating that high-market share, high probability of technical success, and high contribution to manufacturing improvement all contribute to project selection.

As indicated in cell D26, the regression explains nearly 81% of the variance in the director's decisions (the R value in F26 was added manually; it is not part of the standard regression output).

Column G shows the *computed* results, obtained by multiplying the coefficients by the appropriate project values, and adding the regression constant from cell D24. The block in double lines shows the formulas in Column G. The formula in G5 was entered manually, then copied to the rest of the column. Note that the constant term is included as $D$24, and the coefficients are indicated by a column label and $30. These absolute references are needed so that when the formula is copied, the constant and the coefficient references are not incremented by the spreadsheet in the same way the project row references are incremented in Column G.

As would be expected, the regression does not give exactly 0 or 1 for the "decision." However, all those projects selected by the R & D director had a computed regression value greater than 0.5. All those not selected by the R & D director had computed regression values less than 0.5. Thus the constant and coefficients from the regression could be used as a scoring model. If the resulting score was greater than 0.5, the project should be selected. If less, the project should not be selected. Such a rule would replicate very closely the decisions the R & D director would have made had they made the decisions themselves. Moreover, use of the scoring model would eliminate problems of fatigue or inconsistency on the part of the R & D director. In a sense, the scoring model would do a better job of "representing" them than they could themselves.

It might be asked, is this simple linear regression adequate to capture the thinking of an individual? Is it not possible that the mental model the R & D director uses to make decisions is nonlinear? Experience with cognitive modeling has shown that simple linear regression seems to do an adequate job of capturing the thinking of the person or group being modeled, so long

TABLE 7.2 Regression Analysis of R & D Director's Decisions

example1	A	B	C	D	E	F	G	H
1								
2			Market	Prob. Tech.	Mfg. Improv.	Xmpl1		
3	Project	Cost	Share	Success	Rating	Selected		
4		($1000)	(Pct.)	(Pct.)				
5	1	48	11	32	3	0	0.1359	+$D$24+C5*D$30+D5*E$30+E5*F$30+F5*G$30
6	2	38	12	36	10	1	0.7800	+$D$24+C6*D$30+D6*E$30+E6*F$30+F6*G$30
7	3	40	10	79	3	0	0.4681	+$D$24+C7*D$30+D7*E$30+E7*F$30+F7*G$30
8	4	43	13	60	9	1	0.8038	+$D$24+C8*D$30+D8*E$30+E8*F$30+F8*G$30
9	5	35	28	48	4	1	0.8361	+$D$24+C9*D$30+D9*E$30+E9*F$30+F9*G$30
10	6	25	28	27	9	1	1.1853	+$D$24+C10*D$30+D10*E$30+E10*F$30+F10*G$30
11	7	26	20	79	2	1	0.7989	+$D$24+C11*D$30+D11*E$30+E11*F$30+F11*G$30
12	8	41	15	93	10	1	1.1216	+$D$24+C12*D$30+D12*E$30+E12*F$30+F12*G$30
13	9	53	10	40	3	0	0.0952	+$D$24+C13*D$30+D13*E$30+E13*F$30+F13*G$30
14	10	81	12	31	7	0	0.0184	+$D$24+C14*D$30+D14*E$30+E14*F$30+F14*G$30
15	11	97	10	96	3	0	-0.1420	+$D$24+C15*D$30+D15*E$30+E15*F$30+F15*G$30
16	12	51	13	63	9	1	0.7215	+$D$24+C16*D$30+D16*E$30+E16*F$30+F16*G$30
17	13	89	16	43	1	0	-0.3327	+$D$24+C17*D$30+D17*E$30+E17*F$30+F17*G$30
18	14	78	16	45	7	0	0.2222	+$D$24+C18*D$30+D18*E$30+E18*F$30+F18*G$30
19	15	97	23	62	5	0	0.1030	+$D$24+C19*D$30+D19*E$30+E19*F$30+F19*G$30
20	16	90	21	57	6	0	0.1848	+$D$24+C20*D$30+D20*E$30+E20*F$30+F20*G$30
21								
22	Example 1							
23			Regression Output:					
24			Constant	0.1000916				
25			Std Err of Y Est	0.2616009				
26			R Squared	0.8088164	R	0.89934		
27			No. of Observations	16				
28			Degrees of Freedom	11				
29								
30	X Coefficient(s)	-0.012329	0.0226316	0.005451	0.06806			
31	Std Err of Coef.	0.0027316	0.0113182	0.003154	0.02287			
32								
33	Student-t value	4.5135326	1.9995697	1.728399	2.97632			
34	(5% critical value)	1.796						
35	(10% critical value)	1.363						
36								
37		58.25	16.125	55.6875	5.6875		0.4375	
38								
39		0.100092	-0.71818	0.3649346	0.303553	0.3871	0.4375	

as the data used as input to the model is itself consistent with the decision maker(s) mental model. Hence, while linear regression might not capture the decision maker(s) mental model perfectly, it does well enough to be used in practice.

7.2 EVALUATION

Since cognitive modeling captures the mental model used by a decision maker to reach a decision, it can serve another purpose besides allowing us to mimic that decision. It also allows us to evaluate the factors that went into the decision. For instance, we can ask, did the R & D director faithfully follow the company president's policy about how R & D projects should be evaluated?

Consider Table 7.2 again. Row 33 shows the Student-t values for the coefficients of the four factors that were to be considered (these are simply the coefficients divided by their own standard errors). Are the coefficients significantly different from zero? That is, do we have evidence to believe that the R & D director really took each factor into account? The 5% critical value for the Student-t distribution with 11 degrees of freedom (see cell D28) is 1.796. (This value is obtained from Table A3.3, in the column for 90% confidence interval width, i.e., 10% probability in the tails, divided equally between the two tails.) The coefficients of cost, market share, and manufacturing improvement rating are all significant at the 5% level (i.e., < 5% chance that the coefficient is as large as it is purely by chance). The coefficient of probability of technical success is nearly significant at the 5% level, and clearly significant at the 10% level. Hence, we can conclude that these coefficients are not the result of sheer chance, but do show that the factors to which they apply were taken into account in the R & D director's decisions.

We can look at the results another way, as well. Row 37 shows the *averages* of the values of the original data. Columns C–F show the averages of the data in Columns B–E, respectively, and Column G shows the average of the data in Column F. Row 39 shows the product of the average value in row 38 multiplied by the coefficient above it in row 30. That is, the entries in row 39, Columns C–F, are the *average* contributions of each factor to the *average* value of the dependent variable. All seem to contribute, with three contributing about equally and cost contributing more strongly than any of the other three. Cell B39 replicates the constant term of the regression, and cell G39 is the sum of B39–F39. By definition, the result of substituting the average values of the independent variables in the regression formula must produce the average value of the dependent variable, as is the case in cell G39.

Now consider Table 7.3. This is like Table 7.2 except that a different set of projects has been selected, as shown in Column F. The regression result is

TABLE 7.3 Regression Analysis of Alternative Decisions

example2	A	B	C	D	E	F	G	H
1								
2					Mfg.	Xmpl2		
3			Market	Prob. Tech.	Improv.	Selected		
4	Project	Cost ($1000)	Share (Pct.)	Success (Pct.)	Rating			
5	1	48	11	32	3	0	0.1523	+$D$24+C5*D$30+D5*E$30+E5*F$30+F5*G$30
6	2	38	12	36	10	0	0.3203	+$D$24+C6*D$30+D6*E$30+E6*F$30+F6*G$30
7	3	40	10	79	3	1	0.6900	+$D$24+C7*D$30+D7*E$30+E7*F$30+F7*G$30
8	4	43	13	60	9	1	0.5189	+$D$24+C8*D$30+D8*E$30+E8*F$30+F8*G$30
9	5	35	28	48	4	1	0.9682	+$D$24+C9*D$30+D9*E$30+E9*F$30+F9*G$30
10	6	25	28	27	9	1	0.8750	+$D$24+C10*D$30+D10*E$30+E10*F$30+F10*G$30
11	7	26	20	79	2	1	1.1738	+$D$24+C11*D$30+D11*E$30+E11*F$30+F11*G$30
12	8	41	15	93	10	1	0.9191	+$D$24+C12*D$30+D12*E$30+E12*F$30+F12*G$30
13	9	53	10	40	3	0	0.1329	+$D$24+C13*D$30+D13*E$30+E13*F$30+F13*G$30
14	10	81	12	31	7	0	-0.3018	+$D$24+C14*D$30+D14*E$30+E14*F$30+F14*G$30
15	11	97	10	96	3	0	0.0743	+$D$24+C15*D$30+D15*E$30+E15*F$30+F15*G$30
16	12	51	13	63	9	0	0.4385	+$D$24+C16*D$30+D16*E$30+E16*F$30+F16*G$30
17	13	89	16	43	1	0	-0.1487	+$D$24+C17*D$30+D17*E$30+E17*F$30+F17*G$30
18	14	78	16	45	7	0	-0.0099	+$D$24+C18*D$30+D18*E$30+E18*F$30+F18*G$30
19	15	97	23	62	5	0	0.1062	+$D$24+C19*D$30+D19*E$30+E19*F$30+F19*G$30
20	16	90	21	57	6	0	0.0909	+$D$24+C20*D$30+D20*E$30+E20*F$30+F20*G$30
21								
22	Example 2							
23		Regression Output:						
24	Constant			0.19929299				
25	Std Err of Y Est			0.27878598				
26	R Squared			0.77201658	R	0.87864474		
27	No. of Observations			16				
28	Degrees of Freedom			11				
29								
30	X Coefficient(s)		-0.0137013	0.02867402	0.00971834	-0.0052307		
31	Std Err of Coef.		0.00291107	0.01206175	0.00336097	0.02436992		
32								
33	Student-t value		4.70663219	2.37726854	2.89153179	0.21463856		
34	(5% critical value)		1.796					
35	(10% critical value)		1.363					
36								
37			58.25	16.125	55.6875	5.6875	0.375	
38								
39		0.19929299	-0.7981021	0.46236861	0.54119022	-0.0297497	0.375	

74

much different from that of Table 7.2. Here the coefficient of manufacturing improvement rating (cell F30) is not significant at all, and as shown in cell F39, it contributes very little to the average of the dependent variable. We can conclude that the person who made these selections paid no attention to manufacturing improvement in making the selections shown. Thus while the model captures that person's decision making process, it also shows that the company president's policy was honored more in the breach than the observance.

Thus cognitive modeling not only allows us to mimic the decision processes used by an individual or group, but also to identify the factors that went into the decisions, and their relative strengths.

7.3 SUMMARY

In some cases we may have a set of decisions to use as a model. These decisions were made on a limited set of cases. Our intent is to mimic these decisions on a larger set of cases. Cognitive modeling allows us to calibrate a model on the limited set, and apply the results to the larger set. This calibration is done by using linear regression, with the data about the cases as the independent variables, and the selection or nonselection (1 or 0, respectively) as the dependent variable. A spreadsheet can be used to carry out the linear regression, as well as to evaluate the results.

7.4 QUESTIONS FOR CLASS DISCUSSION

1. Use the projects from Project Menu 1 of Appendix 2, and the variables employed in the analyses in the chapter. You are told that Projects 2, 3, 4, 8, 11, 12, 15, and 16 have been selected for funding. Develop a model of the decision process by which this selection was reached. Which factors were significant? Apply the model to the projects of Project Menu 2 of Appendix 2. Which projects from that menu are selected?

7.5 FURTHER READINGS

Fox, E. F. and N. R. Baker (1985). Project Selection Decision Making Linked to a Dynamic Environment. *Management Science*. **31**(10), October, 1272–1285.

Schwartz, S. L. and I. Vertinsky (1977). Multi-Attribute Investment Decisions: A Study of R & D Project Selection. *Management Science*. **24**, November, 285–301.

Stahl, M. J. and A. M. Harrell (1983). Identifying Operative Goals by Modeling Project Selection Decisions in Research and Development. *IEEE Transactions on Engineering Management*. **30**(4), November, 223–228.

Stahl, M. J., T. W. Zimmerer, and A. Gulati (1984). Measuring Innovation, Productivity, and Job Performance of Professionals: A Decision Modeling Approach. *IEEE Transactions on Engineering Management*. **31**,(1), February, 25–29.

_____8
CLUSTER ANALYSIS

In Chapter 5 we examined methods for selecting portfolios of projects to maximize income. However, there may be other reasons for selecting portfolios of projects than maximizing some measure of income. One possible alternative is to select projects according to how they support the strategic positioning of the firm. The issue of strategic positioning itself will be taken up in Chapter 13. Here we will examine means for selecting portfolios of projects that support specific strategic positions.

Mathieu and Gibson [1993] present a method, based on cluster analysis, which groups projects according to their support for specific objectives. The groupings can then be rated according to the importance of their strategic positioning. That is, the projects in a group support a strategic position, and derive their importance (and desirability for support) from the importance of the strategic position.

8.1 CLUSTERING EXAMPLE

This process is best explained by carrying through an example. Consider a large, multi-division corporation, which has multiple product lines in the commercial and military electronics, aerospace, and automotive areas. The corporate director of R & D has been presented with a list of projects, proposed by the various division laboratories and the central R & D laboratory, which support various technologies or applications in the corporation's product lines. All of these have already survived screening for technical soundness and market acceptability. Because of resource limitations, he/she cannot approve the entire list. He/she wishes to approve those projects that

76

**TABLE 8.1   Technology / Application Areas
in Which the Corporation Is Active**

TA1.	Synthetic Aperture Radar
TA2.	Satellite Electrical Power
TA3.	Aircraft Navigation
TA4.	Microcomputer CPUs
TA5.	Microcomputer memories
TA6.	Microcomputer graphics circuits
TA7.	Videophone
TA8.	Television displays
TA9.	Satellite ground stations
TA10.	Air-to-air communications
TA11.	Air-to-ground communications
TA12.	Point-to-point communications
TA13.	Ground-to-air communications
TA14.	Cellular telephones
TA15.	Satellite antennas
TA16.	Modems
TA17.	Portable computers
TA18.	Mobile radios
TA19.	Automotive radio receivers
TA20.	Automotive electric power
TA21.	Satellite transponders
TA22.	Cellular phone base stations
TA23.	Digital switching circuits
TA24.	Military tactical communications
TA25.	Military strategic communications
TA26.	Airborne command and control
TA27.	Digital X-ray imaging
TA28.	Quality control sonogram imaging
TA29.	Medical sonogram imaging

support the corporation's strategic objectives, as were established by the company president and the board of directors.

Table 8.1 is a list of technology/application areas in which the corporation's various divisions are currently active. Table 8.2 is the list of projects that have been proposed to the director of R & D. How can these projects be identified or described as supporting various strategic objectives?

Table 8.3 shows which of the technology/application areas is supported by each proposed project. Technically, this is an "incidence matrix." An entry of 1 in a cell indicates that the project (row) supports the technology/application area (column). An entry of 0 in a cell indicates the project does not support that technology/application area.

What is now needed is some means for identifying patterns in the incidence matrix. That is, we need means for grouping together those

TABLE 8.2   **Projects Proposed for Approval**

P1.	Digital signal processor
P2.	Digital image processor
P3.	Speech synthesizer
P4.	Low-voltage computer chip
P5.	High-efficiency solar cell
P6.	Digital-to-analog converter
P7.	Analog-to-digital converter
P8.	Frequency converter module
P9.	Conformal phased-array antenna
P10.	Radio frequency mixer
P11.	Signal converter
P12.	High-speed encryption circuit
P13.	Lightweight dc-to-dc converter
P14.	High-energy-density battery
P15.	Improved coding algorithm
P16.	Optical materials for solar cells

projects that are similar in the sense that they support the same technology/application areas. To start with, we can compare two projects at a time with each other. There will be some technology/application areas that are supported by both, some that are supported by only one or the other, and some that are supported by neither project. Arbitrarily label the two projects 1 and 2. We then define variables a, b, c, and d as follows:

a = number of technology/application areas both 1 and 2 support

b = number of technology/application areas that 1 supports but 2 does not

c = number of technology/application areas that 2 supports but 1 does not

d = number of technology/application areas that neither support

The "measure of similarity" between the two projects is then defined as:

$$S = \frac{a + d}{a + b + c + d}$$

This is known as the Jaccard coefficient. Essentially, it is the number of agreements between the two divided by the maximum possible number of agreements. (Note that the Jaccard coefficient implies that joint failure to support a technology/application area indicates a similarity between the two projects. In some situations, the fact that neither project supports a technology/application area will have no significance for grouping them. In such

TABLE 8.3   Project Support for Technology / Application Areas

incidmat		A	B	C	D	E	F	G	H	I	J	K	L	M	N	O	P	Q	R	S	T	U	V	W	X	Y	Z	AA	AB	AC	AD
		incidma	TA1	TA2	TA3	TA4	TA5	TA6	TA7	TA8	TA9	TA10	TA11	TA12	TA13	TA14	TA15	TA16	TA17	TA18	TA19	Ta20	TA21	TA22	TA23	TA24	TA25	TA26	TA27	TA28	TA29
1		P1	1	0	1	0	0	0	1	1	1	1	1	0	1	1	0	1	0	1	0	0	1	0	0	1	1	1	1	1	1
2		P2	1	0	0	0	0	0	0	1	0	0	0	1	0	0	0	0	1	0	0	0	0	0	0	0	0	1	0	1	1
3		P3	0	0	0	0	0	1	1	1	0	1	1	1	1	1	0	1	1	1	1	0	0	1	1	1	1	0	1	0	0
4		P4	0	1	1	0	1	1	1	0	0	1	1	1	1	1	0	1	1	1	1	1	1	1	1	1	1	1	1	1	1
5		P5	0	1	1	1	1	1	1	0	0	0	1	0	0	0	0	0	0	0	0	0	0	1	0	0	0	0	0	0	0
6		P6	0	1	0	0	0	0	0	0	0	1	0	1	1	1	0	1	1	1	1	0	0	1	0	0	1	1	0	0	1
7		P7	1	0	1	0	0	1	1	1	1	1	1	1	1	1	1	1	1	1	1	1	1	1	1	1	1	1	1	1	1
8		P8	1	0	1	0	0	1	1	1	0	1	1	1	1	1	0	0	0	1	1	0	1	0	0	1	1	1	1	1	0
9		P9	1	0	1	0	0	0	0	0	0	0	1	0	0	0	0	0	0	1	1	0	0	0	0	0	1	1	0	0	0
10		P10	1	0	1	0	0	0	1	0	1	1	1	1	1	1	1	0	0	1	1	0	1	1	0	1	1	1	0	0	0
11		P11	1	0	1	0	1	1	1	0	1	1	1	1	1	1	1	0	1	1	1	1	0	1	0	1	1	1	0	0	0
12		P12	0	0	0	0	0	0	1	0	0	1	1	0	0	1	0	0	1	1	0	1	1	1	0	0	0	1	0	0	0
13		P13	1	1	1	0	0	1	0	0	0	0	1	1	0	1	1	1	1	1	1	1	1	0	0	1	0	1	0	0	0
14		P14	0	1	0	0	0	0	0	0	0	0	0	0	1	1	0	1	1	1	1	1	0	1	0	0	1	1	0	0	0
15		P15	0	0	0	0	0	0	0	0	1	1	1	1	1	1	1	0	0	0	0	0	1	0	0	1	1	1	0	0	0
16		P16	0	0	0	0	0	0	0	0	0	0	1	0	1	1	0	0	0	1	0	0	0	1	0	1	1	1	0	0	0
17			0	0	1	0	0	0	0	0	1	0	0	0	0	1	0	0	1	1	0	0	0	1	0	0	0	0	0	0	0

situations, the variable d should be eliminated from the definition of the similarity coefficient S. This is no longer the Jaccard coefficient, but an unnamed variant.)

By computing the Jaccard coefficient for each pair of projects, we can construct a "similarity matrix" for them. Since the designation of 1 and 2 for the projects was arbitrary, and the value of S would be the same regardless of which project was designated as 1 and which was designated as 2, it is customary to present the similarity matrix as a lower triangular matrix. This is shown in Table 8.4. The diagonal elements are of course 1, since each project is identical with itself. The missing elements, above the diagonal, would be symmetrical with those below the diagonal. There is no need either to compute them or to display them, since they add no information to what is already in the table.

Note that the analog-to-digital converter and the digital-to-analog converter projects had identical entries for support of technology/application areas, and therefore their Jaccard coefficient is 1.0. The same is true for the radio frequency (RF) mixer and signal converter. Other pairs have Jaccard coefficients between 0 and 1.0, indicating varying degrees of similarity.

After having obtained a similarity matrix for the projects, we next construct a "dendogram." This construction is done as follows. The two projects most alike are "joined" into a cluster. Then either the next-most-alike pair is joined into a cluster, or the project most like the first pair is added to their cluster. This procedure is continued. At each step, one project is either joined with another project to form a cluster, or one project is joined with an existing cluster, or two existing clusters are joined. At each step, then, the number of clusters, including "unjoined" projects, is reduced by one. Finally, all projects are joined into one big cluster.

The clustering is portrayed graphically as a tree diagram, with all projects at the left, and the "joins" as branches toward the right of the diagram. Each "join" is plotted on the horizontal axis according to the degree of *dissimilarity* between the two clusters merged at that "join." In effect, the plot displays the amount of "shoe-horning" required to merge projects into a larger cluster, with the degree of "shoe-horning" required shown by the position on the diagram of each "join."

Figure 8.1 shows the dendogram for the similarity matrix of Table 8.4.* The dissimilarity is shown as stretching from -2 to $+2$. The digital-to-analog converter and analog-to-digital converter projects are the earliest merged, since they are completely similar. Likewise, the signal converter and RF mixer projects are merged at the same dissimilarity level as the analog-to-digital converter and digital-to-analog converter. Other pairs are merged at greater degrees of dissimilarity, and then pairs are merged with other pairs to form larger clusters. Ultimately, all projects are merged into one large cluster.

---

*The cluster analysis, and preparation of this dendogram, was performed using SYSTAT[tm]. Other statistical programs are available, which can also perform cluster analysis.

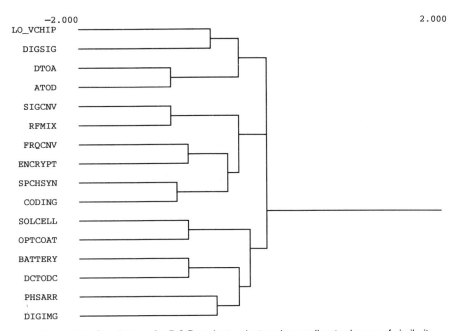

Figure 8.1. Dendogram for R & D projects, clustered according to degree of similarity.

From the analyst's standpoint, the object is to identify clusters that are large enough that there are significantly fewer of them than there are initial projects, but not so large that the projects joined to form them are not really very much alike. This amounts to a selection of a point on the dissimilarity scale such that all clusters formed to the left of it are accepted as internally similar, while those formed to the right of it are regarded as insufficiently similar. Selection of such a point is partly subjective. The analyst cannot appeal to any statistical rules regarding magnitude of the dissimilarity measure to justify selection of any specific dissimilarity value as the "cutting value."

In examining Figure 8.1, it appears that there are three major clusters among the projects:

Cluster 1: Low-voltage chip, digital signal processor, digital-to-analog converter, and analog-to-digital converter.

Cluster 2: Signal converter, RF mixer, frequency converter, high-speed encryptions circuit, speech synthesizer, and improved coding algorithms.

Cluster 3: High-efficiency solar cell, optical materials for solar cells, high-energy-density battery, dc-to-dc converter, conformal phased-array antenna, and digital image processor.

TABLE 8.4 Similarity Matrix for Projects

E	A	B	C	D	E	F	G	H	I	J	K	L	M	N	O	P	Q
		DIGSIG	DIGIMG	SPCHSY	LO-VCHIP	SOLCELL	DTOA	ATOD	FRQCNV	PHSARR	RFMIX	SIGCNV	ENCRYPT	DCTODC	BATTER	CODING	OPTCOAT
1	DIGSIG	1															
2	DIGIMG	0.414	1.000														
3	SPCHSYN	0.655	.414	1.000													
4	LO-VCHIP	0.586	.345	.448	1.000												
5	SOLCELL	0.345	.586	.552	.276	1.000											
6	DTOA	0.759	.586	.621	.621	.172	1.000										
7	ATOD	0.759	.586	.621	.621	.172	1.000	1.000									
8	FRQCNV	0.759	.310	.828	.483	.517	.655	.655	1.000								
9	PHSARR	0.483	.517	.690	.414	.517	.586	.586	.724	1.000							
10	RFMIX	0.724	.276	.793	.448	.483	.621	.621	.966	.759	1.000						
11	SIGCNV	0.724	.276	.793	.448	.483	.621	.621	.966	.759	1.000	1.000					
12	ENCRYPT	0.621	.379	.897	.483	.517	.586	.586	.793	.586	.759	.759	1.000				
13	DCTODC	0.483	.448	.621	.621	.517	.586	.586	.724	.724	.690	.690	.586	1.000			
14	BATTERY	0.31	.552	.655	.517	.621	.483	.483	.552	.655	.517	.517	.621	.828	1.000		
15	CODING	0.69	.379	.966	.483	.586	.586	.586	.862	.655	.828	.828	.862	.655	.621	1.000	
16	OPTCOAT	0.379	.552	.655	.379	.828	.345	.345	.552	.552	.517	.517	.690	.621	.793	.621	1.000

Cluster 1 appears to be focused on digital circuitry. Cluster 2 appears to be focused on radio communications. Cluster 3 is less well defined. The first four projects in it are clearly related to electric power generation and control, while the last two projects, respectively, involve radio communications and digital processing. The common thread among the projects in this cluster seems to be their relation to communications satellites. Hence, this cluster could be designated a space satellite cluster.

At this point, how can the director of R & D utilize the information in the dendogram? The projects to be supported should be selected from the cluster(s) that are most closely aligned with the strategic goals of the corporation. For instance, if the corporate strategy is to become heavily involved in space technology, the projects in Cluster 3 should be supported. If the corporate strategy is to focus on digital computers and digital control systems, the projects in Cluster 1 should be supported. If the corporate strategy is to emphasize the radio communications market, the projects in Cluster 2 should be supported. If resources permit, of course, more than one cluster could be supported. The point is, however, that the projects selected for support should be those in the cluster(s) that are most directly supportive of the overall corporate strategy.

This example involved a large, multi-division corporation. However, use of the technique is not restricted to such organizations. Even small firms might need to identify projects according to how they support the firm's strategic objectives. The only difference in using the technique would be that the technology/application areas would be more narrowly defined. The process would still be the same: generate an incidence matrix between projects and products or market areas; compute the similarity matrix; carry out a cluster analysis; evaluate the resulting dendogram. The end result will be the same: clusters of projects that can be ranked according to the importance of the strategic objectives that they support.

8.2 SUMMARY

The method of cluster analysis does not directly rank projects, or relate them to measures of payoff or income. Instead, it identifies groups or clusters of projects that are related or are "similar" in some sense. Having identified clusters of "similar" projects, the decision maker then approves the projects in those clusters that support the most important objectives of the organization. In principle, clusters would be ranked from most important to least important, based on their support for the organization's strategic objectives. Entire clusters would be funded, then, from most important to least important, until resources were exhausted. The projects in the clusters that supported only the least important strategic objectives might not be funded at all.

8.3 QUESTIONS FOR CLASS DISCUSSION

1. Prepare an incidence matrix similar to Table 8.3 for projects and technology or application areas in your organization. Carry out a cluster analysis. How many groups of projects are there?

8.4 FURTHER READING

Mathieu, R. G. and J. E. Gibson (1993). A Methodology for Large-Scale R & D Planning Based on Cluster Analysis. *IEEE Transactions on Engineering Management*. **40**(3), August, 283–292.

____9
AD HOC

This chapter presents several project selection methods that do not fit neatly into any of the categories presented in the earlier chapters. The techniques presented here are largely pragmatic in nature. Included are profiles and interactive methods.

9.1 PROFILES

Profiles amount to a crude form of scoring model. A project is given a score on each of several characteristics. If a score on some characteristic falls below a preset cutoff, a project may be rejected. Projects that dominate others on all or most characteristics are then selected. If funds remain after all undominated projects have been selected, then projects with the "best'" profiles are selected from those remaining, where "best" is largely subjective.

This process can be illustrated with Project Menu 1 of Appendix 2. Assume that the factors to be taken into account are project cost, market share, market size, probability of technical success, and probability of market success.

Figure 9.1 shows bar charts of each of these factors for each project. Assume that the following thresholds have been set for ruling out projects:

Cost: Reject all projects costing over $75K.

Market share: Reject all projects with market share less than 15%.

Market size: Reject all projects intended for markets less than $500K.

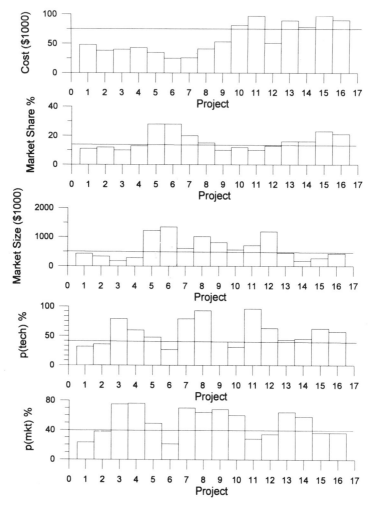

Figure 9.1. Profiles of projects.

Probability of technical success: Reject all projects whose probability is less than 40%.

Probability of market success: Reject all projects whose probability is less than 40%.

These limits are illustrated by the horizontal lines in the figure. If these rules are applied, the only projects to be selected are 5, 7, and 8. All the remaining projects fail at least one of the criteria.

Raising or lowering the thresholds will alter the number of projects excluded by each criterion. Setting the various thresholds reflects the decision maker's trade-offs between the factors. For instance, if market size is more important than market share, the threshold for market size might be raised to exclude more projects, while the threshold for market share would be lowered to include more projects. Cost, of course, works the other way. If cost is very important, the threshold for cost should be lowered, to reject more high-cost projects.

The method of profiles is easy to display. When bar charts are used, of the type presented in Figure 9.1, the viewer can readily see the effect of a specific threshold, and the effects of adjusting the threshold up or down. The profile method can thus be an effective starting point for negotiations about where the thresholds should be. It can also be an effective means for reporting to higher management, since the profiles directly show the effects of each threshold in selecting projects in or out.

9.2 INTERACTIVE SELECTION

The methods presented earlier in this book have all depended on explicit factors being identified at the outset, then using them to rank, rate, or otherwise evaluate projects. Alternatively, interactive project selection works by having the R & D director interact with subordinate managers to determine what the selection factors should be.

The process begins with the R & D director requesting project proposals from their subordinate project managers. The director may give whatever guidelines are deemed appropriate. The project managers then submit proposed projects which, in their best judgment, conform to the guidelines.

The director selects only one of the projects from the set of proposals. He/she then explains what led him/her to that decision. The project managers then revise their proposals to conform more closely to what in effect become modified guidelines. This process of revising proposals and selecting one project from the revised list continues until the director's budget is exhausted, or some other resource constraint becomes binding. At each stage, the project managers "improve" their project proposals in an effort to more closely align them with the director's objectives.

The key feature of this interactive, "back-and-forth" process of project selection, is that the selection criteria become better and better articulated as the process continues. Even if the R & D director's criteria are not at first well defined, they become better defined as successive projects are selected and reasons are given for the selection. Moreover, the project managers have an incentive to make their projects more attractive by identifying and emphasizing features that seem to fit the desires of the director.

One of the risks of this procedure is that all the project proposals will begin to "look alike." This would result from improper use of the method. The object is to develop and refine projects so they more nearly fit the strategic and tactical objectives of the R & D director. If the objectives are spelled out in terms that are too concrete and short ranged, many potentially rewarding projects will never be proposed because they do not fit the "strait jacket" of narrowly defined objectives.

9.3 SUMMARY

The methods described in this chapter do not fit any of the categories discussed earlier. To some extent they are not formal methods at all, but methods for display and aids to negotiation. These methods can be used when none of the methods presented earlier seem to be appropriate. In particular, they can be used when the true criteria for project selection are not well defined, since they assist in defining criteria more clearly.

9.4 QUESTIONS FOR CLASS DISCUSSION

1. Develop profiles of the projects on cost, market share, market size, probability of technical success, and probability of market success by using Project Menu 2 of Appendix 2. Assume you have a budget of $500K to spend on R & D projects. Select thresholds for the factors such that the projects selected use as much of the budget as possible. What is your rationale for each threshold? What arguments would you use to defend the thresholds you have set?

9.5 FURTHER READING

Hall, D. L. and A. Nauda (1990). An Interactive Approach for Selecting IR & D Projects. *IEEE Transactions on Engineering Management*. **37**(2), May 126–133.

PART II
FACTORS TO BE CONSIDERED

Each of the project selection methods requires that projects be evaluated on the basis of certain criteria. The evaluation criteria are not peculiar to any particular method. Any of the methods can use almost any criteria. The criteria that have been utilized in the past can be grouped into technical, marketing, political, and stage of innovation. Appropriate criteria can be selected from any or all of these groups for inclusion in a selection procedure. The chapters in Part II describe the factors in the various groups.

─────10
TECHNICAL

Technical factors are those that are related to the content of the project itself and its management. This chapter discusses the technical factors relevant to decisions about project selection.

The technical factors that have been described in the literature include:

1. Probability of technical success.
2. Existence of a product champion.
3. Competence in the required disciplines.
4. Degree of internal commitment.
5. Degree of internal competition for resources.
6. Intrinsic merit of the research.
7. Potential for strategic positioning.
8. Stage of innovation.
9. Source of project proposal.

Some or all of these may need to be taken into account in evaluating a project or a portfolio of projects.

10.1 INDIVIDUAL FACTORS

The nature of each factor is described in more detail in the following sections.

Probability of Technical Success

Clearly, no conscientious R & D manager would decide to support a project that had no chance of success. At least implicitly, then, any project approved by a responsible manager is assumed to have some chance of success. In attempting to rationalize project selection, however, the criterion of probability of technical success should be made explicit rather than allowed to remain implicit. Unfortunately, there is no way to measure probability of success, either at the outset of the project or after the project is carried out.

Ex post, the project was either a technical success or a technical failure. Once a project is completed, one cannot speak of a "probability that it was a success." Moreover, the outcome (success or failure) provides no information about what the estimated probability of success *should have been* at the outset. Even a project with a "true" probability of success of 90% might fail; a project with a "true" probability of success of 10% might succeed.

Ex ante, one does not know whether the project will be technically successful or not. While it is meaningful to talk of a probability of success, there is no objective way to determine the numerical value of the probability. Even if the analyst tries to evaluate the ratio of successes to attempts in previous "similar" projects, the assessment of "similar" is subjective.

Ultimately, then, the probability of technical success must be evaluated subjectively. Methods for doing this will be presented in Chapter 19. At this point we simply note that if the R & D manager wishes to incorporate an explicit measure of probability of success into a project selection procedure, the actual number must be obtained as a subjective judgment. This judgment is usually obtained from the responsible project leader.

How good are subjective probability estimates of project success? Meadows [1968] evaluated a set of estimates of the probability of project technical success, made at the outset of the projects. The evaluation process was carried out as follows. The projects were grouped according to estimated probability of success (e.g., 90–100%, 80–89%, etc.). If the estimates were accurate, and for a large sample of projects, all those projects that were estimated to have probability of success of (say) 80–89%, approximately 85% would be successful. For each such group, Meadows [1968] took the actual fraction of successful projects, then used the binomial distribution to estimate a 50% confidence bound on the "true" (but unknown) probability of success for that group. If for one-half of the groups, the actual fraction of successes fell within the 50% confidence band, then "the initial estimates have not been proved inaccurate" (p. 113).

How well did the estimators do? Meadows found that the initial estimates, made at the outset of the project, were "not accurate enough to be employed in project evaluation formulas."

Souder [1978] conducted a related study, in which 30 projects were analyzed. These were selected to include 15 "research" and 15 "development" projects. Moreover, any projects thought to be "politically sensitive" were eliminated from the study, to avoid any possible distortion of the estimates. The researchers obtained probability of success estimates from the project managers at the outset, and at 6-month intervals during the course of the 30-month projects.* Final success or failure judgments (whether the project met technical and cost goals) were made by higher level management.

How well did the estimates turn out? The initial and 6-month estimates were negatively correlated with actual project outcome (Pearson product moment correlation), but were not statistically significant. Correlations at 12 months were positive but still not statistically significant. Estimates made at 18 and 24 months, however, were statistically significant and correlated well with actual outcome (0.67 at 18 months, 0.75 at 24 months, for estimates made on the assumption of continued full project funding).

This result agreed with Souder's [1969] earlier results in which project leaders were requested to make estimates of probability of success at several points during the course of a project.

It appears, then, that initial estimates of project probability of success may not be reliable, but those made later in the project are highly reliable. Thus estimates of probability of success may not be very useful in selecting which projects to initiate, but can be very useful in selecting projects to continue or terminate.

Existence of a Product Champion

R & D projects do not exist in a vacuum. These projects exist in an organizational context. There is the project team itself, including people with different skills and personalities. There are other projects whose leaders may require the same resources as does the project in question. The project will be reviewed periodically by higher management, who will be seeking answers as to whether to continue or terminate it.

This social context means that a project needs a champion. Without such a champion the project may become an orphan. It will not be supported enthusiastically during reviews by higher management. Its staffing and equipment use will not be defended vigorously against other project leaders who wish to raid its resources. The project team will not be motivated to put forth their best efforts.

Because of these considerations, many researchers have concluded that existence of a project champion is a critical factor in deciding whether to approve a project for funding. In the absence of a champion who is committed to project success, the project is likely to fail.

---

*Souder [1978] notes that the probability estimates he collected during the research were not utilized by management at any of the laboratories taking part in the study.

Lockett et al. [1986] list the following questions that should be asked about a project champion:

1. Is there an obvious leader for the project?
2. Is he/she respected by his/her staff, colleagues, and supervisors?
3. Is he/she capable of presenting his/her case forcefully, persuasively, and with authority?
4. Can he/she fight off criticism?
5. Does he/she usually get his/her own way?

If these questions can be answered "yes," a champion exists for the project. If the answers are in the negative, the chances of project success are much lower. If the project leader does not have "fire in his/her belly" for the project, the team will not be motivated, and the project will not be defended vigorously against alternative demands on its resources. In the absence of a project champion, the risk of failure increases, and approving the project may be a poor decision.

Competence in the Required Disciplines

If a project is proposed by the laboratory staff, it is reasonable to expect that the staff already has the required competence to carry it out. However, in some cases projects are proposed by the marketing staff, in response to a perceived customer need or a competitor's offering; or are proposed by manufacturing in response to a problem or a need for cost reduction; or are requested by a customer. In these cases the proposers may not be aware of the limitations to the technical competence available within the R & D organization. Hence, an otherwise desirable project may be impossible to undertake because the R & D organization does not have the necessary skills or competence.

In evaluating this factor, the decision maker needs to determine whether the required competence already exists. If so, is it available now, or is it already committed to some other project? When can it be available for the proposed project? If it is not currently available, can some of the existing staff be retrained? How long will that take? Will new staff have to be recruited? How long will that take? What will the new staff members be utilized for when the project is completed? Will there be further requirements for the same competence, or is this a one-shot project? The answers to these questions will help determine whether the project should be undertaken, and when.

Degree of Internal Commitment

Project success requires commitment, even in the face of discouraging results or setbacks. The project workers may need to identify alternative approaches if the first attempts do not work. Management may be asked to continue the project even though progress is slow or initial results are not favorable.

The decision maker will need to ask, are the project workers themselves committed to the success of the project? How about the workers in other projects associated with the proposed one (e.g., testing, fabrication, or support)? Is the project supported by higher management? Is the project supported by outside consultants and experts? A lack of commitment to the project, by any of the parties on which it depends, may lower the likelihood of success.

Degree of Internal Competition for Resources

The resources required by the proposed project may also be required by other projects. This requirement will certainly be true of the budget itself. It may also be true of specialized or unique resources, such as particular research skills, particular pieces of equipment, or limited resources, such as computer time and fabrication or instrument shop hours. The competing uses for limited resources must be taken into account in making decisions about whether to approve a project.

The decision maker will need to ask, What resources are required by the proposed projects? Are any of these resources outside the control of the project leader? Must they be shared with other projects? Do any of these shared resources represent bottlenecks or constraints? What other projects compete for them? How much "slack" is available in the critical resources? What are the relative priorities of the competing projects and the proposed project? If the proposed project is approved, what is the likelihood that it will have to be "put on hold" or terminated because of competition for resources by other projects?

A limitation on critical resources may lead the decision maker to reject an otherwise attractive project.

Intrinsic Merit of the Research

Most projects are thought of in terms of generating newer improved products or processes. However, projects also result in increased competence of the research staff. Even a project that fails to achieve its technical or commercial objectives may enhance the skills of the research staff, opening the way to projects that will generate new products or processes.

One of the important technical considerations about a proposed project, then, is its intrinsic merit in terms of enhancing staff competence. While a laboratory cannot afford many projects that are "intrinsically meritorious" but fail to achieve their technical and commercial objectives, this consideration may be a "tie breaker" in deciding between projects that otherwise appear to be equally attractive.

Potential for Strategic Positioning

Projects should be evaluated, not only in terms of their immediate payoff in new products or processes, but also in terms of their fit with the firm's long-term strategy. In particular, they should be evaluated in terms of the extent to which they develop a capability for future work. Does the project lead to other things besides its specific objectives, or is it essentially a dead end once its objectives have been achieved?

Vepsalainen et al. [1988] describe a procedure for selecting project portfolios that enhance the likelihood of winning a subsequent government or commercial contract. They argue that projects should be selected that enhance product performance criteria that are valued by the customer, and that provide an advantage over competitors. This requires an evaluation of customer preferences, and the strengths of competitors. The analytic hierarchy process (AHP) is used to carry out the evaluation and project ranking.

This is a clear example of selecting projects to achieve strategic positioning. In many cases, however, the exact customer may not be as clear, and customer requirements may be more vague, than in the case of competition for a specific contract. Nevertheless, the idea is sound and a project's potential for enhancing the strategic position of the firm should be considered.

Morris et al. [1991] present an argument that projects should be considered in the light of the firm's long-term strategy, not simply as isolated projects. They claim that high-risk projects have a wider range of possible outcomes than do low-risk projects, that is, not only is the downside risk greater, but the upside payoff is also greater. Put another way, if the high-risk project is successful, it will have a greater payoff when implemented than would a successful low-risk project. They argue that a proper R & D project portfolio should contain some high-risk, high-payoff projects. If the projects are chosen so that their uncertainties are independent, or better yet negatively correlated, the overall risk associated with the portfolio need not be greater than with a portfolio composed entirely of low-risk projects. The high-risk portfolio will include more failures, but the successes will have a higher payoff. As Matthews [1991] puts it, "If you want to find a prince, you have to be prepared to kiss a lot of frogs!"

Meadows [1968] presents figures on overruns and market payoff for the projects he evaluated. Those proposed by the laboratory had an average overrun of 120% (i.e., cost 220% of initial estimate), those proposed by marketing had an overrun of 102%, and those proposed by the customer had an overrun of only 27%. Of those projects proposed by the laboratory, fully two-thirds produced no increase in sales, and none achieved a "large" increase in sales. "Small" and "medium" increases were each achieved by 17%. For projects proposed by marketing, the figures are 58, 14, 14, and 14% for non, small, medium, and large, respectively. For those projects proposed by the customer, the respective percentages were 33, 33, 13, and 20%. Thus projects proposed by the customer lead to smaller overruns and greater increases in sales than do projects proposed by either the laboratory or marketing.

Unfortunately, Meadows does not cross-tabulate payoffs and overruns with initial estimates of probability of technical success. If we assume that those projects proposed by the research laboratory were the most risky, those proposed by the customer least risky, and those proposed by marketing had an intermediate risk, we can conclude that the upside payoff to risky projects may be exaggerated. However, this should be evaluated carefully in each case. It should not be assumed that risky projects automatically have high payoff, but if they do the risk may be worth taking, in light of the potential long-term strategic positioning.

Stage of Innovation

Conventionally, projects may be categorized as basic research, applied research, prototype, and commercial development. The boundaries between these categories are somewhat fuzzy, but nevertheless these are distinct categories. Basic research is usually understood as phenomenon-oriented activity. The object of the research is to understand some phenomenon, not to solve some problem.

Reich [1985] points out that a major function of Bell Laboratories in the first several decades after its founding was to investigate the physical and chemical phenomena involved in the devices utilized by the American Telephone and Telegraph (AT & T) Company. The research was not intended to lead to a product, it was intended to lead to understanding of the products the company already made and used. Despite its device orientation, this was high-quality research, resulting in seven Nobel prizes. The central research laboratory at General Electric pursued a similar approach and likewise resulted in a Nobel prize as well as other honors and awards.

Applied research is still phenomenon-oriented, but is typically focused on problems or difficulties that have arisen in the firm's products or processes. The intent is to understand the phenomena involved, in order to craft solutions. However, the research is not itself intended to produce a solution.

The building of prototypes is a problem-oriented activity. It is intended to result in a product or process that solves some problem or meets some need. The prototype's design may rest on knowledge gained in basic and applied research, but its focus is on application of knowledge to problem-solving rather than on gaining knowledge as such. However, a prototype is not necessarily intended for commercial use or operational deployment. Instead, it is intended to demonstrate the practicality of a solution to some problem.

Commercial development is intended precisely to lead to something that can be marketed or deployed. Commercial development is the only technical activity that leads directly to revenue for the firm. However, if commercial development is not founded on knowledge from basic and applied research, and on the experience gained from prototypes, it runs a high risk of technical failure.

An industrial laboratory should be conducting a mix of projects, at all stages of innovation. Too great a focus on commercial development runs the risk of technological surprise, as competitors exploit new knowledge from research. Too great an emphasis on research will lead to a withering of revenue from lack of products, and possibly even to other firms bringing out products that utilize the knowledge the firm has gained through its basic research, and published in the scientific literature.

Source of Project Proposal

Ideas for good projects can come from any of several sources. The laboratory staff will generate many good ideas. However, other company departments, such as manufacturing and marketing, can also be fruitful sources of ideas for new products and processes, and can identify areas in which basic or applied research would lead to improved products and processes. Customers, likewise, can often be fruitful sources of ideas for new products. Laboratory-generated project proposals tend to be technically interesting and challenging. Customer-generated project proposals tend to be oriented to immediate market needs. A laboratory should have a balanced mix of projects from all sources. Projects suggested by marketing tend to be responsive to customer demands and to competitive offerings of other firms. Projects suggested by other internal groups, such as manufacturing, tend to be oriented towards solving current problems.

10.2   EXAMPLE

Table 10.1 presents the technical factors for the projects in Project Menu 1 of Appendix 2. Clearly, these are not the only factors that should be taken into consideration in selecting projects. For instance, project cost is not a technical factor, yet it should be considered. Likewise, potential market is not a technical factor, yet it should be considered. However, since the focus in this chapter is on technical factors, the nontechnical factors will be omitted from the discussion.

Any of the methods discussed in Part I could be utilized to select individual projects, or a portfolio of projects, from this menu. Without going into the specifics of those methods, however, some qualitative evaluations are still possible. For instance, Project 7 would require that personnel be hired, since the required skills are not available within the firm. However, the effect on the firm's strategic position is indicated as LOW. One might question the desirability of hiring someone to engage in a basic research project that, even though customer-suggested, will not result in a strong strategic position.

TABLE 10.1   Technical Factors for Selected Projects

Project	Cost ($1000)	Prob. Tech. Success (Pct.)	Stage of Innovation	Skills Available	Project Source	Product Champion	Strategic Position
1	48	32	Bas. Rsch.	TRAIN	R & D Lab	NO	LOW
2	38	36	Bas. Rsch.	YES	Production	YES	HIGH
3	40	79	Com'l Dev.	HIRE	Customer	YES	HIGH
4	43	60	Com'l Dev.	YES	Marketing	NO	LOW
5	35	48	Com'l Dev.	TRAIN	R & D Lab	YES	HIGH
6	25	27	Com'l Dev.	YES	Production	NO	LOW
7	26	79	Bas. Rsch.	HIRE	Customer	NO	LOW
8	41	93	Bas. Rsch.	YES	Marketing	YES	HIGH
9	53	40	App. Rsch.	YES	R & D Lab	NO	HIGH
10	81	31	App. Rsch.	TRAIN	Production	YES	LOW
11	97	96	Prototype	YES	Customer	YES	LOW
12	51	63	Prototype	HIRE	Marketing	NO	HIGH
13	89	43	Prototype	YES	R & D Lab	YES	LOW
14	78	45	Prototype	TRAIN	Production	NO	HIGH
15	97	62	App. Rsch.	YES	Customer	NO	HIGH
16	90	57	App. Rsch.	HIRE	Marketing	YES	LOW

Project 8, by contrast, results in a strong strategic position, skills are available, and there is a product champion. Even though this project is basic research, it is recommended by marketing, hence it might be expected to result in a profitable product.

These examples illustrate the point that the technical factors may be used to screen out less-desirable projects, before the more elaborate methods described in previous chapters are applied.

10.3 SUMMARY

Many of the factors that affect desirability of R & D projects can be described as "technical" in nature, in that they deal with the content of a project and its management. These factors can be used to screen projects before more elaborate selection methods are applied, or they can be utilized as factors in scoring, ranking, or portfolio selection.

10.4 QUESTIONS FOR CLASS DISCUSSION

1. Assume the laboratory budget for the coming fiscal period is $500K. Use Project Menu 2 of Appendix 2. Considering technical factors only (i.e., do not consider

market share or revenue), select a project portfolio that includes at least one project from each stage of innovation, at least one project from each source that maximizes the number of projects with HIGH strategic position, and that does not exceed the budget. What is the probability that at least one project in this portfolio will be a technical success? (*Hint*: what is the probability that all projects in the portfolio will be technical failures?)

2. Same as Question 1 except that the portfolio should minimize the number of new hires required.

3. Same as Question 1 except that the portfolio should maximize the number of projects that have a product champion.

10.5 FURTHER READINGS

Cooper, M. J. (1978). An Evaluation System for Project Selection. *Research Management*. **21**, July, 29–33.

Lockett, G., B. Hetherington, and P. Yallup (1986). Modeling a Research Portfolio Using AHP: A Group Decision Process. *R & D Management*. **16**(2), April, 151–160.

Matthews, W. H. (1991). Kissing Technological Frogs: Managing Technology as a Strategic Resource. *European Management Journal*. **9**(2), June, 145–148.

Meadows, D. L. (1968). Estimate Accuracy and Project Selection Models in Industrial Research. *Industrial Management Review*. **9**, 105–119, Spring.

Mehrez, A. (1988). Selecting R & D Projects: A Case Study of the Expected Utility Approach. *Technovation*. **8**, 299–311.

Morris, P. A., E. Olmsted Teisberg, and A. L. Kolbe (1991). When Choosing R & D Projects, Go With Long Shots. *Research-Technology Management*. **34**(1), 35–40, January–February.

Reich, L. (1985). *The Making of American Industrial Research*. New York: Cambridge University Press.

Souder, W. E. (1978). Analytical Effectiveness of Mathematical Models for R & D Project Selection. *Management Science*. **19**(8), April, 907–923.

Souder, W. E. (1969). The Validity of Subjective Probability of Success Forecasts by R & D Project Managers. *IEEE Transactions on Engineering Management*. **16**(1), February, 35–49.

Vepsalainen, A. P. J. and G. L. Lauro (1988). Analysis of R & D Portfolio Strategies for Contract Competition. *IEEE Transactions on Engineering Management*. **35**(3), August, 181–186.

___11
MARKETING

The R & D staff of the firm tend to think in terms of technical success of a project: If it achieves its technical goals it will result in a product or process that then can be taken to the market. Brockhoff and Pearson [1992] note that inventors are often falsely convinced that their inventions will not need intensive marketing to become successful.

However, the market represents yet another hurdle beyond the technology itself. A technically successful product may still be a commercial failure. Brockhoff and Chakrabarti [1988] summarize several studies, which present data on both technical and commercial success of R & D projects. Rates of technical success are typically greater than 50%, and in several studies exceeded 75%. Rates of commercial success, however, were much lower, typically less than 50%. The discrepancy between the two figures indicates that a significant proportion of projects that meet their technical goals still fail when introduced into the market. Thus marketing considerations must play an important role in R & D project selection.

Marketing factors are those that involve the potential commercial success of the project. The marketing factors that have been discussed in the literature on R & D project selection include:

1. Degree and nature of anticipated competition for the product resulting from the project.
2. Size of the market for the product.
3. Probability of market success of the product.
4. Length of product life cycle.
5. Availability of raw materials that would be required to manufacture the product.

Some or all of these factors may need to be taken into account in selecting projects for funding.

11.1 INDIVIDUAL FACTORS

The individual factors are described in the following sections.

Competition

The study by Cooper [1975] found that the most common specific cause of commercial failure of an innovation was that the competitor was already firmly entrenched in the market. This does not mean that a new product cannot displace an older one. Many firms have found, to their dismay, that their "firm" market position has been eroded by some new product offered by a competitor. Mechanical watches, mechanical cash registers, reciprocating aircraft engines, slide rules, and vacuum tubes are all products that at one time were a dominant technology, and that have been displaced either largely or completely by new technologies. In virtually all cases, the firms that were identified with the old technology were unsuccessful in making the transition to the new technology.

Nor is it necessary that a newcomer to an industry completely replace the old technology. Lower cost, higher performance, or some combination of the two, may allow one firm to erode the market share of another firm, even with the same technology and with a virtually identical product.

In evaluating an R & D project, then, an important marketing factor will be the current state of the market. If a competitor is firmly entrenched, then the question would be, In what way can the proposed project lead to something that will displace the market leader? Will it lead to a replacement for the current technology? Will it allow the firm to bring what is essentially the current technology on the market at some attractive combination of price and performance? If the project will not either undercut or replace the product of the current market leader, the project may not rank very high from a marketing standpoint.

Size of Market

The Cooper [1975] study found that the second most common specific cause of commercial failure of an innovation was an overestimate of the number of potential users. Poensgen and Hort [1983] found that an intermediate degree of influence over R & D by marketing lead to increased return on capital for the firm. While they did not investigate the detailed nature of marketing's influence, it is reasonable to conclude that marketing would steer R & D away from projects where the market is small. (A high degree of influence by marketing on R & D led to lower return on capital, probably because of too-great focus on the short term.)

The size of the potential market, then, should be an important marketing factor in evaluating an R & D project. The size consideration must be relative to the size of the firm, of course. A market that is "too small to bother with" for a large firm might well be appropriate for a small firm that can focus its efforts on that market. In any case, however, market size should be sufficient that if the project is commercially successful, R & D costs will be recovered and the project will be profitable for the firm. If the market is too small for costs to be recovered, it is not appropriate for even a small firm.

Probability of Market Success

As used in the literature, the term "market success" is ambiguous. To some writers, it means the product will be adopted by potential users. To other writers, the number of potential users is also part of "success." That is, some may consider the innovation a failure if the potential users adopt a competing product instead, or do without the product entirely. Others would consider the innovation a failure even if it is adopted by potential users, if the total number of such users is too small to provide a reasonable return on the investment made in bringing the product to market.

The issue is not that one definition is more "correct" than the other, but that both elements of success must be taken into account. An innovation must be adopted by potential users if the project is to be counted as a commercial success. In addition, the total sales must not only be sufficient to recoup R & D and marketing costs, but should exceed the revenues from alternative investments, including not only alternative R & D projects but alternative investments in manufacturing and marketing.

Regardless of definition, aggressive marketing is crucial to sales growth. However, Brockhoff and Pearson [1992] found that harmony between R & D and marketing does not correlate well with sales growth. Marketing aggressiveness counts for more than R & D aggressiveness in increasing sales. However, harmony between the two groups was greatest when neither was aggressive, but sales growth was low with this combination. Considerations of probability of success must take the degree of marketing aggressiveness into account.

As with probability of technical success, probability of market success must be obtained through subjective judgment. Methods for doing this will be described in Chapter 19. In obtaining the estimates, however, there must be agreement on what constitutes market success. Does it consist only in capturing the market of potential users, or does it also require that the market of potential users be a large one?

Product Life Cycle

How long will it take for the product to go from introduction to obsolescence? This question is a critical marketing issue. The shorter the life cycle of the product, the less opportunity there is to recoup the costs of bringing it to the market. A good current example is the short-life cycle of central process-ing units (CPUs) for personal computers. A CPU may be "top of the line" for only two or three years. Among other things, this means there are no "repeat buyers" for a given CPU. A computer owner may "upgrade" when machines with a new CPU are available, but there is no "replacement" market in which machines with a given CPU wear out and are replaced with essentially identical machines.

In evaluating the life cycle of a potential product or process, the analyst must determine the length of time during which the product or process will be competitive for its intended purpose, whether repeat sales are possible, and the alternatives open to possible buyers.

Raw Materials

The availability of raw materials for the product or process may be an important marketing factor in deciding whether to fund an R & D project. This consideration can be very important in the pharmaceutical industry if the starting point for a product is some biological material. It may also be a consideration in the chemical industry, in those cases where the starting point is actually a byproduct or waste product from some other process. The supply of raw material may then be limited by the extent of use of the other process. Limitations on the availability of a needed raw material can affect the marketability of a product in two ways. First, the total production will be limited by the availability of the raw material, which may make the product relatively scarce. While this may drive up the market price of the product, it will also drive up the price of the scarce raw material. In effect, the firm making the final product will simply be a conduit for funds to the source of the scarce raw material. Second, a shortage of the product resulting from scarcity of the raw material may lead other firms to develop substitute products that do not depend on that raw material. This will drive the price down, but sales will still be limited by the supply of the raw material, hence total revenues from the product will likewise decline. Availability of the needed raw materials should therefore be considered when the R & D project is evaluated for funding.

11.2 EXAMPLE

Table 11.1 shows market factors extracted from Project Menu 1 of Appendix 2. Other factors would also be taken into account in selecting projects. The technical factors discussed in Chapter 10 would also be important. However, discussion here will focus on market factors.

Any of the methods discussed in Part I could be utilized to select individual projects, or a portfolio of projects, from this menu. Instead of

TABLE 11.1   Market Factors for Selected Projects

Project	Cost ($1000)	Market Share (Pct.)	Market Size ($Mill.)	Prob. Market Success (Pct.)	Stage of Innov.	Strategic Position
1	48	11	430	26	Bas. Rsch.	LOW
2	38	12	340	28	Bas. Rsch.	HIGH
3	40	10	180	63	Com'l Dev.	HIGH
4	43	13	290	68	Com'l Dev.	LOW
5	35	28	1220	30	Com'l Dev.	HIGH
6	25	28	1340	24	Com'l Dev.	LOW
7	26	20	610	52	Bas. Rsch.	LOW
8	41	15	1010	78	Bas. Rsch.	HIGH
9	53	10	810	78	App. Rsch.	HIGH
10	81	12	560	50	App. Rsch.	LOW
11	97	10	710	43	Prototype	LOW
12	51	13	1180	25	Prototype	HIGH
13	89	16	460	55	Prototype	LOW
14	78	16	180	75	Prototype	HIGH
15	97	23	270	21	App. Rsch.	HIGH
16	90	21	430	23	App. Rsch.	LOW

dealing with the specifics of such methods, however, some general considerations will be examined.

Projects 5, 6, 8, and 12 all have large potential markets. Of these, however, only Project 8 has a really high probability of market success. Other factors would have to outweigh probability of market success if the other projects were to be attractive. For instance, Project 5 has high strategic position, and Project 6 is intended for an unregulated market. These other factors might make up for lack of market size.

Project 1 is basic research, that is, very early in its life cycle, has low strategic position, and only modest estimated market size. From a marketing standpoint, this might not be a desirable project.

Depending on the objectives of the firm, marketing considerations may be used to screen out projects that do not fit the firm's marketing strategy, before applying the more elaborate project selection techniques described in previous chapters.

11.3   SUMMARY

Many of the factors that affect desirability of R & D projects are related to marketing of the final product or process. These factors can be used to screen projects before more elaborate selection methods are applied, or they can be utilized as factors in scoring, ranking, or portfolio selection.

11.4 QUESTIONS FOR CLASS DISCUSSION

1. Use Project Menu 2 of Appendix 2. Assume a budget for basic and applied research of $150 K. Select a portfolio of basic and applied projects that includes the maximum number of projects with high strategic position while remaining within the budget.

11.5 FURTHER READINGS

Bard, J. F., R. Balachandra, and P. E. Kaufmann (1988). An Interactive Approach to R & D Project Selection and Termination. *IEEE Transactions on Engineering Management*. **35**(3), August, 139–146.

Brockhoff, K. and A. K. Chakrabarti (1988). R & D/Marketing Linkage and Innovation Strategy: Some West German Experience. *IEEE Transactions on Engineering Management*. **35**(3), August, 167–174.

Brockhoff, K. and A. Pearson (1992). Technical and Marketing Aggressiveness and the Effectiveness of Research and Development. *IEEE Transactions on Engineering Management*. **39**(4), November, 318–324.

Cooper, R. G. (1975). Why New Industrial Products Fail. *Industrial Marketing Management*. **4**, 315–326.

Poensgen, O. H. and H. Hort (1983). R & D Management and Financial Performance. *IEEE Transactions on Engineering Management*. **30**(4), November, 212–222.

_____12
POLITICAL

The primary political concern in project selection is government regulations. These may include:

1. Regulations regarding product safety to users.
2. Regulation of effectiveness.
3. Safety regulation of the industry using the product or process.
4. Economic regulation of the industry using the product or process.
5. Regulations regarding workplace safety during manufacture.
6. Regulations regarding environmental hazards.
7. Regulations regarding disposability or recyclability.

Each of these types of regulation may influence product acceptance and profitability, and may need to be considered in project selection.

12.1 PRODUCT SAFETY REGULATION

Safety regulation of a product to be utilized by the firm's customers can add significant costs to the process of bringing the product to market. The usual requirement is that the product must be demonstrated to be safe when used for its intended purpose. In the case of pharmaceuticals, for instance, this means demonstrating that among the various effects produced by a drug, none are detrimental to the person taking the drug.* Safety must be demonstrated through elaborate testing. Until the responsible regulatory agency is

107

satisfied that the product is safe, it will refuse to permit the product to be marketed. The need to meet safety regulations must be taken into account in planning the project. Despite the most extensive testing, of course, a product may still turn out to have some safety hazard once it is introduced. The existence of such a hazard may call for expensive modifications (recall) or may lead to the product's removal from the market. The risk of such a safety problem must be taken into account when evaluating the effects of government regulation on product planning.

12.2   PRODUCT EFFECTIVENESS REGULATION

Some products are regulated for effectiveness as well as for safety. This is particularly true of pharmaceuticals. The product must be shown to achieve the purpose for which it is marketed. The U.S. Food & Drug Administration interprets this to mean that a new drug that is less effective than one already on the market (treats a smaller percentage of cases) will not receive marketing approval. Thus in selecting projects for funding, one consideration must be whether the resulting product or process will have an effectiveness that is competitive with products or processes already available.

12.3   SAFETY REGULATION OF THE USING INDUSTRY

Some industries are subject to regulations to enhance safety. This regulation may take two forms. One is workplace safety, discussed below, the other is the kind of regulation to which the airline industry is subjected, which is intended to ensure safe operation. This kind of safety regulation concerns itself with operational and maintenance procedures, and is intended to ensure that the product does not fail in operation. Projects intended to lead to products or processes that might be regulated for safety must take the effects of regulation into account. In particular, the extent to which they make meeting regulatory requirements easier or more difficult will have an effect on their marketability.

12.4   ECONOMIC REGULATION

Economic regulation often takes the form of setting rates that may be charged customers. Industries subject to economic regulation may have either maximum rates (e.g., electric utilities) or minimum rates (e.g., taxis) estab-

---

*In this regard it must be remembered that there are no such things as "side effects." A drug will produce several effects, some of which we want and some of which we do not want, but "nature" does not care. The effects come as a package.

lished. In either case, the adoption of new technology is likely to be influenced by the regulatory agencies involved. Historically, some regulatory agencies have encouraged technological innovation while others have discouraged it. Under the former Civil Aeronautics Bureau, the airlines were encouraged to adopt technological innovations. Under the Interstate Commerce Commission, railroads were often discouraged from adopting technological innovations, particularly those that would reduce costs and thereby improve the competitive position of the railroads vis-a-vis trucks. If the R & D project is intended to develop a product or process to be used by an industry subject to economic regulation, the attitude of the regulatory agency toward technological innovation in the industry must be taken into account.

12.5 WORKPLACE SAFETY

Regulation of workplace safety has become a major concern in many industries. Safety is becoming a significant cost factor for many firms. Workplace hazards arise from two major sources. The first is the manufacturing process uses; the second is the materials used.

Manufacturing processes that are highly energetic, such as those that involve high-temperatures, high-pressures, high-speed machinery, high-noise levels, and high-impact forces, are inherently hazardous. Workplace safety requires that workers be separated as much as possible from the energetic processes. Achieving this separation may require a higher degree of automation, or remote control allowing greater physical separation of the worker and the process, or protective equipment for the worker.

The materials used in a process may themselves be hazardous, such as toxic chemicals or radioactive materials. In some cases the purpose of the process is to produce such materials or incorporate them into a product. In other cases, these materials are ancillary to the process, such as plasticizers, degreasers, cleaning fluids, solvents, and lubricants. Whether these materials are basic to the process or are merely ancillary, there are two approaches to workplace safety. One is to protect the worker, either by isolating the process by means such as enclosing it, or by providing the worker with protective equipment. The other is to eliminate the hazard by redesign of the process. If the use of toxic or hazardous intermediate products, or ancillary materials, can be eliminated entirely, workplace safety becomes much easier to achieve.

R & D projects that find replacement materials or less hazardous processes may be very important means to enhance workplace safety. The regulations bearing on workplace safety, then, may influence the selection of R & D projects. An additional consideration is that R & D projects that eliminate safety hazards at the same time eliminate the cost of protecting against those hazards. Thus the cost reduction potential of a project should be taken into account in evaluating it. A cost reduction arising from eliminating a hazard may provide the firm with a significant competitive advantage over other firms depending on isolation or other protective measures to safeguard workers from hazards.

12.6 ENVIRONMENTAL HAZARDS

Some production processes result in environmental hazards either through emission of hazardous materials during production, or in disposal of waste materials following production. It is important to recognize that "the material balance balances." Every gram of material brought on site must leave the site, as either product, packaging, or pollution. Pollution may leave the site as uncontrolled emissions during the production process, or as contained waste at the end of the process. Clearly, the former must be reduced to negligible levels, and the latter must be reduced as much as practicable.

Dealing with environmental hazards is in some ways similar to dealing with workplace hazards. The public must be shielded from the hazardous materials. However, this always means enclosing or otherwise containing the hazardous material. Attempting to shift the burden to the public, by requiring people to utilize protective equipment, is not an acceptable solution.

R & D projects intended to reduce or eliminate environmental hazards will focus on replacing hazardous materials with nonhazardous ones, or on neutralizing the hazardous materials before they leave the plant site. Properly enclosing or containing hazardous materials is costly. R & D projects that eliminate the hazard can thereby result in significant savings to the firm. These savings should be taken into account in evaluating the project. Moreover, cost savings from the elimination of hazardous waste may give the firm a competitive advantage over other firms that incur the cost of enclosing or containing hazardous materials.

12.7 DISPOSABILITY OR RECYCLABILITY

There is growing concern about problems of disposing of no-longer-needed products and materials. The "automobile graveyard" is perhaps the most notable example of the problems of disposing of scrap materials. However, other concerns focus on paper and plastics. Even greater concern is focused on hazardous or toxic materials.

To the extent that products can be designed to be recyclable or biodegradable, disposal problems can be reduced or eliminated. While there is not yet significant regulation of this issue, it is one that may become a significant topic for regulation. Producers may eventually be faced with requirements to "build in" biodegradability or recyclability.

Disposability and recyclability of manufactured products are generally seen to hinge on two factors: ease of disassembly into different materials, and use of materials that are biodegradable or are readily recyclable. Should regulations that impose these requirements become common, greater importance must be placed on R & D projects that enhance the reusability, disposability, or recyclability of the products that a firm produces.

12.8 SUMMARY

Political considerations involving regulation of products, processes, or materials may be important in selecting R & D projects. R & D projects that will lead to products or processes subject to regulation should take the regulations into account. Will the product or process actually meet or satisfy the regulations? Can the R & D project reduce the cost of satisfying the regulations, thus providing a competitive advantage to the firm using or selling the resulting product or process? The barriers imposed by regulations, and the cost savings arising from cheaper ways of satisfying regulations, should be included explicitly as factors in the decision about funding a project.

12.9 QUESTIONS FOR CLASS DISCUSSION

1. Use Project Menu 2 of Appendix 2. Assume a maximum R & D budget of $350K. Assume that all products subject to extensive regulation will go to markets in which the regulatory agencies set minimum prices to assure profitability, and encourage technological innovation. Select a portfolio of projects intended for these markets that maximizes expected revenue (product of market share, market size, and probability of market success) while remaining within the budget.

12.10 FURTHER READINGS

Henderson, D. R. (Ed.) (1993). *The Fortune Encyclopedia of Economics*, Chapter 7, Economic Regulation. Warner Books, New York.

Henderson, D. R. (Ed.) (1993). *The Fortune Encyclopedia of Economics*, Chapter 8, Environmental Regulation. Warner Books, New York.

____13
STAGE OF INNOVATION

The stages of innovation have been discussed in several of the preceding chapters. In this chapter we will look at the project selection considerations that are most important at each stage of innovation. The stages of innovation to be considered here are

1. Basic research.
2. Applied research.
3. Prototype/pilot plant.
4. Commercial development.

Different selection criteria may be appropriate for each of these different stages of innovation.

From the standpoint of product or process development, the very purpose of R & D is to reduce uncertainty. One conducts an R & D project to reduce the uncertainty about some question. There are two types of uncertainty that R & D addresses. The first type is technical uncertainty: Can something be done, and if so, how? Can the goals be met? The second type is target uncertainty: Have the goals been set properly?* Throughout the progression from basic research to commercial development, the focus shifts from technical uncertainty to target uncertainty.

---

*There is a third type of uncertainty, process uncertainty, which involves the question of whether the project has been organized in such a manner as to achieve the goals that have been set for it. However, it is not among the purposes of an R & D project to reduce this uncertainty. This is a management issue.

13.1 BASIC RESEARCH

Basic research is a phenomenon-oriented activity. Its goal is to gain increased understanding of some phenomenon. A firm may support basic research in a particular scientific area because the phenomenon to be studied is important to its products or processes. However, the key point is that the basic research .   not of itself lead to a product or process. It will instead lead to greater .   .erstanding of the phenomena that are involved in the product or process.

The phenomena being investigated in basic research may be those that are utilized in current products or processes, with the intent of learning how to improve those products or processes. Alternatively, the phenomena being investigated may be thought to lead to new products or processes, which may either replace the firm's current line of business, or lead to new business.

An example of the first type of investigation is that done by Irving Langmuir at General Electric (GE). Once the tungsten filament lamp was in mass production, it turned out to have several problems, including short lifetime and darkening of the bulb. Langmuir decided he would make progress faster if he understood the phenomena taking place at the surface of the filament, rather than focusing on the problems themselves. He conducted a series of experiments which, as he put it, "would have seemed quite useless, or even foolish, to a man who was making a direct and logical attack on the problem of improving tungsten lamps" (Reich [1975] p. 121). He not only solved the immediate problems plaguing the tungsten filament lamp, but gained knowledge that could be applied to vacuum tubes and other GE products. In 1932 he received the Nobel prize in chemistry for his fundamental work on surface phenomena on heated filaments.

An example of the second type of investigation is that of Wallace Carothers at DuPont (Hounshell and Smith [1988], p. 232ff). A disputed question in chemistry during the 1920s was whether large polymers were single molecules held together by chemical bonds, or loosely bound aggregations of small molecules. Carothers decided to address the issue by synthesizing ever larger molecules, one step at a time, so that there would be no question of how the molecule was held together. His work demonstrated that polymers were in fact single molecules. His work led to methods for synthesizing polymers. An outgrowth of his work was the development of nylon, and particularly of the methods for producing it. Carothers' work, unrelated to any existing DuPont products, opened up an entirely new line of business for DuPont.

In evaluating basic research projects, market considerations must receive much lower weight than technical and scientific considerations. Basic research is almost entirely directed at resolving technical uncertainty. If the work is to lead to new markets, it may not even be possible to identify those markets in any detail at the outset of the research. The selection of basic research projects, then, should focus primarily on the significance of the work itself, the competence of the researcher to conduct the work, and the availability of the necessary equipment. With regard to equipment, the evaluation should take into account whether existing or currently available instrumentation is adequate to make the measurements needed during the research.

13.2 APPLIED RESEARCH

In applied research, the focus is still on gaining understanding of phenomena, but there is more of a product orientation. The researcher undertakes the project with the specific intent of gaining understanding of a phenomenon because that understanding is needed to improve a current product or process, or to make a new product or process feasible.

An example of applied research is William Coolidge's work at GE on the development of ductile tungsten for incandescent lamp filaments (Reich [1975], p. 80). Tungsten was seen as a desirable material for lamp filaments because of its high-melting point. The problem was that it was brittle and could not be drawn into fine wires for use as filaments. Coolidge and co-workers focused on gaining an understanding of tungsten's internal structure, and how to change that structure through heat treatment and mechanical impact. They finally achieved the desired ductility in tungsten metal, permitting its use in mass-produced incandescent lamps. In 1914 Coolidge received the Rumford medal of the American Academy of Arts and Sciences for his work on ductile tungsten.

In evaluating applied research projects, the significance of the work and the competence of the researcher remain critical factors. However, market factors receive somewhat more weight than they do in evaluating basic research projects. Because applied research is intended to gain understanding needed to improve a product or develop a new product, some concern must be given to the question of whether there is or would be a market for the product or process. At this stage of innovation, however, it is still too early to try to take market size and revenue into account. Emphasis should be placed on suitability and feasibility, rather than on financial return. At this stage, the emphasis is still on resolving technical uncertainty.

13.3 PROTOTYPE / PILOT PLANT

By this stage, technical uncertainty should have been resolved favorably. Manufacturability, reliability, and customer suitability become the most important questions. That is, target uncertainty becomes more important. The issue becomes, can it be done in a way to suit a customer, at a price the customer is willing to pay?

An example of this stage of innovation is the follow-up work Coolidge did once ductile tungsten was demonstrated in the laboratory (Reich [1975] p. 116). In the laboratory, Coolidge demonstrated that tungsten could be made ductile. He had produced short filaments of tungsten wire through conventional wire-drawing processes. However, at this point the method was not suitable for mass production of thousands of lamps per day. It was necessary to develop methods for preparing ingots of pure tungsten, as the starting point for the process. Then it was necessary to develop methods for controlling the temperature of both the tungsten itself and the machines that applied pressure to it, as well as the level of pressure applied. It was necessary to develop special lubricants to reduce die wear as the wire was drawn to smaller and smaller sizes. And, to cure a problem of short filament life, it was discovered that precise amounts of refractory materials, added to the tungsten, prevented the growth of crystals that would lead to fracture. The end result was a manufacturing process for tungsten wire, a process that could be scaled up to commercial size.

While basic and applied research projects usually are fairly low in cost, prototype or pilot plant projects are much more expensive. In evaluating projects at this stage of innovation, market factors become very important. Political factors may also be important.

13.4 COMMERCIAL DEVELOPMENT

At this stage, technical uncertainty and target uncertainty should both have been resolved. If a project survives to this stage, there should be confidence that it is technically feasible and that customer issues have been identified. At this point, the remaining issues are those of design. The design should meet identified customer needs, should satisfy customer expectations for reliability and durability, should be readily manufacturable, should be readily maintainable in service, and should meet whatever safety and environmental regulations apply to it. Production costs should be known fairly closely, and market size known with a high degree of confidence.

At this stage, costs and revenues become the most important considerations in project selection. A commercial development project should be treated as an investment, similar to other investment alternatives open to the firm. Thus net present value or internal rate of return may be the most important selection criteria.

13.5 SUMMARY

The stage of innovation for the project will significantly affect the criteria that should be utilized in evaluating the project. At early stages of innovation, technical criteria are the most important. At later stages of innovation, market criteria become more important. It is important not to impose selection criteria that are inappropriate to the stage of innovation. At the basic research stage, it may not even be clear what product or process will result, let alone what the size of the market will be. At the prototype or commercial development stage, technical elegance should not be allowed to overshadow questions of whether there are customers, and how much they are willing to pay.

13.6 QUESTIONS FOR CLASS DISCUSSION

1. Use Project Menu 2 of Appendix 2. Develop a scoring model for the basic research projects. What factors should be included? What should be their weights? Present a justification for including factors and assigning weights.

13.7 FURTHER READINGS

Albala, A. (1975). Stage Approach for the Evaluation and Selection of R & D Projects. *IEEE Transactions on Engineering Management*. **22**(4), November, 153–164.

Clarke, T. E. (1974). Decision-Making in Technologically Based Organizations: A Literature Survey of Present Practice. *IEEE Transactions on Engineering Management*. **21**(1), February, 9–23.

Hounshell, D. A. and J. K. Smith Jr. (1988). *Science and Corporate Strategy*, New York: Cambridge University Press.

Reich, L. S. (1975). *The Making of American Industrial Research*, New York: Cambridge University Press.

PART III
DATA REQUIREMENTS

Each of the project selection methods requires data about the criteria included in the model or profile. There may be problems obtaining this data to the accuracy demanded by some project selection methods. Some of the data can be obtained as objective facts. Other kinds of data may need to be obtained subjectively. Therefore the availability of data, or of an expert to provide subjective judgments, may influence choice of project selection methods. The chapters in this section discuss the various data types. Methods are presented for obtaining objective data or scaling subjective data.

III.1 FURTHER READING

Meadows, D. L. (1967). Estimate Accuracy and Project Selection Models in Industrial Research. *Industrial Management Review*. **9**, 105–119.

___14
TECHNICAL DATA

Technical factors, those related to the content of the project itself and its management, were described in Chapter 10. In this chapter we will discuss means for estimating the values of these factors, for inclusion in project selection methods. The technical factors described earlier are

1. Probability of technical success.
2. Existence of a product champion.
3. Competence in the required disciplines.
4. Degree of internal commitment.
5. Degree of internal competition for resources.
6. Intrinsic merit of the research.
7. Stage of innovation.
8. Source of project proposal.

Clearly, Item 2 is a binary, yes–no, event and no estimation is required. Items 7 and 8 likewise do not need to be estimated. The rest, however, do require estimation.

Methods for estimating the remainder of the technical factors will be discussed below. In all cases, it will be assumed that the analyst wishes the estimates to be made on a 0–10 scale. One effective method for improving the quality of estimates is to use anchored scales. These are scales in which specific, discrete events or situations are assigned scale values. Vague or indefinite events or situations cannot provide useful anchor points for a scale.

The events or situations must be such that an observer can determine unambiguously whether the event or circumstance actually exists.

Choosing the events to be used to anchor the scale, and assigning scale values to them, are the essence of the scale design task. Once the scales are designed, however, it becomes much easier for individuals to compare two projects or other entities on the same factor, and for two different individuals to reach agreement on the numerical value to be assigned to a specific entity on a given factor. The rating scales presented below are all based on use of anchored scales.

14.1 PROBABILITY OF TECHNICAL SUCCESS

Discussion of methods for estimating probabilities will be deferred to Chapter 20. However, factors that affect probability of technical success, and that should be taken into account in estimating probabilities, will be discussed here.

Technical success must be defined in terms of achieving a specified goal. If the goal is not well defined, probability of technical success is low. Hence, the goal must be defined before the probability of reaching it can be estimated.

For a product development project, the goal may be specified in terms of a set of technical objectives for the product, such as size, weight, power consumption, speed, and so on. (Note that the "correctness" of these goals, in terms of customer desires, is a marketing issue, not a technical issue.) For a basic research project, the goals may be expressed in terms of making a certain measurement, synthesizing a certain compound, or detecting presence or absence of a certain phenomenon.

Probability of success depends on the extent to which uncertainties and unknowns still exist with regard to the goals. Clearly, if the project has no uncertainties or unknowns, it is probably not R & D. It is simply construction (although even construction may face uncertainties). The very nature of an R & D project, then, implies that some uncertainties and unknowns exist. The probability of success depends on how well these uncertainties and unknowns have been identified. The probability of success also depends on the extent to which the design of the project permits the uncertainties and unknowns to be evaluated. This involves issues such as: Can the instrument to be used make the necessary measurements? Will the synthesis process used achieve the desired product? Can the necessary power density be achieved by the planned approach?

In general, the probability of success will be higher, the less the departure from previous experience. Similarly, the probability of success will be higher, the better the theoretical understanding of the goal. That is, even a significant departure from previous practice may have low risk if the theory used to predict behavior is well founded.

While the probability of success is a subjective estimate, and must be obtained as a judgment of the people most knowledgeable about the project, the various factors affecting probability of success must be evaluated as objectively as possible.

14.2 COMPETENCE IN THE REQUIRED DISCIPLINES

The issue here is whether or not the skills and knowledge to conduct the R & D project already exist within the organization. Note that if the skills do exist within the organization but are assigned to other tasks, the skills may actually be unavailable. This possibility will be considered under "competition" below. However, since the proposed project may be assigned a higher priority than competing projects, the skills should be rated as "available" even if the staff members are assigned to other tasks.

If the skills do not exist within the organization, then there are two possibilities: retraining existing staff or hiring new staff. Retraining is a realistic possibility only if some members of the existing staff have related skills, so that the needed skills can be acquired readily. If extensive retraining is required, it may be better to hire new staff, since the retraining would take considerable time and delay start of the project.

The first step in assessing this factor is to identify the skills that will be required to carry out the work. This task should certainly include the scientific and engineering disciplines that are expected to be needed. In addition, the assessment should include instrument makers, laboratory technicians, data reduction technicians, computer programmers, glass blowers, and any other skills needed to support the project.

Despite the manager's best efforts to identify the needed skills, it may turn out once the project is under way that one or more skills are required, which were not anticipated, or the mix of skills is somewhat different from original expectations. To some degree, this will be inevitable. However, a thorough evaluation should be made at the outset, to minimize the amount of "surprise" that will be encountered during the course of the project.

Once the needed skills have been identified, the next step is to determine their availability within the firm. This determination should include personnel from other divisions of the laboratory, or other departments in the firm. It may be possible to transfer these people to the project, or to borrow them temporarily, and a promising project should not be abandoned simply because the needed people work in another department.

After the available skills have been identified, the degree of availability must be converted into a scale suited for use in the project selection method to be employed. Figure 14.1 shows an example of a scale that might be used to obtain judgments for a scoring model. It is a 0–10 scale, which is "anchored" with descriptive statements. Such a scale could be used to evaluate one or more projects on this factor.

```
10┬ All skills in ample supply
 9┼ All skills available with no excess
 8┼
 7┼ All professional skills available, some technical skills retraining needed
 6┼
 5┼ Some professional retraining needed
 4┼ Extensive technical retraining needed
 3┼ Extensive professional retraining needed
 2┼ All technical skills must be hired
 1┼ All technical skills and some professional skills must be hired
 0┴ All professional and technical skills must be hired
```

Figure 14.1. Example of scale for availability of skills.

One assumption behind this particular scale is that technical skills are easier both to retrain and to hire than are professional skills. If this assumption is not valid in specific cases, the anchor points on the scale would have to be revised. In addition, the numerical values of the anchor points may need to be adjusted up or down, if they do not properly reflect the situation in the particular laboratory for which the evaluation is being performed.

By identifying the skills needed for a project, and comparing them with the skills available or potentially available, it is possible to estimate a numerical value for the organization's degree of competence in the disciplines required for a particular project.

14.3 DEGREE OF INTERNAL COMMITMENT

As noted in Chapter 10, internal commitment to the project includes not only the researchers conducting the project, but those other workers whose support will be required (e.g., testing, fabrication, or data reduction), and higher management. If any of these groups are not really committed to the project, their support will not be forthcoming when it is needed. If the project workers themselves are not committed to the project for some reason, they will not be aggressive in pursuing leads, looking for ways around problems, and seeking alternatives if their current approach turns out to be fruitless. If supporting groups are not committed to the project, they will be unwilling to put out extra effort or provide rapid response when the project gets in trouble or must meet a tight deadline. If higher management is not really committed to the project, it will not receive high priority, its resources will be "borrowed" when other projects get in trouble, and support will disappear when the project itself gets in trouble.

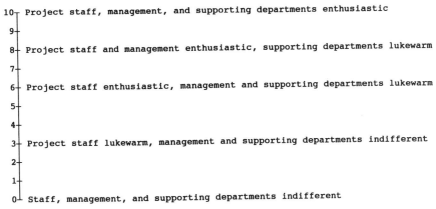

Figure 14.2. Example of scale for degree of commitment.

The problem that the manager encounters in estimating degree of internal commitment is that everyone may *say* at the outset that they are committed, when in reality they are not. This need not be deliberate deception. The people involved may be willing to "go along," but do not really take the project seriously.

This means that the manager who has to make the final decision about approving the project may need to make his/her own estimates of other people's degree of commitment, and these may differ from the publicly stated positions of the people involved. The manager may thus need to keep these estimates secret from the people involved. However, if (say) a scoring model shows a low score for a project about which no one is really enthusiastic, it is unlikely that anyone will ask about the factors that went into the score. Hence the decision maker may be able to use his/her own estimates of other people's degree of commitment without ever revealing what those estimates were.

A possible scale is shown in Figure 14.2. It is shown only as an example, and can be adjusted to tailor it to specific cases.

14.4 DEGREE OF INTERNAL COMPETITION FOR RESOURCES

In assessing the degree of internal competition for resources, the decision maker must identify those resources required for the project. Project staff and supporting department requirements will already have been identified if the factors listed above have been evaluated. Beyond these requirements, the decision maker should identify resources that must be shared with other projects, such as specialized test equipment required for the project, model shop and instrument shop effort, supercomputer time, environmental test chamber time, and any other required resources that are not under the direct

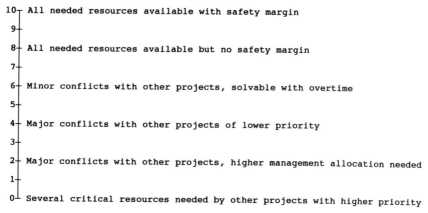

Figure 14.3. Example of scale for competition for resources.

control of the project manager. This evaluation should also include other projects with a higher priority, which may generate an unexpected demand for resources if they get in trouble.

Once the potential resource conflicts are identified, the decision maker then must assess the magnitude of the potential conflicts. It is possible that total demand for some resource may exceed capacity within the planning horizon? If so, what is the potential extent of the excess demand? How likely is that excess demand? What are the relative priorities of the projects that might create excess demand on limited resources?

With the potential conflicts identified, the decision maker can then estimate a value for this factor. A possible scale is shown in Figure 14.3. This scale is shown as an example only, and may need to be revised to fit actual cases.

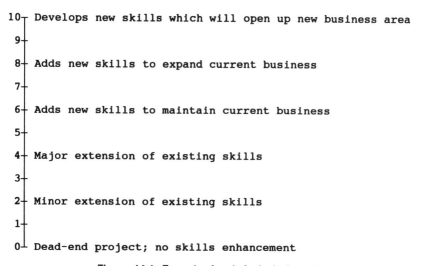

Figure 14.4. Example of scale for intrinsic merit.

14.5 INTRINSIC MERIT OF THE RESEARCH

This factor describes the extent to which a project enhances the skills of the research staff. The enhanced skills may lead to new business areas, they may lead to new projects in current business areas, or may simply be refinements of existing skills. An example of a possible rating scale for intrinsic merit is shown in Figure 14.4. It can be adjusted to tailor it to specific cases.

14.6 SUMMARY

Technical factors are important in the evaluation of an R & D project. Unfortunately, most of the relevant technical factors cannot be measured directly. It is necessary to rate them subjectively. The reliability of this subjective rating can be improved by using properly developed scales, in which specific events or situations serve as anchor points for the scale. These scales ordinarily will need to be tailored to fit the specific circumstances of the decision maker responsible for project selection. However, by applying the general approach of anchored scales, reliable estimates can be derived.

14.7 QUESTIONS FOR CLASS DISCUSSION

1. Which of the following descriptors would be suitable as anchor points for a scale for rating technical feasibility of a development project? For each descriptor, state why it is suitable or unsuitable.

   Adaptation of technique used in related field.
   Computations based on accepted theory.
   Design specifications based on experimental results.
   Easy extension of current state of the art.
   Laboratory model successfully demonstrated.
   Modest extension of current state of the art.
   Working prototype already built.
   Within current state of the art.

14.8 FURTHER READINGS

Cooper, M. J. (1978). An Evaluation System for Project Selection. *Research Management*. **21**, July, 29–33.
Lockett, G., B. Hetherington, and P. Yallup (1984). Modeling a Research Portfolio Using AHP: A Group Decision Process. *R & D Management*. **16**(2), April, 151–160.

Meadows, D. L. (1968). Estimate Accuracy and Project Selection Models in Industrial Research. *Industrial Management Review*. **9**, Spring, 105–119.

Mehrez. A. (1988). Selecting R & D Projects: A Case Study of the Expected Utility Approach. *Technovation*. **8**, 1988, 299–311.

Reich, L. (1985). *The Making of American Industrial Research*. New York: Cambridge University Press.

Souder, W. E. (1978). Analytical Effectiveness of Mathematical Models for R & D Project Selection. *Management Science*. **19**(8), April, 907–923.

Souder, W. E. (1969). The Validity of Subjective Probability of Success Forecasts by R & D Project Managers. *IEEE Transactions on Engineering Management*. **16**(1), February, 35–49.

———15
MARKET DATA

Marketing factors are those factors that involve the potential commercial success of the project. The marketing factors that were identified in Chapter 11 as being important were

1. Degree and nature of anticipated competition for the product resulting from the project.
2. Size of the market for the product.
3. Probability of market success of the product.
4. Length of product life cycle.
5. Availability of raw materials that would be required to manufacture the product.

Most of the project selection techniques presented in Chapters 2–9 require information about the market or payoff for the project. However, at an early stage of innovation for a product or process, it may be difficult to obtain realistic market data. This fact will be particularly true of basic and applied research projects, for which the final form of product or process is not really known. For projects at the prototype or commercial development stage, however, reliable market information should be more readily available.

Each of the market factors is discussed in the following sections. For each factor, it will be assumed that the analyst wishes to estimate a value on a 0–10 scale. Example scales, using anchor points based on the market factors, are shown.

15.1   COMPETITION

A commercial product or process is intended to perform some function or solve some problem for a user. The user may have alternative means of performing that function or solving that problem. In fact, the user may have alternatives that eliminate the problem entirely, replacing it with some other problem. As a homely example, a householder can eliminate the problem of scrubbing and waxing floors by installing wall-to-wall carpeting, thereby changing the problem to one of sweeping the carpet. In considering the competition for the product or process that results from an R & D project, then, it is insufficient to look only at direct alternatives. It is necessary to look more broadly, to include alternatives that represent completely different ways of achieving the same objective.

The ability to evaluate the degree of competition will vary with the stage of innovation. The closer the project is to market, the more readily the competition can be identified.

When a project is at the product development stage, the competing products or processes are already available to customers (i.e., on the market), or are likewise in final stages of development. These alternatives may even have already been evaluated in the process of selecting the project that is being conducted. Thus they are likely to be well understood. However, the analyst must beware of looking only at direct alternatives. As noted above, alternative ways of achieving the same function compete with the product or process.

When a project is at the basic research stage, it may not be possible to determine what will compete with any products or processes that eventually result. Indeed, basic research is usually undertaken to find something better than the current method of performing some function or solving some problem. Moreover, if the function to be achieved is important, and the current method is seen to have serious shortcomings, it is likely that others will also devote much effort to finding superior solutions. Thus while the current method can be looked upon as a competitor, it is highly likely that additional competing products or processes will emerge by the time a marketable product or process is finally developed from the findings of the basic research.

In general, then, the competition must be viewed in terms of the function to be performed for the user. What is the user's problem? Are there alternative ways of solving it? Are there ways of "trading" it for some other problem? The farther away the project is from the ultimate market, the more broadly it is necessary to look for competing products or processes.

Figure 15.1 shows an example of a scale that might be used to obtain judgments for a scoring model. A scale such as this could be used to evaluate one or more projects on degree of competition. (Note that a condition of little or no competition receives a high score on the scale, to be compatible

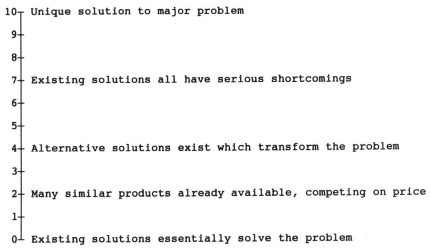

Figure 15.1. Example of a scale for rating degree of competition.

with other scales in which a larger number represents a more desirable situation.)

15.2 MARKET SIZE

The size of the market can be expressed in several ways, such as number of potential customers or monetary value of sales. Ultimately the concern with market size is to assure that if the product is successful, it can recoup R & D costs and provide a profit for the firm. One current instance in which this is an issue is so-called "orphan drugs." These are drugs that treat diseases that afflict only a comparatively few people, or that primarily afflict people who cannot afford much medical treatment. The cost of developing a drug, testing it for effectiveness and safety, and bringing it to market, is not only quite high but is almost independent of the number of people who need it. Thus a drug with only a small potential market is unlikely to be brought to market, since the costs of development cannot be recouped.

In general, the earlier the stage of innovation, the more difficult it is to estimate market size. This is not always true, of course. In the case of basic medical research intended to lead to treatment of some disease, the size of the market (number of sufferers) is often known at the outset. Indeed, the size of the market may be a critical factor in determining whether to approve the project. Nevertheless, it is usually easier to determine the size of the market for product development projects than it is for basic research projects, since the latter are not intended to result directly in a product, but instead are intended to gain the understanding needed for subsequent product-oriented efforts.

A major problem with high-technology projects is that they may be based on technology push rather than on market pull. The technologists' enthusiasm for some "neat" technical solution may lead them to overlook the question of whether anyone really needs the final product. Thus the market size may be overestimated. Even if there is a need for the product, technology push may lead to its being "user hostile," since it may be loaded with technical features that display the virtuosity of the designer but that do not respond to the actual needs of the customer. Thus the product may not achieve the full market that actually exists. A later model, or a competitor's product, more attuned to actual user needs, may be more successful.

Conversely, the market for even a high-technology product may be underestimated. Certainly no one in 1973 foresaw the eventual market for personal computers. The first such machines brought on the market were marketed to hobbyists through electronics magazines, and it was assumed the market would be a small one. As it turned out, the market was far larger than anyone anticipated. Personal computers turned out to meet many needs people did not realize they had, not only in business offices and research laboratories, but in households.

Market size can be a critical issue in determining whether to approve a project. At the product development stage, market size is often relatively easy to determine. At the basic research stage, market size is much more difficult to determine. Indeed, it may not be particularly relevant, since the cost of basic research is much smaller than the cost of product development. At the basic research stage, the anticipated utility of the information to be gained, in terms of making more informed choices regarding product development or strategic positioning, may be of more significance than the size of any eventual markets. Nevertheless, even basic research is expected to lead eventually to a marketable product or process, hence market size must in some way be taken into account.

Market size is usually estimated in terms of number of potential users and the amount they are willing to pay to obtain the benefits of the product or process under development. Number of buyers may be estimated in a variety of ways, such as:

1. Number of persons facing some problem for which no solution exists (e.g., number of people suffering from a disease for which there is no current cure).

2. Number of persons already using a complementary product (e.g., number of TV set owners is the maximum market for VCRs).

3. Number of persons already using a less satisfactory solution to the same problem (e.g., number of offices using typists represents potential market for word processors).

4. Number of persons already using lower performing version of the product or process, who therefore represent a market for an upgrade.

Amount buyers are willing to pay may be estimated in several ways, such as:

1. Savings to be achieved by adopting the new product or process.
2. Price of less-satisfactory solutions to the same problem.
3. Price of complementary or related products (e.g., price of a VCR should not exceed the price of a TV set).
4. Price of alternative solutions to the same problem (e.g., an electric car should not cost more than a gasoline car of comparable performance).

Estimates of market size should be made at all stages of innovation. The earlier the stage of innovation, however, the more difficult it is to define the market, let alone estimate its size. At any stage of innovation, efforts must be made to avoid either the error of assuming that customers will buy a product simply because of its technical elegance, or the error of assuming that a product, which offers a radically new capability, will find little market because "people never bought anything like that before."

15.3 PROBABILITY OF MARKET SUCCESS

Discussion of methods for estimating probabilities will be deferred to Chapter 20. This section will discuss those factors that may affect probability of market success.

Probably the most critical factor affecting market success is the extent to which the product or process meets an identified need of the potential user. Thus the probability of market success depends on the extent to which user needs have been identified. If they have not been identified clearly, the product or process may have a low probability of market success, since meeting those needs would happen almost entirely by accident rather than through design.

If user needs have been properly identified, the next consideration is the alternatives open to the potential user. Are there other solutions available to the same problems? If so, are they cheaper? Are they easier to use? Are they more aesthetically satisfactory? Are their shortcomings more acceptable than the shortcomings of the proposed product?

In making estimates of probability of market success, the analyst must take into account the extent to which the proposed product or process meets user needs, and the alternatives open to the user.

15.4 PRODUCT LIFE CYCLE

As noted in Chapter 11, the length of the product life cycle, from introduction to obsolescence, can affect the profitability of the product, and thus the worth of a project that might eventually lead to marketing the product.

In evaluating the product life cycle, the analyst must consider: Is the product a one-time-use item, such that there will be repeat sales? Is it reusable or long lived? If so, will it become obsolete before it wears out, or will users instead purchase identical replacements? If it becomes obsolete before it wears out, so there are no repeat purchases, for how long will it be marketable?

If the life cycle is very short, then development costs must be recouped from first-time purchasers. If the life cycle is comparatively long, especially if it is long enough to permit repeat purchases, then long-term profits can be high, and comparatively high development costs can be tolerated. The rate of obsolescence thus becomes an important consideration in determining whether to approve a project.

Figure 15.2 presents an example of a scale that could be used to rate product life cycle. It can be modified to suit particular circumstances.

15.5 AVAILABILITY OF RAW MATERIALS

The intent of an R & D project is to provide some product or process that satisfies a need of the ultimate user. If the product or process successfully meets that need, but production is limited by the availability of some raw material, then the market may turn out to be small even though the number of potential users is much larger. A recent real-life example of this situation was the discovery that a naturally occurring compound, taxol, was an effective

```
10┬ One-time-use item; many repeat purchases possible before obsolescence

 9┼

 8┼ Rapidly consumed in use; frequent replacement needed

 7┼

 6┼ Wear-out expected before obsolescence; some repeat purchases possible

 5┼

 4┼ Slow obsolescence; worn-out items replaced with modestly-improved models

 3┼

 2┼ Rapid obsolescence; frequent upgrades to improved models

 1┼

 0┴ Fad item; high risk of being left with large unsold inventory
```

Figure 15.2. Example of a scale for length of product life cycle.

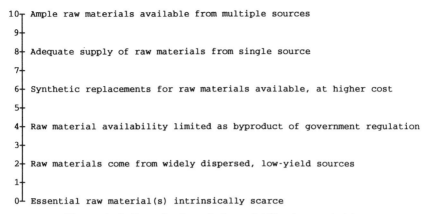

Figure 15.3. Example of a scale for availability of raw materials.

treatment for certain types of cancer. The problem was that it could be obtained only from the bark of a comparatively rare species of yew tree, thus drastically limiting the supply. It appeared that the full market could not be served because there was simply not enough raw material. Eventually, however, taxol was synthesized, and the raw material problem disappeared.

While this situation, raw material shortage, is not an every-day occurrence, it should be considered in evaluating the market for the product or process coming from the R & D project. That is, the usual concern is, "How big is the market? How many buyers are there?" The possibility of a raw material limitation, however, reverses the situation. The question then becomes, "How many customers can be served?" If the available supply of a needed raw material is limited, the actual market for the product or process is thereby constrained to be less than the number of would-be buyers. If the constraint is severe enough, the rewards for bringing the product or process to market may not be sufficient to justify the project.

Figure 15.3 presents an example of a scale for rating availability of raw materials. It can be modified to suit individual circumstances.

15.6 SUMMARY

Marketing considerations are of critical importance in R & D projects that are intended to lead to commercial application. However, it may be difficult to evaluate marketing factors at an early stage of innovation. During basic and applied research, the focus should be on verifying that there is a demand for the product or process, and casting a wide net to identify alternatives that are or might be available to potential buyers. At the prototype or product development stages, the market should be fairly well defined, and its evaluation much easier. At any stage, the use of anchored scales can help improve the quality of estimates of marketing factors.

15.7 QUESTIONS FOR CLASS DISCUSSION

1. Which of the following descriptors would be suitable for use as anchor points in a scale for probability of market success? State why each descriptor is or is not suitable.

More customer benefit per dollar than competing products.

More features than competing products.

Production cost lower than for competing products.

Service life longer than that of competing products.

Tests show easier to learn to use than competing products.

Uses less expensive raw materials than competing products.

15.8 FURTHER READINGS

Bard, J. F., R. Balachandra, and P. E. Kaufmann (1988). An Interactive Approach to R & D Project Selection and Termination. *IEEE Transactions on Engineering Management*. **35**(3), August, 139–146.

Brockhoff, K. and A. K. Chakrabarti (1988). R & D/Marketing Linkage and Innovation Strategy: Some West German Experience. *IEEE Transactions on Engineering Management*. **35**(3), August, 167–174.

Brockhoff, K. and A. Pearson (1992). Technical and Marketing Aggressiveness and the Effectiveness of Research and Development. *IEEE Transactions on Engineering Management*. **39**(4), November, 318–324.

Cooper, R. G. (1975), Why New Industrial Products Fail. *Industrial Marketing Management*. **4**, 315–326.

Poensgen, O. H. and H. Hort (1983). R & D Management and Financial Performance. *IEEE Transactions on Engineering Management*. **30**(4), November, 212–222.

_____16
POLITICAL CONSIDERATIONS

As noted in Chapter 12, government regulation can be a significant factor in selection of R & D projects. These regulations may include:

1. Regulations regarding product safety to users.
2. Regulation of effectiveness.
3. Safety regulation of the industry using the product or process.
4. Economic regulation of the industry using the product or process.
5. Regulations regarding workplace safety during manufacture.
6. Regulations regarding environmental hazards.
7. Regulations regarding disposability or recyclability.

Each of these factors is described below. For each factor, an example scale is presented, to illustrate how this factor might be rated in practice. These scales can be tailored to meet individual requirements.

Note that on all scales, the condition of "no regulation" is given a scale value of 1.0. This value allows the comparative evaluation of projects, some of which are affected by regulation and some of which are not. Those that are not affected simply receive a rating of 1.0, and their overall score is unaffected by concerns about legal regulation.

16.1 PRODUCT SAFETY

Given a choice among several R & D projects, the product safety issues can be an important one. Products that present hazards to users in normal

135

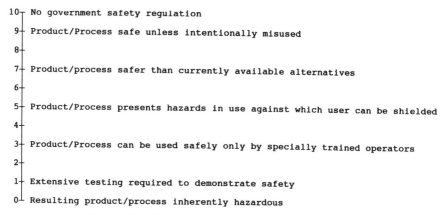

Figure 16.1. Example of a rating scale for product safety.

operation may be subject to government regulation. A project that reduces the hazards of an existing product or process can reduce costs to users, resulting in improved sales. Reduction or elimination of a hazard can also provide a competitive edge, if competing products continue to present the previous hazards.

If a product or process must demonstrate that it meets safety regulations before it can be marketed, it will be more costly to bring to market than an otherwise equivalent project, which does not face such regulations. Hence the need to demonstrate safety can be a negative factor in making a decision among several possible projects.

Figure 16.1 presents an example of a scale for rating projects that may face government regulation for product safety. This scale can be modified to suit individual circumstances.

16.2 PRODUCT EFFECTIVENESS

If the product or process resulting from the R & D project must demonstrate effectiveness before the relevant regulatory agency will permit it to be marketed, this factor should be taken into account before the project is selected. In some cases (e.g., pharmaceuticals), the product or process will not even be approved by the Food & Drug Administration (FDA) if it is inferior to existing methods. In other cases, a product or process may be approved for use even if its overall effectiveness is inferior to that of existing methods, particularly if it can be effective in cases not covered by the existing methods.

In any case, if regulation for effectiveness is a consideration, all projects competing for support should be evaluated on this criterion. An example of a

```
10┬ No regulation for effectiveness

 9┤

 8┤ Product/process superior in all respects to those currently available

 7┤

 6┤ Product/process superior in some respects, equal in others, to those currently
   │    currently available
 5┤

 4┤ Product/process superior in some respects, inferior in others, to those
   │    currently available
 3┤

 2┤ Product/process essentially matches those currently available

 1┤ Extensive demonstration of effectiveness required

 0┴
```

Figure 16.2. Example of scale for product effectiveness.

scale for rating effectiveness is shown in Figure 16.2. This scale can be modified to suit individual needs.

It should be noted that concerns about effectiveness cannot be limited only to project selection. If regulation for effectiveness is a consideration, each project should be evaluated periodically to determine whether its original evaluation is still valid. Indications that the resulting product or process will be less effective than originally estimated, or that effectiveness may be more expensive to demonstrate than originally estimated, may be cause for termination of the project.

16.3   INDUSTRY SAFETY

Some industries, such as transportation (airlines, railroads, trucking, etc.), are regulated to increase safety in operation. Products or processes that are utilized in these industries may be required to demonstrate that they will not create a hazard in normal operation.

A variety of considerations may affect the safety of a product or process in operation. Some possible considerations are

1. Fail-safe design (provision of alternate load paths or back-ups).
2. High-confidence detection of incipient failures (real-time detection, or periodic inspections for "slow" failures).
3. Known safe operating period, allowing replacement before failure.
4. Operating environments that shorten safe lifetimes (sand, dust, saltwater).
5. Protection against known hazards (e.g., explosion-proof enclosures or grounding of static electricity charges).

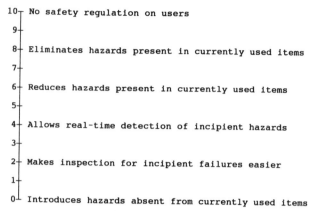

Figure 16.3. Example of a scale for conformance to safety regulation.

Incorporation of features that enhance safety may make a product more attractive to buyers in an industry subject to safety regulation. Conversely, failure to incorporate safety-enhancing features may reduce the competitiveness of a product or process.

Figure 16.3 provides an example of a scale that could be used to rate a project for the extent to which it makes it easier for potential users to meet safety regulations. This scale is general in nature. It should be refined to meet the specific requirements of the industry or group expected to use the product or process that will result from the R & D project.

16.4 ECONOMIC REGULATION

The purported goals of economic regulation are two: to protect buyers against unfairly high prices, and to assure sellers of "fair" prices. The former goal is usually pursued by setting maximum or "ceiling" prices. Public utility regulation is an example of this type of regulation. The latter goal is usually pursued by setting minimum prices. Farm price supports are an example of this type of regulation.

Many economists doubt the value of either type of regulation. See, for instance, Chapter 7 of Henderson [1993] for a series of essays on various types of economic regulation. However, from the standpoint of R & D project selection, the arguments of the economists are irrelevant. Economic regulation exists, including price floors in some industries and price ceilings in others. The question, then, is how to take this into account in selecting among projects, some of which may be intended for use in industries facing economic regulation.

If an industry is regulated to maintain prices above a minimum level (price floor), this price level is obviously set above the market price (otherwise the price floor makes no sense). The inevitable result, however, is that the excess profits generated by prices above the market level will attract other firms to the industry. Thus there must be barriers to entry to prevent new firms from entering and competing the price down (legal price floors can often be circumvented by price-cutters by various means, such as rebates, discounts for "quantity orders" or "prompt payment," and extension of credit at below-market interest rates). In many cases the barriers to entry are legal ones, created as part of the regulations establishing floor prices: examples include limiting the number of licenses (taxicab licenses and acreage restrictions on growing cotton or peanuts); requiring would-be entrants to demonstrate that there is a "need" for their services, which is not being met by the existing firms (used by the trucking industry prior to deregulation); requiring an "industry council" of existing firms to approve or new entrants (also used in the trucking industry prior to deregulation). However, these political barriers to entry can sometimes be overcome by political means. It is far more satisfactory to the firms in the industry if the barriers to entry can be based on technological means, such as machinery requiring a large capital investment, which discourages firms from entering. Thus an R & D project that promises to shield those firms already in an industry by increasing the barriers to entry may be very profitable.

Another problem facing industries subject to price floor regulation is that the workers in the industry may attempt to capture some of the industry's excess profits by obtaining above-market-level wages (i.e., above those obtained by workers with equivalent skills in other industries). This is often done by restricting the supply of workers, either through occupational licensing requirements or the need for special skills (trucking and airlines, before deregulation, are examples of industries where workers captured much of the industry's excess profits through above-market wages). That is, the workers themselves may benefit from legal or technical barriers to entry into the industry's work force. Innovations that reduce these barriers to entry into the work force will benefit firms in the industries enjoying price floor regulation. Likewise, "labor-saving" innovations, which reduce the size of the work force, can greatly benefit industries enjoying price floor regulation.

Figure 16.4 provides an example of a scale for rating R & D projects that are intended for use in an industry subject to price floor regulation. This scale can be modified to fit individual situations.

Firms in industries subject to price ceilings face a somewhat different set of problems stemming from regulation. They usually must convince a regulatory agency that they "need" an increase in the ceiling, usually by showing that their costs have increased, or that their rate of return on investment is

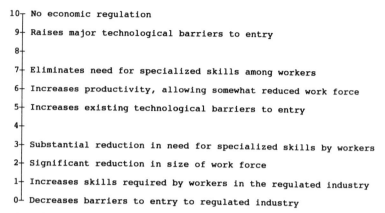

10┬ No economic regulation

9┤ Raises major technological barriers to entry

8┤

7┤ Eliminates need for specialized skills among workers

6┤ Increases productivity, allowing somewhat reduced work force

5┤ Increases existing technological barriers to entry

4┤

3┤ Substantial reduction in need for specialized skills by workers

2┤ Significant reduction in size of work force

1┤ Increases skills required by workers in the regulated industry

0┴ Decreases barriers to entry to regulated industry

Figure 16.4. Example of scale for products / process used by industries subject to minimum price regulation (price supports).

"unfairly" low (laws establishing public utility regulation often place a floor under the firm's rate of return). The "hearings" before a regulatory commission are often highly politicized, with political influence having more weight than either economics or technology. Once a rate is established, however, it is rarely revisited. That is, if costs decrease, the rate is not subject to new "hearings," to establish a lower rate.

While cost-reducing innovations are important to any industry, they are especially important to industries subject to ceiling price regulation. As noted earlier, they do not usually cause a reopening of the issue of "fairness" of the current rates, thus increasing the firms' profitability. A cost-reducing innovation also can extend the time between requests for a rate increase, thus reducing the effectiveness of opposing arguments and enhancing the likelihood of getting the increase (We haven't asked for an increase in five years; inflation during that time has increased the general price level X%; we're lagging behind and we need a rate increase).

Industries subject to price ceiling regulation are often "protected" by floors on their rate of return on investment. The floor provides them with an incentive to replace workers with machinery, since wages are a pure cost, while capital investment increases their "rate base," allowing greater total profits at a given minimum rate of return.

Innovations that decrease the skill levels required of workers also increase the size of the pool from which workers can be drawn, thus holding down wages in the industry. While this represents a cost saving, it is different in nature from simply increasing workers productivity or replacing workers with machinery.

Figure 16.5 is an example of a scale for rating innovations to be used in industries subject to ceiling prices. It can be modified to fit individual cases.

```
10┬ No economic regulation

 9┤ Significantly increases rate base, replacing workers with machinery

 8┤

 7┤ Major increase in worker productivity

 6┤

 5┤ Decreases operating costs from maintenance and consumption of raw materials

 4┤

 3┤ Minor increase in worker productivity

 2┤

 1┤ Minor decrease in operating costs

 0┴
```

Figure 16.5. Example of scale for products / process used by industries subject to maximum price regulation (price ceilings).

16.5 WORKPLACE SAFETY

As noted in Chapter 12, workplace hazards can arise from either energetic processes or hazardous materials. These workplace hazards raise costs in several ways: workers may require premium pay before accepting hazardous jobs; accidents raise operating and insurance costs; workers must be shielded from hazards.

Innovations that make it easier to shield workers from hazards can reduce costs due to accidents, and may reduce the wage premium required to attract workers. While such innovations are useful, they still do not eliminate the hazard, which continues to exist behind the shield. In those cases where the

```
10┬ No safety regulations

 9┤ Completely replaces hazardous material/process with non-hazardous one

 8┤

 7┤ Replaces current process with less hazardous one

 6┤

 5┤ Replaces current process with one easier to shield

 4┤

 3┤ Reduces need for workers' safety equipment

 2┤ Improves workers' safety equipment

 1┤ Introduces new hazard, but reduces costs

 0┴ Introduces new hazard with no cost saving
```

Figure 16.6. Example of a scale to rate products or processes for changes in workplace safety.

hazard arises from the materials used in production, it may not be possible to eliminate the hazard. Hence, processes that are easier to shield can be important to the user.

Innovations that eliminate the hazard by replacing the hazardous material with a less hazardous one, or replace an energetic process with a less energetic one, may be superior to innovations that merely neutralize the hazard. Even if the new processes or materials are more expensive, this added cost may be offset by eliminating the costs resulting from the hazard.

Figure 16.6 is an example of a scale to rate R & D projects that alter the workplace safety of the using industry. It can be modified to suit individual circumstances.

16.6 ENVIRONMENTAL HAZARDS

R & D projects that have the effect of reducing environmental hazards can employ one or a combination of three methods: replacing a hazardous material with a less-hazardous one; improving the containment of hazardous materials; or improving the ability to neutralize hazardous materials before they are shipped from the site as waste. This latter method may involve an improved processing technique, or it may involve use of a substitute material, which is easier to process. Clearly, replacing a hazardous material is the best approach, but it may not be possible. In such a case, development of better containment or neutralizing methods can decrease the costs of the industry faced with the environmental hazard.

Figure 16.7 is an example of a scale for rating R & D projects for their suitability for an industry subject to environmental regulation. This scale may be modified to suit individual circumstances.

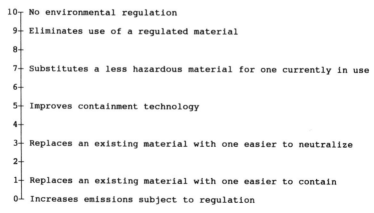

```
10┬ No environmental regulation

 9┼ Eliminates use of a regulated material

 8┼

 7┼ Substitutes a less hazardous material for one currently in use

 6┼

 5┼ Improves containment technology

 4┼

 3┼ Replaces an existing material with one easier to neutralize

 2┼

 1┼ Replaces an existing material with one easier to contain

 0┴ Increases emissions subject to regulation
```

Figure 16.7. Example of a scale for rating R & D projects on reduction of environmental hazards.

```
10┬ No recycling regulation

 9┤

 8┤ Replaces current material with a completely biodegradable material

 7┤

 6┤ Replaces current material with one which is readily recyclable

 5┤

 4┤ Enhances ability to disassemble into homogeneous components for easier recycling

 3┤

 2┤ Replaces some components with recyclable ones

 1┤

 0┴ Increases difficulty of recycling or disposing
```

Figure 16.8. Example of a scale for rating R & D projects on disposability / recyclability.

16.7 DISPOSABILITY / RECYCLABILITY

An R & D project may allow the replacement of materials that are not biodegradable, or that cannot readily be recycled, with materials that do biodegrade or can be recycled. This replacement would enhance the ability of the product to satisfy regulations requiring built-in disposability or recyclability. If the product is a complex one, involving two or more components with different properties, it may be necessary to disassemble it and treat the separate components differently. An R & D project that facilitates disassembly of some product can enhance the disposability or recyclability if that product. For instance, a current product may require a component containing multiple layers of materials with different properties in order to achieve some desired effect (e.g., low-moisture permeability combined with high-dielectric constant). An R & D project that results in a single material that combines all the desired properties means the component can be made of that single material, resulting in easier disassembly for recycling or disposal, as well as lower costs for assembly in the first place.

Figure 16.8 is an example of a scale for rating R & D projects on the extent to which they enhance the recyclability or disposability of products and materials. This scale can be modified to suit particular situations.

16.8 SUMMARY

Government regulations, on either the process by which something is manufactured, the materials of which it is made, the hazards it presents, or on the prices of the industry using it, can affect the market value of the product or process resulting from an R & D project. The impact on these government regulations should be taken into account in selecting projects for support.

Scales can be devised that allow the user to rate a project in terms of how it affects or is affected by government regulation, and that allow comparison with projects that are not affected by government regulation. Such scales should be utilized for rating projects that are expected to lead to products or processes subject to regulation.

16.9 QUESTIONS FOR CLASS DISCUSSION

1. Assume your company has manufacturing plants in several countries around the world, with each plant manufacturing products for sale in the country where it is located. Assume each country has strong "domestic content," laws, requiring that all products sold have at least a certain percentage of locally manufactured materials or components. Assume that a central R & D laboratory develops products for manufacture in each of the factories. Devise a rating scale for R & D projects that can help evaluate the conformance of the resulting products to these domestic content laws. Consider use of locally produced raw materials, locally manufactured components, and "value added" in your firm's factories.

16.10 FURTHER READINGS

Henderson, D. R. (Ed.) (1993). *The Fortune Encyclopedia of Economics*, Chapter 7, Economic Regulation. Warner Books, New York.

Henderson, D. R. (Ed.) (1993). *The Fortune Encyclopedia of Economics*, Chapter 8, Environmental Regulation. Warner Books, New York.

___17
COST DATA

Costs of R & D projects can be categorized as development (or nonrecurring), capital, manufacturing, and sales costs. Accurate estimates of these costs are required by project selection methods, which involve cash flow or portfolio optimization. Estimating of capital, manufacturing, and sales costs are important disciplines in their own right, and are not covered here. The focus here will be on estimating the nonrecurring costs associated with research, development, and testing. The methods to be considered are bottom up estimating, regression analysis, and cost modeling.

Regardless of the method used for cost estimating, the first issue to be resolved is, "What is the question to be answered?" That is, why is the estimate being made? For what purpose will the information be used? The answer(s) to these questions will determine the level of detail needed in the cost estimate, and the accuracy required.

17.1 BOTTOM UP ESTIMATING

Bottom up cost estimating is based on identifying what actually needs to be done during the course of the project, then determining the cost of those activities. A bottom up estimate, then, requires a detailed work breakdown structure for the project. Within each work package, several sources of cost must be evaluated.

Figure 17.1 shows an illustrative work breakdown structure for a space instrument package. The package is to contain several instruments. Each instrument has several major components. For each component, there is a set

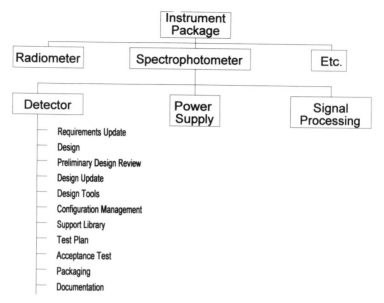

Figure 17.1. Work breakdown structure for space instrument package.

of discrete tasks that must be carried out. These tasks are identified as separate activities. Each of these individual tasks must then be costed separately.

Fundamentally, all the costs associated with each task are based on either labor or materials, since these are the things the firm pays for. However, these two categories may need to be examined in more detail. The following considerations should be taken into account in estimating the cost for each work package.

Labor Hours

Direct labor hours must be estimated for the completion of the work package. If necessary, these may be further broken down by pay grade or worker classification. However, the analyst should also take account such considerations as overtime. For instance, if an attended test must be run long enough to include a weekend, overtime pay for the test operations must be included. In addition, allowances for rework of fabricated items, or repetition of unsatisfactory tests or experiments, may be needed. Allowances for such "excess" items should be based on experience with similar prior projects.

Purchase of Materials

Direct costs of purchased materials are an obvious item to be included in the cost estimate. However, it may also be necessary to include costs of incoming inspection or any other processing required. Material costs should include allowances for waste, spoilage, fabrication errors, and incoming defects.

Length of Project

Some costs are based upon calendar time for completion of the work package rather than on level of activity in the work package. Obvious examples of this category of cost are leased equipment, project-unique security guards (if required), and administrative support. The analyst should identify all costs related to the project that are calendar-time based, and therefore depend on the duration of the work package rather than on total effort. Estimating these costs for a specific task requires an estimate of the calendar duration of the task.

Special Considerations

Not all costs can be handled as suggested above. There will be cases that need special handling. Typical examples of these special cases are as follows:

1. Specialized test equipment is purchased, which will be used for several tasks on the project. How should its cost be allocated among the tasks? Should it be treated as a single cost item charged to the project as a whole?
2. What cost, if any, should be assigned to a life test in the natural environment (i.e., no special environmental test chambers, just place the item outdoors)?
3. What cost, if any, should be assigned to approval of shop drawings?
4. Should overhead be computed in the same way for all tasks?
5. Should cost for activities, such as purchasing, subcontract negotiation, and approval of shop drawings, be included in direct costs or in overhead?
6. Should costs for project management be included in direct costs or in overhead?

Cost-Reducing Considerations

After the work breakdown structure has been developed and individual activities costed, the entire cost package should be reviewed to see if there are cost reduction possibilities. The following issues should be examined:

1. Are there common items or identical elements in several work packages that could be standardized to reduce cost?
2. Are there any items for which similar or identical designs have already been accomplished for other projects?
3. Are there off-the-shelf or commercial components or subsystems available, which could be substituted for items in the design without compromising performance?

A major problem with bottom up costing is that at the beginning of an R & D project, it may not be possible to develop a work breakdown structure in the detail needed to develop costs. Some activities anticipated at the outset will not actually be carried out (e.g., acceptance test of a device that failed at the brassboard stage). Some activities not anticipated at the outset will actually occur (e.g., tests of a replacement material when the original choice fails an accelerated life test). However, when bottom up costing can be done, it is likely to be the most accurate method. Moreover, it is relatively easy to explain and defend.

17.2   MULTIPLE LINEAR REGRESSION

Bottom up costing is based on identifying the activities that must be carried out, and determining the cost of each. An alternative approach is based on project goals rather than on project resource inputs. The assumption is that it is the project goals that drive costs, and the activities that are carried out flow from the goals, not vice versa. Therefore the idea is to base the cost estimate on what the project is to accomplish, rather than basing it on the activities needed to accomplish it.

This can be illustrated with an example. Consider Project Menu 7 of Appendix 2. The data presented are costs of software development projects. The analyst has determined that three variables are the primary influences on costs. One is source lines of code (SLOC), which is the direct output of the programmers' effort. Another is the number of modules. Breaking the code down into independent modules simplifies the direct coding effort, but creates problems of integration, increasing costs. The third is the security requirements imposed by the customer. The more stringent the security requirements, the more costly the project. These security requirements are rated on the scale shown in Figure 17.2.

By using the multiple linear regression capability of a spreadsheet, we can compute the regression coefficients for cost as a function of the three variables. The results are

Cost($K) = 3674.40 + 35.64*KSLOC + 0.118*Modules − 285.12*Security

The actual costs from Menu 7 and the predicted costs from this regression equation are shown in Table 17.1. The actual versus predicted costs are plotted in Figure 17.3. A 45° line is also shown in the figure. If all the predicted costs were equal to the actual cost, the points would fall on the 45° line. Those points falling above the line represent overestimates; those points falling below the line represent underestimates.

This regression model, then, could be utilized to estimate the cost of a future software development project, knowing the size of the project and the customer's security requirements. Source lines of code, and number of

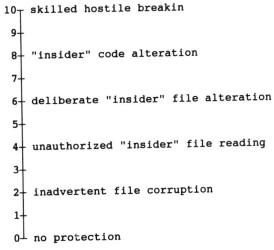

Figure 17.2. Scale for software security.

TABLE 17.1   Actual versus Predicted Costs for Software Projects

Actual	Predicted
5,776.9	7,093.8
4,454.0	4,944.3
5,696.6	5,250.1
2,782.4	2,903.9
10,043.3	10,706.9
5,223.2	6,505.9
4,026.4	3,413.4
2,632.0	3,358.6
28,237.0	27,583.2
22,703.8	20,220.8
9,095.5	9,240.5
33,525.5	34,133.6
27,133.4	28,959.6
23,738.6	21,409.0
49,571.6	50,321.6
15,770.8	14,365.6

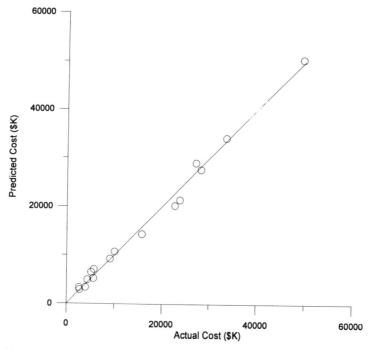

Figure 17.3. Actual versus predicted costs of software development projects.

modules, would have to be estimated on the basis of prior experience with similar projects.

Note that the regression model must be computed for a specific organization, since it is based on past experience. Moreover, the regression model may have to be recomputed from time to time as conditions change. For instance, introducing computer aided software engineering (CASE) tools should increase the productivity of the programmers, reducing cost. Introducing a higher level of design discipline should reduce the integration problems associated with independent modules, also reducing cost. Greater experience with security requirements might reduce the cost of meeting them. Conversely, introducing a new higher order language may raise costs since programmers are not as familiar with it.

This approach is not limited to estimating software development costs. It can be used for any kind of R & D project, provided the important cost drivers are known, and there is an historical data base available from which to compute the regression coefficients.

17.3   COST MODELING

Cost modeling goes beyond the regression analysis of the preceding section to develop more complex models relating cost to performance goals. These models may range in level of detail from productivity of the individual engineer to overall cost of a development project.

Simmons [1992] discusses several models that predict programmer productivity as a function of task size. One typical model is that proposed by Watson and Felix [1977]:

$$KSLOC/MM = 0.192(KSLOC)^{+0.05}$$

This model implies that programmer productivity increases slightly as program size (KSLOC) increases. Other models cited by Simmons have slightly negative exponents, implying that productivity drops as program size increases. Clearly, it would be necessary to fit a model for a particular firm, to determine how productivity varies with total effort. Moreover, this type of model is not limited to software productivity. Engineering productivity in many kinds of development activities could be modeled, if sufficient historical data were available to fit the model.

In Chapter 18 a method will be presented for estimating the time when a particular level of performance should be achieved. As a byproduct of this technique, a particular development project can be characterized as "early" or "late" depending on whether it is ahead of or behind the "expected" time. Moreover, a quantitative measure of the degree of advance or delay is readily available.

Dodson [1985] found that the measure of "early" or "late" development of the device correlates well with the cost of the development project. Thus to apply this method, the analyst must develop a model relating cost to state of the art (SOA) advance. This can be done by regressing costs of past projects (corrected for inflation if necessary) on their degree of SOA advance. The result will be a model similar to that described in Section 17.2, but relating cost to SOA advance, not to specific product characteristics, such as those used in Section 17.2. The analyst should then estimate the degree of advance in SOA required by the project to be costed. The model can then be applied to estimate the cost of the project.

Cost models, such as those described here, are used primarily for preliminary estimates. The estimates they generate should be replaced with bottom up estimates as early in the development cycle as possible.

17.4 DISTORTING FACTORS

Some factors are hard to include in formal cost estimating procedures. However, they can have a significant effect on the accuracy of cost estimates. Some of these distorting factors are listed in Table 17.2. The analyst should attempt to correct the cost estimates arrived at by other means for the effects of these factors, if they are present in the project.

TABLE 17.2   Distorting Factors that Can Affect Cost Estimates

Volatility of customer requirements
Personnel continuity
Management quality
Customer interface quality
Amount of documentation required
Security and proprietary restrictions

17.5   SUMMARY

R & D projects involve nonrecurring costs for research, design, and testing. Estimates of these costs may be required for certain project selection techniques. As the project progresses from basic research through product development, estimates of costs to be incurred through continuing the project become more accurate. This result suggests that early in the project's history, selection methods should be utilized that do not demand high accuracy in cost estimates.

17.6   QUESTIONS FOR CLASS DISCUSSION

1. Using the data from Project Menu 8 of Appendix 2, compute a regression model to be used in estimating software development costs.

17.7   FURTHER READINGS

Dodson, E. N. (1985). Measurement of State of the Art and Technological Advance. *Technological Forecasting & Social Change.* **27**(2/3), May, 129–146.

Helm, J. (1992). The Viability of Using Cocomo in the Special Application Software Bidding and Estimating Process. *IEEE Transactions on Engineering Management.* **39**(1), February, 42–58.

Moder, J. P., C. R. Phillips, and E. W. Davis (1983). *Project Management With CPM, PERT, and Precedence Programming.* New York: van Nostrand-Reinhold Company.

Simmons, D. B. (1992). A Win–Win Metric Based Software Management Approach. *IEEE Transactions on Engineering Management.* **39**(1), February, 32–41.

Watson, C. E. and C. P. Felix (1977). A method of programming measurement and estimation. *IBM System Journal.* **10**(1), 10–29.

─────18
TIME ESTIMATES

Estimates of time to completion or time to market may be required for certain project selection techniques. For instance, those methods involving portfolio optimization subject to constraints dictated by specialized equipment or unique skills may require estimates of time to completion for a project. Time to market may also be required for project selection techniques involving discounted cash flow, net present value, or cash flow payback. An estimate of when a competitor might be expected to have an equivalent product can be helpful in selecting the performance goal for a product development project. The methods presented in this chapter include both methods for estimating the time to complete an activity, and a method for estimating when some performance level will appear on the market.

18.1 PROJECT TIME ESTIMATION

Estimating the time a project will take, from start to finish, is of course a highly subjective activity. Moreover, it necessarily involves uncertainty, since an R & D project represents something never done before, unlike a construction project, which involves a sequence of known activities (but which is still subject to uncertainty). The fact that an estimate is subjective, however, is not a reason to avoid making it, or to make it haphazardly. Time estimates can be sharpened by following certain procedures.

First, it is necessary to analyze the project at as fine grained a level of detail as possible. The project should be dissected into individual tasks. Each task should be a discrete activity, with a defined starting and a defined ending point. Tasks might include such things as making a measurement, fabricating

153

a device, preparing a sample, or running a test. Each of these discrete tasks is similar to tasks that have been carried out before. Prior experience with similar tasks can be used to sharpen the estimate of time for a given task, by comparing the relative difficulty of the task to be done with past similar tasks. If a bottom up estimating procedure has been used, the work breakdown structure developed for it should also be used for time estimates.

Once the times for the individual tasks are estimated, the total time for the project becomes the sum of the times for all activities on the "critical path." The critical path is made up of activities that cannot be started until some other activities are completed, and represents the longest path through the network of parallel and serial tasks required by the project.

Once the tasks are defined, and prior experience with similar tasks called upon, other factors can be taken into account to adjust the time estimates for the tasks. These factors fall under several headings, which are presented below.

Fixed-Time Activities

Some activities take a fixed length of time, which is not under the control of the project manager. Examples of such activities include legal requirements for approval of tests by regulatory agencies and notices of public hearings. These may be fixed by law or regulation and cannot be changed. Other examples are transportation times, technical requirements, and requirements imposed by specifications or standards. Transportation times represent simply the time that may be required to move something from one point to another, as for instance to move a test item to the off-site laboratory or test site where a test is to be conducted. Instances of technical requirements include such things as time to cure a composite material, time to bring a test chamber to a desired temperature, and time to "cook" a composition while some desired reaction takes place. Specifications and standards may impose fixed time requirements, such as specifying that a material is to be tested under certain conditions for a fixed number of hours or days.

These fixed times, while not under the control of the project manager, are at least comparatively easy to estimate. However, even though a test is to take a fixed length of time, setup for the test may vary depending on the skill of the technicians and the complexity of the test. Past experience will again be the best guide to estimating the time for these pre- and posttest activities.

Note that even though the times for these activities are fixed, the project manager may be able to run other activities in parallel with them. Hence, the project itself may not be lengthened by the full amount of time required by the fixed activities. This possibility must be taken into account in estimating total project time.

Uncontrollable Factors

Some tasks may be affected by factors that are not only under the control of the project manager, but are to some extent individually unpredictable. These include weather, natural disasters, strikes, and lead times for critical purchased items.

Weather may affect tasks that must be conducted "outdoors," such as tests in an operating environment—flight tests, road tests, and environmental measurements. Weather may also affect tasks that require construction of new facilities, since the construction activity itself may be delayed by weather.

Natural disasters may disrupt the operating site. Even if the natural disaster occurs somewhere else, it may affect a supplier, or the transportation of some critical component or material.

Strikes may affect the firm directly. However, strikes at suppliers or at transportation companies may also affect a project, as they may delay delivery or shipment of critical materials.

Procurement lead times may change dramatically. Recent examples include sudden increases in lead times for solid rocket fuels, and for certain electronic microcircuits, caused by fires at plants supplying critical materials. Lead times may also change suddenly as demand for some critical components rises or falls.

While these kinds of delays cannot be predicted individually, at least not a long time ahead, they may be predicted in the aggregate, on the basis of past experience. Moreover, many of them are such that some degree of advanced warning is available. This is particularly true of labor disputes and weather. In practice, then, the project manager can revise the project schedule when advanced warning of one of these kinds of delay is received.

Competing or Incompatible Activities

There may be situations in which activities compete with each other, or are incompatible with each other. These must be scheduled in series, thus possibly adding to the length of the project.

Competing activities usually involve requirements for some limited resource: use of a particular measuring instrument or piece of test equipment; time of a technician with a rare skill, such as a glass-blower; computation-intensive activities that overload computing capability; test item fabrication requirements that exceed the capacity of the fabrication shop. These competing requirements should be known as soon as the individual tasks are defined. The project manager can then arrange the overall project schedule to eliminate the conflicts. To the extent possible, these competing demands on critical resources should be scheduled in parallel with noncompeting activities that are on the critical path, in order to avoid having these activities themselves become part of the critical path.

Incompatible activities usually involve tasks that would interfere with each other, or that would increase some hazard, if attempted simultaneously. For instance, if a test item must be tested for both radio frequency (RF) emissions and safe operation in an explosive atmosphere, it would be unwise to run both tests simultaneously if the RF test equipment itself has not demonstrated safety in the explosive atmosphere. Incompatible activities are not always as obvious as are competing activities. Once the project activities are defined, the project manager should examine them carefully for possible incompatibilities, then take these into account in estimating the time for completion of the project.

Project-Related Delays

Some activities that are directly related to a project, or that exist because people are assigned to the project, may contribute to delays or require adjustments in the time estimates for individual tasks. Smith and Mandakovic [1985] present a list of such activities. This list is given in Table 18.1. These are project related in the sense that they occur because of the project, or they are normal activities of the people on the project. They must be taken into account in estimating the time required for individual tasks.

TABLE 18.1   Project-Related Delay Factors

Coffee Breaks
Nonproject related phone calls
Washroom breaks
Travel time
Project-related meetings
Office parties
Availability of required tools and equipment
Changes in work procedures
Learning curve effects
Skill levels
Personal rest, fatigue, and delay
Misinterpretation of activity definition
Relocation time for new employees
Availability of support functions
Communicating instructions
Maintenance
Setup and changeover
Inoperable equipment
Rework of incorrectly made parts
Repetition of questionable or invalid measurements

TABLE 18.2   Non-Project-Related Delay Factors

Vacations
Employee Turnover
Sick leave
Non-project meetings
Attendance at seminars, other non-project professional activity
Maternity leave
Holidays

Nonproject Delays

Some activities that would take place even without the project may contribute to delays or require adjustments in the time estimates for individual tasks. Smith and Mandakovic [1985] present a list of such activities. This list is given in Table 18.2. These activities delay the project because they take time away from it. Past experience can be helpful in estimating the degree to which these activities will contribute to delay.

Calendar Time versus Project Time

Certain activities may be estimated as requiring a specific time to carry out. However, this time may not all be work time. For instance, if an unattended test requires 10 days to carry out, part of the time will include weekends. Thus the actual work time involved may be less than the calendar time required. Task time estimates based on total work hours involved and task team size may need to be adjusted to take into account any differences between work time and calendar time.

Estimating project time, then, requires that individual tasks be identified. The time for these tasks should be estimated on the basis of historical experience. Adjustments to the estimates may be required to take into account unique or special factors related to the project. Finally, the tasks must be organized into a network of serial and parallel activities, with the aim of reducing overall project duration by scheduling as many activities in parallel as possible.

18.2   ESTIMATING THE TIMING OF A PERFORMANCE GOAL

Setting the performance goal for an R & D project involves a trade-off between two opposite risks: the risk of project failure and the risk of early product obsolescence. If the performance goal for the project is set low, the risk of project failure is minimized. However, the risk that a competitor will bring out a somewhat better product shortly after the "easy to achieve" product is marketed becomes quite high. The commercial life of the product will then be short. There may not be enough time to recoup even R & D and marketing expenses, let alone make a significant profit from the product. If the performance goal is set very high, a successful project will result in a product with a long and profitable commercial life. However, setting a high goal increases the risk of project failure. By focusing on a difficult-to-achieve goal, the project team may choose one or more approaches that represent "long shots." If these approaches work at all, they will achieve the desired goal, but their chances of working are low. Thus by setting a goal that demands a "go for broke" attitude on the part of the project team, the risk of failure is increased.

Selecting the right balance between risk of project failure and risk of early obsolescence is of course a management decision. However, a tool is available that can assist managers in assessing the magnitude of the two risks, thereby helping to select the proper balance.

In technological forecasting, it is common to carry out a linear regression of performance on time, to project performance into the future. However, a "reverse regression," of time on performance, can help answer the question of the timing of a given performance level.

To illustrate this technique, we will utilize the data on efficiency of illumination sources (lumens per watt), from Table A3.1 of Appendix 3. We will utilize the data from 1850–1935, to obtain confidence bounds on timing of performance levels. The resulting confidence bounds will then be compared with the actual introduction of the fluorescent lamp in 1942.

Growth in illumination efficiency appears to be exponential. Therefore we would want to regress the year of achievement on the logarithm of efficiency. This could be done using the regression capability of a spreadsheet. Unfortunately, most spreadsheets do not calculate confidence bounds for the predictions from a linear regression. Hence it will be necessary to carry out the regression step by step with the use of a spreadsheet. Before doing this, we need to develop some formulas.

The regression equation is given by

$$\hat{Y} = \beta_0 + \beta_1{}^*X$$

where

$\hat{Y}$ is the *estimate* of the dependent variable Y

X is the independent variable

β_0 is the constant term (intercept) of the regression and

β_1 is the coefficient of the independent variable (X coefficient).

We have N pairs of values for the dependent and independent variables. We can compute the following sums from the data: ΣY, ΣY^2, ΣX, ΣX^2, and

ΣXY. We can also compute the following averages or mean values:

$$Y = \frac{\Sigma Y}{N}$$

$$X = \frac{\Sigma X}{N}$$

In addition, we can compute the following variables:

$$S_{xx} = \Sigma X^2 - (\Sigma X)^2 / N$$

$$S_{yy} = \Sigma Y^2 - (\Sigma Y)^2 / N$$

$$S_{xy} = \Sigma XY - (\Sigma X)(\Sigma Y) / N$$

With these computations made on the data, we can now compute the regression coefficients:

$$\hat{\beta}_1 = \frac{N * \Sigma XY - (\Sigma X)(\Sigma Y)}{N * \Sigma X^2 - (\Sigma X)^2}$$

$$\hat{\beta}_0 = Y - \hat{\beta}_1 X$$

$$\hat{\sigma} = \left[\frac{S_{yy} - \hat{\beta}_1 S_{xy}}{N - 2} \right]^{1/2}$$

where the $\hat{ }$ on the β values indicates an estimate based of the true values, based on sample data. The coefficient of determination of the regression (square of the correlation coefficient) can be computed as:

$$R^2 = \hat{\beta}_1 \frac{S_{xy}}{S_{yy}}$$

When we carry out the regression to obtain the values of the regression coefficients, we obtain the equation of a line or curve. If the equation captured perfectly the relationship between X and Y, all the data points would fall on the line or curve. However, the historical data are found to be scattered around the "best-fit" line or curve. If there is scatter in the historical data, there will be scatter in the future as well. Thus we want to obtain some estimates of how much scatter there will be in the future. The "prediction interval" or confidence bounds on future values of the independent variable can be computed as:

$$\hat{Y}_0 = \pm t_{(\alpha/2, N-2)} * \left[1 + \frac{1}{N} + \frac{(X_0 - X)^2}{S_{xx}} \right]^{1/2} * \hat{\sigma}$$

This is an interval that is symmetrical, in the sense that it is centered on the mean of the distribution of values (in this case the best-fit curve), and the two "tails" (the regions outside the interval) have equal probability. In the equation, X_0 is a specific value of the independent variable, Y_0 is the corresponding bound to the prediction interval, α is the total probability in the tails (one-half on either side of the interval), and t is the Student-t value corresponding to $\alpha/2$ and the number of degrees of freedom, $N - 2$ (we have N data points; in estimating two regression coefficients, we have "used up" two degrees of freedom, leaving only $N - 2$). (Values of t for various numbers of degrees of freedom and selected values of the probability *inside* the confidence interval are given in Table A3.3 of Appendix 3.)

With these formulas, we can now set up a spreadsheet. This is shown in Table 18.3. The efficiencies are shown in Column A. The logarithms (X) are shown in Column B. Values of X^2 are shown in Column C. The values of Y^2 and XY are shown in Columns E and F, respectively. The sums and means are computed below the data values, in rows 17 and 18 (note that the sums for Columns B and G include only rows 2–10, corresponding to actual data in Column D). The regression coefficient β_1 the intercept β_0, and the correlation coefficient, as well as the S values, are computed from the earlier values. The best-fit regression line is shown in Column G, and the residuals (difference between actual values and the regression line) are shown in the Column H.

We want the prediction contours for 5, 25, 75, and 95% likelihood of achieving future values of the illumination efficiency. Suppose we have an *interval* that includes a 90% probability of enclosing future values, and is symmetrical such that there is a 5% probability of being outside the interval on either side (5% in each tail). Then the lower bound of that interval is one such that there is a 5% chance that the performance will be achieved before that date (lower tail). The upper bound of that interval is one such that there is a 95% chance that the performance will be achieved before that date (upper tail). Likewise a symmetrical interval 50% "wide" gives the 25 and 75% bounds on likelihood of achieving the performance. The regression line itself, which splits the prediction intervals in two, provides the line such that there is a 50% chance of the performance occurring before the date given by the regression line. The prediction contours are shown in Columns J–M. Note that the best-fit line and the prediction contours are projected beyond the actual data, to a maximum value of 60 lumens/W.

TABLE 18.3 Spreadsheet for Reverse Regression

	A	B	C	D	E	F	G	H	I	J	K	L	M
	Efficiency	log(Eff)=X	X^2	Year=Y	Y^2	XY	Best Fit	Residuals	Resid^2	5%	25%	75%	95%
2	0.1	-1.000000	1.00	1850	3422500	-1850.00	1853.05	-3.05	9.33	1830.44	1844.57	1861.54	1875.67
3	1.6	0.204120	0.04	1879	3530641	383.54	1887.45	-8.45	71.38	1868.22	1880.24	1894.66	1906.67
4	0.7	-0.154902	0.02	1892	3579664	-293.07	1877.19	14.81	219.23	1857.33	1869.74	1884.65	1897.06
5	2.6	0.414973	0.17	1894	3587236	785.96	1893.47	0.53	0.28	1874.45	1886.34	1900.61	1912.49
6	12.7	1.103804	1.22	1901	3613801	2098.33	1913.15	-12.15	147.57	1893.89	1905.92	1920.38	1932.41
7	10	1.000000	1.00	1907	3636649	1907.00	1910.18	-3.18	10.13	1891.05	1903.00	1917.36	1929.32
8	19.3	1.285557	1.65	1913	3659569	2459.27	1918.34	-5.34	28.51	1898.78	1911.00	1925.68	1937.90
9	20	1.301030	1.69	1928	3717184	2508.39	1918.78	9.22	84.98	1899.19	1911.43	1926.13	1938.37
10	40	1.602060	2.57	1935	3744225	3099.99	1927.38	7.62	58.06	1907.10	1919.77	1934.99	1947.66
11	45	1.653213					1928.84			1908.42	1921.18	1936.50	1949.27
12	50	1.698970					1930.15			1909.59	1922.44	1937.86	1950.70
13	55	1.740363					1931.33			1910.65	1923.57	1939.09	1952.01
14	60	1.778151					1932.41			1911.62	1924.61	1940.21	1953.20
15	65	1.812913					1933.40			1912.50	1925.56	1941.25	1954.31
16	Count		9										
17	Sum	5.756642	9.37	17099.00	32491469	11099.40	17099.00		629.47				
18	Mean	0.639627	1.04	1899.89	3610163	1233.27			9.48				
19													
20	beta1=	28.564429											
21	beta0=	1881.6183											
22	corrcoeff=	0.9383661											
23	t(.05,7)=	1.895											
24	t(.25,7)=	0.711											
25	Sxx=	5.6860745											
26	Syy=	5268.8889											
27	Sxy=	162.41947											
28	sigmahat=	9.4828372											

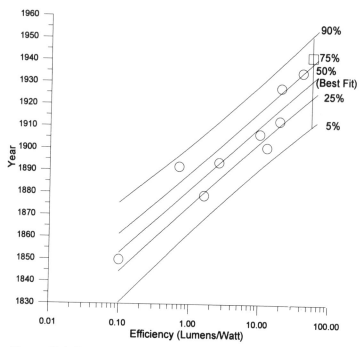

Figure 18.1. Regression of efficiency on time, with prediction contours.

The results of these computations are shown in Figure 18.1. The time of introduction of artificial illumination sources is plotted against their efficiency (lumens per watt), as shown by the circles. The regression line fitted to the logarithms of efficiency, for light sources up to and including incandescent lamps, is shown. The 50 and 90% confidence bounds on the regression are also computed and plotted, giving the 5, 25, 75, and 95% cumulative probability prediction contours. For instance, the lower 90% confidence bound is the contour such that there is only 5% probability that a given performance level will be achieved *earlier* than that time. The upper 90% confidence bound represents a cumulative probability of 95% that a given performance level will be achieved by that time.

A vertical line is drawn between the 5 and 95% contours at the initial performance level of fluorescent lamps, 55 lumens/W. The time of introduction of the fluorescent lamp is plotted as a square. As can be seen, the fluorescent lamp "arrived" later than expected, based on the entire history of innovations in artificial illumination. In fact, according to the analysis, there is a greater than 75% chance that the performance level of the fluorescent lamp would have been achieved earlier than it actually was.

This method can be applied generally, when historical data are available regarding performance and time of introduction of technological devices for carrying out some specified function. Regression time on performance (or logarithm of performance, if appropriate), and computing the prediction bounds, can provide the analyst with an estimate of the likelihood that a specified performance will be achieved by a certain date. This information can then be used to balance the risks of choosing a project goal that is so ambitious as to risk project failure, and choosing a goal that is so easy that it is likely to be superseded shortly after the project is completed.

Note that, as mentioned in Chapter 17, the distance a point falls above or below the trend (best-fit) line is a measure of the degree of advance it represented. A point below the trend line should be more difficult to achieve than one above the line, since it represents an accelerated advance of the state of the art (SOA), while one above the line represents a project that did not fully achieve the SOA advance theoretically possible. Therefore, this reverse regression not only provides an estimate of the trade-off between risk of project failure and risk of early obsolescence, it provides a measure of the difficulty of achieving the project's goals. As noted in Chapter 17, this degree of difficulty has been found to be correlated with project cost. The more ambitions a project, in terms of technical goals, the more expensive it is.

This technique can also be applied to R & D projects in which the performance of the technology is described by multiple parameters instead of by the single parameter used in the example above. Table A3.4 presents data on 56 jet engines introduced between 1943 and 1989. The year of introduction is given, as are the thrust to weight ratio for the engine, the fuel economy (pounds of thrust per pound of fuel per hour), and the maximum thrust of the engine. (Note that engines are usually described in terms of specific fuel consumption, defined as the reciprocal of the fuel economy measure given in the table.) Note that these are all functional parameters, describing the engine in terms of parameters of concern to the user. An engine might also be specified using technical parameters, such as turbine inlet temperature and bypass ratio. In general, it is bad practice to mix functional and technical parameters in the same analysis, since that may lead to double-counting of some parameters. The analysis should either use only functional parameters (those performance parameters that cause it to have value to the user) or use only technical parameters (those that the designer manipulates to achieve the desired performance).

The year of introduction of the engines can be regressed on the functional parameters by using the multiple regression capability of a spreadsheet. The resulting regression equation is

$$Year = 1935.31 + 4.59*Thrust\_to\_Weight + 0.2388*Fuel\_Econ$$

$$+ 0.0004467*Max\_Thrust$$

Table 18.4 presents the actual and predicted years of introduction for the jet engines. These results are also plotted in Figure 18.2. Those points above the line are "early," in the sense that they represent developments that arrived

TABLE 18.4 Actual and Predicted Yearsfor Jet Engine Introduction

Actual	Predicted
1943	1944.844
1944	1945.112
1944	1950.004
1944	1947.407
1944	1947.391
1944	1949.266
1944	1951.308
1946	1948.449
1948	1950.86
1948	1947.249
1948	1951.06
1949	1955.745
1949	1951.064
1949	1949.185
1949	1953.569
1949	1951.496
1950	1950.814
1952	1954.358
1952	1950.972
1953	1953.682
1953	1951.766
1954	1956.476
1955	1956.754
1956	1953.878
1957	1952.503
1958	1965.492
1960	1963.316
1960	1966.804
1962	1962.833
1962	1964.125
1962	1963.062
1963	1963.062
1963	1963.062
1963	1965.758
1963	1968.43
1966	1969.848
1967	1962.836
1967	1964.812
1967	1964.585
1968	1963.118
1968	1966.819
1969	1967.138
1969	1980.439
1971	1975.561
1972	1972.055
1972	1987.902
1973	1981.84

1974	1965.299
1974	1969.268
1981	1967.648
1981	1967.062
1983	1981.721
1985	1954.632
1985	1979.974
1987	1981.263
1989	1966.952
1989	1985.073

sooner than predicted by the regression equation. Those points below the line are "late," in that they arrived later than predicted. Again, the distance above or below the line can be used as a measure of how "difficult" or "easy," respectively, the development projects were. This relative ease or difficulty may be useful in estimating the cost of the development project. Note that the scatter in the data might be reduced by including additional

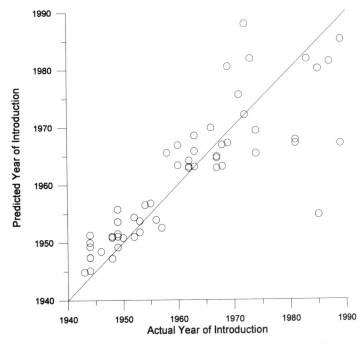

Figure 18.2. Actual versus predicted years of jet engine introduction.

parameters, which capture aspects of jet engine performance not captured by the parameters used, such as engine durability (time between overhauls) or resistance to damage from ingestion of runway debris or birds (foreign object damage).

18.3 SUMMARY

Time estimates are sometimes required for selection of projects. Either of two kinds of estimates may be required. One is the length of time the project itself will take. The other is the time by when a specific performance might be achieved. The former is needed for computations of present value of the project. The latter is needed for setting project goals. While there is uncertainty associated with both kinds of estimates, this chapter has presented techniques by which the estimates can be sharpened, to reduce uncertainty and improve their quality.

18.4 QUESTIONS FOR CLASS DISCUSSION

1. Use the data on aircraft speed records from Appendix 3. Regress time of the speed record (Y) on the logarithm of speed (X), for aircraft speed records between 1919 and 1939. Compute the 50 and 90% confidence bounds for this regression, out to 1955. Plot the time interval between 5 and 95% cumulative probability for a speed record of 606 miles/h (the first record set by a jet aircraft). Where did actual achievement of that speed record fall in the time interval? Was it early? Late? Do you conclude that the project that achieved it was relatively high risk or relatively low risk? How long did the record stand?

18.5 FURTHER READINGS

Martino, J. P. (1992). *Technological Forecasting for Decision Making*. New York: McGraw-Hill.

Moder, J. J., C. R. Phillips, and E. W. Davis (1983). *Project Management with CPM, PERT, and Precedence Diagraming*, 3rd ed., New York: Van Nostrand-Reinhold Company.

Smith, L. A. and T. Mandakovic (1985). Estimating: The Input into Good Project Planning. *IEEE Transactions on Engineering Management*. **32**(4), November, 181–185.

Wadsworth, H. M. (1990). *Handbook of Statistical Methods for Engineers and Scientists*. New York: McGraw-Hill.

____19
STRATEGIC POSITION

The immediate objective of an R & D project is to achieve a set of specified technical goals. However, the technical goals themselves should be chosen in the light of some higher set of goals dealing with the firm's overall objectives. That is, the project's technical goals should be chosen so that successful completion of the project strengthens the firm's position relative to existing competitors in the firm's current business areas, or makes it possible for the firm to enter new businesses. In evaluating a project, then, the potential for strategic positioning should be considered. Even if a project meets its technical goals, if it does not enhance the strategic position of the firm, or at least maintain that position, the project may not be justified.

The strategic considerations to be considered in project selection are

1. Core competencies.
2. Successor technologies.
3. Gap analysis.
4. Projects as options.
5. Targeting specific contracts.

Each of these strategic issues is discussed in the following sections.

19.1 CORE COMPETENCIES

The concept of "core competencies" focuses on the factors that distinguish a firm from its competitors, and that give it a competitive advantage. The idea is that firms should identify their core competencies, then act to enhance them. From the standpoint of R & D project selection, projects that enhance a core competency of a firm can be looked upon as maintaining or improving the firm's strategic position.

Some writers distinguish among base, key, and pacing technologies. In this categorization, base technologies are those that are available to all firms in an industry. Key technologies are those that give a firm a competitive edge. Pacing technologies are those that will become the key or base technologies of the future.

This categorization can be misleading if it is considered too narrowly. A firm's success may be due in part to competence in marketing, or in manufacturing, or in the ability to integrate a great many technologies into a product. Focusing only on technologies, narrowly defined, can cause a firm to overlook some things that contribute significantly to its strategic position.

Figure 19.1 illustrates a categorization due to Dr. Keith Pavitt, which may be more useful in helping to select R & D projects. This method involves a two-way categorization according to whether a firm devotes a large or small share of its resources to a given technology, and whether the firm's activities represent a large or small share of the total activity in a given technology. In Pavitt's work, the "shares" are measured by share of total patents. However, other measures might also be used, such as share of total expenditures, or (for basic research) share of papers in scientific journals.

The upper right quadrant in the figure represents technologies to which the firm devotes a large share of its resources, and in which the firm is a dominant actor, accounting for a large share of the total activity in those technologies. Technologies that would be plotted in this quadrant can be characterized as "core-distinctive" technologies. They are core technologies for the firm, and they help distinguish the firm from other firms.

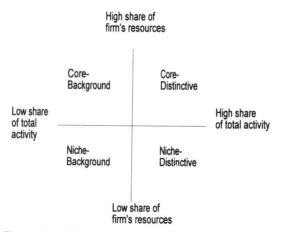

Figure 19.1. Categorization of a firm's technological activity.

The upper left quadrant in the figure represents technologies to which the firm devotes a large share of its resources, but in which the firm is not a dominant actor. These are technologies that are important to the firm (accounting for the share of its resources), but in which many other firms are also active. They may represent technologies that support or complement the technologies that are distinctive for the firm. If several of the firm's technologies are plotted in this area, it suggests that one of the firm's competencies is integration of many technologies. This is an important competency that would not be discovered simply by looking at the technologies in isolation. Moreover, it tends to cast doubt on the idea of "technological focus" for a firm.

The lower right quadrant represents those technologies in which the firm maintains a dominant position despite putting only a small share of its resources into those technologies. If one or more technologies are plotted in this quadrant, it suggests that the firm dominates some market niche with a unique or proprietary technology.

The lower left quadrant represents those technologies in which the firm puts little effort, and in which it is only a minor actor. A firm may maintain a minor presence in some technology simply to keep in touch with developments in other firms or in universities, or as a hedge against the possibility that this technology might become a pacing technology.

From the standpoint of selecting R & D projects according to their contribution to the firm's strategic position, projects falling in either the upper left or upper right quadrants should be given preference, since these support the firm's core technological activities. Projects in the lower right quadrant should be selected only to maintain the firm's dominant position in a niche market (assuming the firm's strategy is to maintain dominance in that niche). Projects in the lower left quadrant need to be justified individually as contributing something to the firm such as early warning of significant developments elsewhere.

Table 19.1 presents a hypothetical example of a firm's patenting position in a number of technologies. The table shows the number of patents the firm received in one year in each of several technology areas, and the percentage of total patents in those areas that the firm's patents represent. The mean values for the each technology area's percent of firm patents, and the firm's percent of industry patents, are also shown.

The data from Table 19.1 are plotted in Figure 19.2, using the labels from Column E of Table 19.1. The axes intersect at the mean values of the two variables. An argument could be made to locate the intersection at the median values, since the median is less affected by extreme values. However, in this example the changes would be minor.

Technologies 6 (fuel injection) and 10 (internal combustion engines) fall in the upper right quadrant. These technologies are not only important to the firm, but their location indicates that the firm is a major player in these technologies. The upper left quadrant holds technologies 3 (cutting tools), 8

TABLE 19.1 Patenting Activity of Hypothetical Firm

A	A	B	C	D	E
1	Technology	Patents	% of Firm	% of Industry Total	Label
2	Aluminum alloys	5	2.48	7	1
3	Ceramics	10	4.95	11	2
4	Cutting tools	25	12.38	15	3
5	Ferroalloys	8	3.96	18	4
6	Flat Panel Displays	10	4.95	2	5
7	Fuel Injection	22	10.89	40	6
8	Glass	7	3.47	8	7
9	Hydraulic Servomechanisms	30	14.85	15	8
10	Injection Molding Machinery	25	12.38	13	9
11	Internal Combustion Engines	27	13.37	35	10
12	Numerical Machine Controls	15	7.43	20	11
13	Paints	18	8.91	10	12
14					
15	Total	202			
16					
17	Mean		8.33	16.17	

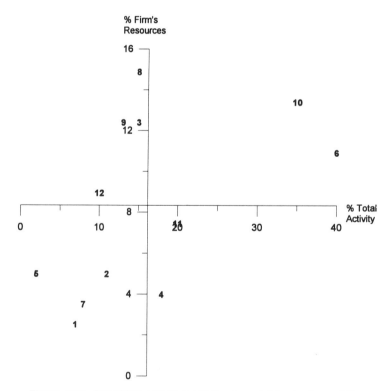

Figure 19.2. Plot of firm patenting activity versus total patenting activity.

(hydraulic servomechanisms), 9 (injection molding machinery), and 12 (paints). These technologies are important to the firm, but the firm is not a major player in these areas. Technologies 4 (ferroalloys) and 11 (numerical machine controls) fall in the lower right quadrant. These technologies are of minor importance to the firm, but its level of activity makes it a major player in these areas. Finally, the lower left quadrant includes technologies 1 (aluminum alloys), 2 (ceramics), 5 (flat panel displays), and 7 (glass). These are areas in which the firm has little activity, and also is a minor player.

Following Pavitt, we might conclude from this analysis that the firm's strategic positioning requires continued emphasis on technologies 6 and 10, and that strength in 3, 8, 9, and 12 is important. Moreover, the disparate nature of the technologies in the upper left quadrant implies that the firm is competent at integrating different technologies. This might not have been so apparent without the analysis. The firm should determine whether technologies 4 and 11 are really important to its strategic goals despite their "niche" status. If so, it should continue to support them at the present level. If not, it should consider abandoning them. Projects supporting each of the technologies in the lower left quadrant should be examined carefully, to determine whether there is strategic merit in pursuing them. Are these potential pacing technologies? If so, continued pursuit may be justified. Are they technologies that are important to the firm, so that it must maintain some competence in them? If so, is the present level of activity sufficient to maintain that competence? If there is no current need or future potential for these technologies, the firm should consider abandoning them.

One of Pavitt's conclusions, based on his analysis of patenting patterns of large firms, it that it is difficult for a firm to change its core technologies rapidly. A firm's ability to build competency in a new field is heavily constrained by its accumulated prior competencies. In particular, the directions in which a firm searches for additional competencies will be constrained by its past activities. This helps explain why a large firm may buy a small firm with competence in a particular technology, rather than trying to build that competence from scratch in its own laboratories. The accumulated weight of past activity is too much to overcome easily. This result suggests that if a firm intends to move into a new area (as discussed in the next section), strong efforts must be made to overcome the constraints imposed by past successes.

19.2 SUCCESSOR TECHNICAL APPROACHES

Every technology is intended to achieve some purpose; to perform some function. It does not exist for its own sake. The performance level of a technology is defined in terms of how well it performs the function for which it is utilized. For instance, according to the laws of thermodynamics, energy cannot be destroyed. Every erg of energy supplied to a machine must come out as energy, even if in a degraded form. However, "efficiency" of a machine is defined as "energy out divided by energy in." According to the laws of thermodynamics, by this definition the efficiency of every machine must be 100%. The given definition of efficiency, however, has an unstated condition: "energy out" *in a form useful to human beings*. The vibration and the frictional heat from a machine are "energy out" in the thermodynamic sense, but they are not *useful*, hence they are not counted as output when efficiency is being computed.

This point becomes important because any single technical approach to performing some function has a limit to its performance, a limit set by the fundamental physics and chemistry of its principle of operation. The degree to which devices using that principle of operation can be useful to human beings cannot exceed this fundamental limit. Indeed, the devices may only be able to approach that limit asymptotically, never actually reaching it.

Levels of performance higher than those set by the principle of operation of a technical approach can be achieved only by utilizing a new principle of operation. The speed of propeller-driven aircraft, for instance, is limited by the speed of sound. To exceed that speed, it was necessary to go to a new propulsion mechanism, the jet engine, which employed a different principle of operation.

Table 19.2 presents a list of considerations that may set a limit to the performance of a technical approach. This list is not intended to be exhaustive but only suggestive. In any given case, it is necessary to identify the principle of operation of the technical approach being used, and determine what limits to its performance (i.e., its use to human beings) are set by the fundamental physics and chemistry of that approach.

The demand for the function being performed is not likely to vanish, nor is it likely to be satisfied by static or stagnant levels of performance, when a technical approach reaches its limit. What usually takes place is that the technical approach that has reached its limit is supplanted by a new technical approach, using a different operating principle, which can surpass the limit of the old technical approach. This new technical approach will have its own fundamental limit, and will eventually be supplanted in turn.

Figure 19.3 shows an illustration of this phenomenon of successive technical approaches. While aircraft speeds maintained an exponential trend for about 50 years, this trend was actually made up of a sequence of growth curves. As each successive technical approach to aircraft structures or propulsion reached its fundamental limits, it was replaced by a successor approach.

When the currently used technical approach is reaching the upper limit of its performance, the firm selling products or processes utilizing that approach is faced with a choice. One possible course of action is to find alternative uses for the core technical competencies that led to its current market position. The other possible course of action is to move to the successor technical approach.

**TABLE 19.2   Some Factors that Set Limits
to Growth of Technical Approaches**

Absolute zero
Atomic dimensions
Black-body radiation
Breakdown voltage
Carnot cycle
Chemical reaction rates
Compressive strength
Efficiency limits (always 100%)
Electrochemical potential
Graininess of electric charge
    charge of electron
Graininess of matter at atomic size
    minimum dimensions required for matter continuity
    limit on surface smoothness
Graininess of radiation at single quanta
    radiation pattern no longer uniform
Heat transfer rates
    conduction
    convection
    radiation
Mass-energy equivalence
Phase change of materials
    freezing point
    melting point
    boiling point
    thermal decomposition
Shear strength
Speed of light
Speed of sound
Tensile strength

The problem, of course, is that the successor approach will be based on an entirely different operating principle from the current approach. This difference is necessary if the successor approach is to exceed the performance limits of the current approach. What this means to the firm, however, is that a totally new technology, including a new science base, will be required if the firm is to make the transition to the new technical approach. Thus the firm whose product line is based on the current approach may need to undertake basic research projects to establish the necessary science base in-house. Eventually, it will need to undertake projects to develop prototypes, and projects to develop marketable products.

Projects aimed at developing the firm's capabilities in the successor approach represent efforts at strategic positioning. Since there may be

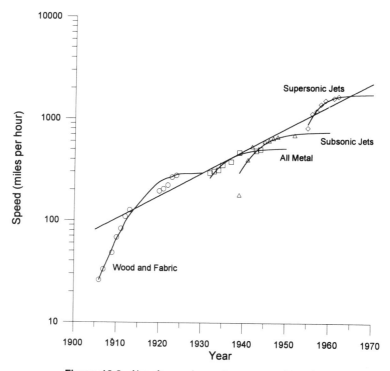

Figure 19.3. Aircraft speed, growth curves, and trend.

several alternative candidates for the successor approach, with no way to identify the "winner" until extensive research is undertaken, the firm may need to establish a strategic position in each candidate approach.

There are many examples of formerly successful firms that failed to make the transition to a new technical approach. For instance, none of the American firms, which were major manufacturers of steam locomotives, successfully transitioned to manufacturing diesel locomotives. The diesel market came to be dominated by firms that had never manufactured a steam locomotive.

If the firm's core competencies have ready applications in other products or processes, the firm may choose to abandon a particular market when the technical approach dominating that market is replaced by a successor approach. Thus when mechanical watches were replaced by digital electronic watches, some watch companies retreated from the general consumer market, and instead pursued a prestige market with products that were valued more as jewelry than as timepieces.

With adequate advanced warning, however, a firm may successfully make the transition to a new technical approach, thus continuing to capitalize on its reputation, its distribution system, and its experience with a particular market and a particular set of customers. R & D projects that create competence in the new technical approach can support a firm's strategy of staying with a market rather than abandoning it.

19.3. GAP ANALYSIS

Gap analysis is used to identify gaps in the firm's technology base, relative either to competitors or to its strategic goals. What is required is a systematic audit of the firm's current technologies, including those in its products, those in its manufacturing processes, and those in its marketing and administrative activities. Questions for such an audit would include:

Does the firm utilize the same technologies across its product lines?

Does the firm use different technologies in related products? If so, is there an opportunity for commonality or standardization?

Are any of the firm's important technologies equally available to competitors?

Do competitor's products incorporate technologies superior to those in the firm's products?

Do competitors utilize superior manufacturing processes? If so, are these obtained from outside vendors or are they proprietary to the competitors?

Have new technologies been developed outside the industry, which could give a competitive advantage to firms in the industry that adopt them?

Where gaps are identified, the firm then must determine whether they hinder the achievement of the firm's strategic goals. Does a gap leave the firm vulnerable to competition on features? On performance? On price? If a gap that has strategic implications is identified, this fact can then be taken into account in evaluating R & D projects. Those projects that help close a significant gap should receive a high rating on strategic positioning.

19.4 PROJECTS AS OPTIONS

Graham Mitchell [1988] pointed out a serious problem with the linkage between R & D projects and the strategic plans of firms. The problem is that "even when the potential impact of a new technology is recognized at the conceptual or strategic level, overreliance on short-term measurement and justification ... often biases the implementation process against some of the more strategically important technical programs" (p. 199).

At the product development stage, an R & D project can be treated as a business investment. Costs and returns can be estimated with reasonable accuracy at that point (although serious mistakes are sometimes made). Hence, the project can be evaluated using conventional investment criteria, such as net present value (NPV) or internal rate of return (IRR). At the basic research stage, an R & D project is intended primarily for knowledge building. The costs of the project, even if not estimated accurately, are still comparatively small. Most firms recognize they can carry basic research as an overhead cost, with individual projects being evaluated on the basis of contribution to the firm's knowledge base rather than being evaluated using investment criteria.

The problem occurs at intermediate stages, where the project is too expensive to carry as overhead, but too far from a marketable product to use investment criteria. It is at this stage that strategic positioning becomes important. R & D projects at this stage should be evaluated in terms of how they affect the firm's strategic position. Projects should support several product lines, or should prepare the firm to enter a significant new line of business.

It is at this stage that Mitchell argues for treating an R & D project as an *option*, analogous to financial options. A financial option is the right to buy (or sell) a security at a specified price at any time during a specified period. If the price of the security changes in a direction favorable to the holder of the option, the option can be exercised and the security immediately traded at a profit. The purchaser of the option, then, has purchased the *opportunity* to make a profitable investment at a later time. Of course, if the security price does not change in a favorable direction before the option expires, the purchaser is out the price of the option. The important point, however, is that for the option purchaser, the "downside" risk is only the price of the option, while if the price of the security is very volatile, the "upside" potential can be quite high.

R & D projects at a stage suited for strategic positioning can likewise be considered as options. The "downside" risk is the cost of the project, which can be terminated at any time it begins to look bad. The "upside" potential, however, is the payoff from a successful product or process. This an R & D project at this stage represents the purchase of an *opportunity* to make a profitable investment at a later time. The range of uncertainty in the payoff of the project corresponds to volatility in a security price. The greater the range of possible payoffs, the greater the upside potential for the project.

In the case of financial options, the greater the volatility in the price of the security, the greater the expected value of the return. Likewise, in the case of an R & D project, the greater the range of possible payoffs, the greater the expected value of the return on the project. Applying the theory of options to strategic positioning, then, suggests that a portfolio of R & D projects should be selected from among those with the greatest range of potential payoff (low to high). Certainty of payoff is neither possible nor required. So long as the cost of the project is small compared with the maximum *potential* payoff, the project is a good *option*. While not every project in the portfolio will achieve its potential (indeed most may be failures), the expected payoff from the entire portfolio will be quite high, and a high payoff will be realized in practice. A crucial *caveat*, however, is that as soon as such a project turns sour, it must be terminated, just as a financial option is allowed to expire if price changes are not favorable to the option holder.

19.5 TARGETING SPECIFIC CONTRACTS

Some firms operate in industries where large but infrequent contracts are a way of life. Firms in the defense industry, for instance, face this situation. Firms that specialize in constructing major technologically oriented projects, such as chemical plants and hydroelectric dams, likewise face this situation. The business is usually highly competitive, and firms can gain an advantage by being able to offer greater technical capability at a price the customer considers acceptable. That is, the customer is often willing to accept higher than the lowest bid, if the extra cost is compensated for with extra benefit.

Firms facing this type of competition are usually aware well in advance that a specific contract will be put out for bids. Thus there is often time to conduct some internally funded R & D that will put the firm in a better position to win the contract. The problem for choosing such R & D projects is that there may be many influences on the contract award, and each source of influence may have a different agenda. For instance, contracts for major military systems must ultimately satisfy a military service, the Administration, and Congress. The military service will prefer the bidder who promises the most military capability, even at high cost. Individual members of Congress will prefer the bidder who will put the most jobs into their district. The Administration may seek to gain favor with some constituency by preferring the bidder who will confer some social or economic benefit on that constituency, such as by putting jobs in an area of high unemployment. In addition to the preferences of the customers, the strengths and weaknesses of other competing firms must be considered.

Vepsalainen and Lauro (V & L) [1988] present an approach to R & D project selection that takes into account the differing customer agendas, and the competitive status of other potential bidders. They argue that "the firm should identify activities that enhance the [system] in performance criteria which are desirable to the customer and which, by virtue of the quality achieved or technology acquired, can generate a recognizable advantage over competitors." In particular, R & D projects that cannot generate a recognizable advantage should not be pursued.

They propose the use of the analytic hierarchy procedure (AHP) to take into account the preferences of the several "customers" whose varying agendas must be satisfied, and the ability of the candidate R & D projects to satisfy these preferences. This will be illustrated by means of an example.

TABLE 19.3   Selection Criteria and Customer Priorities

19_3	A	B	C	D	E	F
1	Customer	PCE		˙Priorities		Composite
2	Criterion	Benchmark	Finance	Production	Marketing	Customer
3	Reliability	+15%	0.11	0.10	0.11	0.106
4	Consruction Cost	-15%	0.22	0.10	0.35	0.198
5	Operating Cost	-20%	0.44	0.70	0.35	0.526
6	Product Purity	+10%	0.23	0.10	0.19	0.170
7						
8	Sums		1.00	1.00	1.00	1.000

Consider a multinational construction company, ChemCon, which is in the business of constructing chemical plants. A petrochemical company has announced plans to construct a new plant in a tropical country. ChemCon would like to bid on the job. Analysis of the potential customer, including review of previous plants it has purchased, indicates that three staff functions of the customer firm will have an influence on selecting the bidder for the construction contract: finance, production, and marketing. Their relative degrees of influence on the decision are, respectively, 0.4, 0.4, and 0.2.

ChemCon's analysis also indicates that the important decision criteria for the customer are reliability of the new plant, construction cost, operating cost, and product purity. ChemCon's design staff has estimated the best that can be done in the time available, in terms of improving on the current industry standards for each criterion. These potential criterion enhancement (PCE) values are shown in Table 19.3 in Column B.

The three staff functions have different priorities regarding the criteria for the proposed new plant. Table 19.3 displays the relative priorities of the three functions (these must sum to 1.0 for each staff function). For instance, production will value a 20% decrease in operating cost seven times as much as it will value a 15% increase in reliability.

Given the priorities, and the relative influences of the three functions, a "composite customer" can be calculated. This calculation is done by multiplying the row relative priorities for each criterion by the respective column degrees of influence, and summing. The priorities of this "composite customer" are shown in Column F of Table 19.3.

ChemCon can carry out some internally funded R & D projects to enhance its competitiveness for the construction contract. Table 19.4 lists the candidate projects for this enhancement. Each project enhances only one criterion, listed in Column B. The possible degree of enhancement, and the cost, are shown for each project in Columns C and D, respectively. It is assumed that the enhancements are linearly additive, that is, Projects 1 and 2 together will enhance reliability by 11%. If the projects are truly independent technically, and given the small increments in capability associated with each, the assumption of linear additivity is reasonable.

TABLE 19.4   Candidate Projects for ChemCon

19_4	A	B	C	D
1		Criterion		Cost
2	Project	Enhanced	Enhancement	$1000
3	1	Reliability	6%	150
4	2	Reliability	5%	100
5	3	Operating Cost	6%	200
6	4	Operating Cost	5%	150
7	5	Construction Cost	5%	125
8	6	Construction Cost	8%	375
9	7	Operating Cost	6%	250
10	8	Product Purity	5%	100
11	9	Operating Cost	6%	150
12	10	Product Purity	4%	400
13	11	Operating Cost	9%	350
14	12	Reliability	9%	400
15	13	Product Purity	6%	200

Next we need to look at the relative strengths of ChemCon and the other potential bidders. Assume there are three other potential bidders, A, B, and C. Each firm has a unique combination of strengths and weaknesses. Their relative capabilities to improve each of the selection criteria are shown in Table 19.5. For instance, ChemCon estimates it has a relative advantage in reducing construction costs (0.457 compared with 0.220 for the next best two competitors). However, competitor B is seen as being comparatively strong in improving plant reliability (0.449 compared with 0.347 for competitor C and only 0.102 for ChemCon). (Note that in this table, row values sum to 1.0, as shown in Column F.)

These relative ratings can be converted into a competitive advantage rating as follows:

$$CA_{ij} = TA_{ij}/TA_i^*$$

where TA_{ij} is the relative advantage of the jth competitor on the ith

TABLE 19.5   Relative Capabilities of Competitors

19_5	A	B	C	D	E	F	G
1	Selection	Technical Capability Rating					Competitive
2	Criterion	ChemCon	A	B	C		Advantage
3	Reliability	0.102	0.102	0.449	0.347	1.00	0.227
4	Consruction Cost	0.280	0.098	0.442	0.180	1.00	0.633
5	Operating Cost	0.457	0.220	0.103	0.220	1.00	2.077
6	Product Purity	0.098	0.430	0.292	0.180	1.00	0.228

criterion, and TA_i^* is a "reference" competitive advantage on the ith criterion. One possible reference value is the average of all ChemCon's competitors, that is, a "composite competitor." However, a more conservative estimate is based on the "benchmark" criterion, that is, the reference value is the highest relative advantage of any competitor. This measures ChemCon against the market leader in each criterion. For this example, we will use the conservative reference value, that of the "benchmark" competitor. ChemCon's competitive advantages on each criterion area shown in Column G of the table. The entries in the column are a measure of ChemCon's efficiency, relative to its competitors, in achieving the PCE for each criterion. In reducing operating cost, it is about twice as efficient as the next-best competitor. However, in increasing plant reliability, it is less than 25% as efficient as the best competitor.

ChemCon's staff estimates that without any additional R & D, they have a 10% chance of submitting the winning bid. If they were to achieve all the PCEs, they would have a 40% chance of being the winning bidder. Estimated profit if they win the bid is $10 million. Thus achieving all the PCEs would be worth an expected $3 million to the company. This means, of course, that it would not be worth their while to spend more than $3 million to achieve all the PCEs.

The contribution to the ratio of customer benefit to ChemCon from carrying out one of the candidate R & D projects can be evaluated as follows:

$$B_q = E_{iq}{}^* (P_i/PCE_i)^* (\text{Margin}/\text{cost}_q)$$

where

B is the benefit-to-cost ratio for project q
P_i is the priority of the ith criterion for the composite customer
E_i is the enhancement achievable by the qth project
Margin is $3 million
The cost_q is the cost of the qth project

The benefit-to-cost ratios for each of the candidate projects are shown in Column G of Table 19.6.

The contribution to competitive advantage from each project can be prorated as the project's share of the PCE, if the project is successfully completed. That is,

$$A_j = CA_{ij}{}^* (E_{ij}/PCE_i)$$

The project advantage contributions are shown in Column F of Table 19.7.

The competitive advantages and customer benefit-to-cost ratios can be plotted against each other, as shown in Figure 19.4. V & L suggest that this

TABLE 19.6   Ratio of Customer Benefit to ChemCon Cost for Projects

19_6	A	B	C	D	E	F	G
2	Project	Enhanced	Enhancement	Priority	PCE	$1000	Benefit
3	1	Reliability	0.06	0.106	0.15	150	0.848
4	2	Reliability	0.05	0.106	0.15	100	1.060
5	3	Operating Cost	0.06	0.198	0.15	200	1.188
6	4	Operating Cost	0.05	0.198	0.15	150	1.320
7	5	Construction Cost	0.05	0.526	0.20	125	3.156
8	6	Construction Cost	0.08	0.526	0.20	375	1.683
9	7	Operating Cost	0.06	0.198	0.15	250	0.950
10	8	Product Purity	0.05	0.170	0.17	100	1.500
11	9	Operating Cost	0.06	0.198	0.15	150	1.584
12	10	Product Purity	0.04	0.170	0.17	400	0.300
13	11	Operating Cost	0.09	0.198	0.15	350	1.018
14	12	Reliability	0.09	0.106	0.15	400	0.477
15	13	Product Purity	0.06	0.170	0.17	200	0.900

plot be treated as a portfolio plot. They recommend that the intersection of the axes be based on experience. In the figure, the vertical axis is placed at a cost benefit ratio of 1.0. In practice, users may wish to require a higher "hurdle," and move the vertical axis to the right. The horizontal axis is arbitrarily placed at a competitive advantage of 0.40. This placement must be based on judgment and experience with past projects. V & L recommend sizing the circles proportional to the cost of the project. This sizing has not

TABLE 19.7   Project Contributions to Competitive Advantage

19_7	A	B	C	D	E	F
1		Criterion			Competitive	Project
2	Project	Enhanced	Enhancement	PCE	Advantage	Advantage
3	1	Reliability	0.06	0.15	0.227	0.0909
4	2	Reliability	0.05	0.15	0.227	0.0757
5	3	Operating Cost	0.06	0.15	2.077	0.8309
6	4	Operating Cost	0.05	0.15	2.077	0.6924
7	5	Construction Cost	0.05	0.20	0.633	0.1584
8	6	Construction Cost	0.08	0.20	0.633	0.2534
9	7	Operating Cost	0.06	0.15	2.077	0.8309
10	8	Product Purity	0.05	0.17	0.228	0.0670
11	9	Operating Cost	0.06	0.15	2.077	0.8309
12	10	Product Purity	0.04	0.17	0.228	0.0536
13	11	Operating Cost	0.09	0.15	2.077	1.2464
14	12	Reliability	0.09	0.15	0.227	0.1363
15	13	Product Purity	0.06	0.17	0.228	0.0804

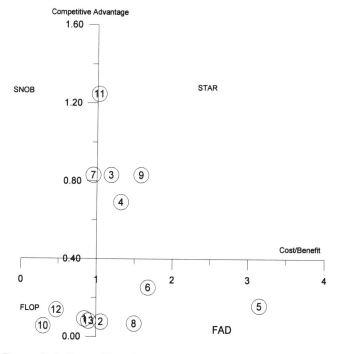

Figure 19.4. Competitive advantage plotted against cost to benefit ratio.

been done in this case, but might convey additional useful information. Note that the competitive advantage figures for the projects may seem low, but this is because each is compared with the "benchmark" for the industry, rather than the average for the industry.

V & L designate the upper right quadrant (high-competitive advantage and high-customer benefit) as star projects. Those in the lower right quadrant (high-customer benefit but low-competitive advantage) are designated as fad projects. Those in the upper left quadrant (low-customer benefit but high-competitive advantage) are designated as snob projects. Those in the lower left quadrant (low-customer benefit and low-competitive advantage) are designated as flops. Clearly in this case Projects 3, 4, 9, possibly 11, are worthwhile projects. Depending on the placement of the horizontal axis, Projects 5, 6, and 12 might be brought into consideration. Project 7 is marginal in any case. The remainder of the projects do not promise enough payoff to justify their cost.

The computations for this method of evaluating strategic positioning for R & D projects are somewhat tedious, but can be carried out readily on a spreadsheet. The major difficulty with use of this approach is obtaining the data, which are largely subjective. Considerable business intelligence activity will be required to evaluate customer preferences. However, a firm should be

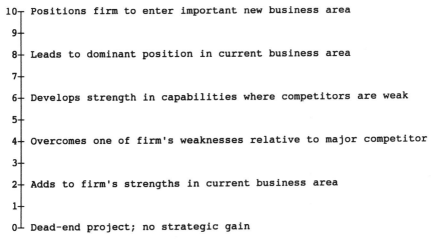

Figure 19.5. Example of scale for strategic positioning.

routinely analyzing its relative strengths and weaknesses relative to competitors, hence obtaining that information should not pose any additional difficulties. If the information can be obtained, this method can make a valuable contribution to the selection of projects intended to put the firm into a strong position to win a specific major contract.

19.6 RATING SCALE

An example of a possible rating scale for strategic position is shown in Figure 19.5. It can be tailored to fit specific circumstances. The tailoring should emphasize those strategic considerations, discussed above, that best reflect the firm's overall strategic objectives.

19.7 SUMMARY

The firm's R & D program does not exist in a vacuum. The goals of the various projects should be selected to further the strategic goals of the firm. However, the degree to which the firm's strategic goals are supported will vary from one project to another. Thus rating a project on its degree of support for the firm's strategic goals can be an important element in project selection. Support for strategic goals can be considered in terms of maintaining core competencies, developing a position in a successor technical approach, filling gaps in the firm's technological coverage, and developing options for future exploitation.

19.8 QUESTIONS FOR CLASS DISCUSSION

1. Obtain data on patents for your organization: number of patents in each area of technological interest, and total number of patents granted in those areas, for the most recent year. Prepare a plot similar to Figure 19.2. What do you conclude about the core competencies of your organization?

19.9 FURTHER READINGS

Lockett, G., B. Hetherington, and P. Yallup (1984). Modeling a Research Portfolio Using AHP: A Group Decision Process. *R & D Management*. **16**(2), April, 151–160.

Martino, J. P. (1992). *Technological Forecasting for Decision Making*. New York: McGraw-Hill.

Matthews, W. H. (1991). Kissing Technological Frogs: Managing Technology as a Strategic Resource. *European Management Journal*. **9**(2), June, 145–148.

Mitchell, G. (1988). Options for the Strategic Management of Technology. In T. M. Khalil, B. A. Bayraktar, and J. A. Edosomwan (Eds.). *Proceedings of the First International Conference of Management of Technology*, Geneva, Switzerland: Interscience Enterprises Ltd., pp. 198–206.

Morris, P. A., E. O. Teisberg, and A. L. Kolbe (1991). When Choosing R & D Projects, Go With Long Shots. *Research-Technology Management*. **34**(1), January–February, 35–40. (Strategic positioning.)

Patel, P. and K. Pavitt (1994). Technological Competencies in the World's Largest Firms: Characteristics, Constraints and Scope for Managerial Choice. Fourth International Conference on the Management of Technology. Industrial Engineering and Management Press, Norcross, Georgia.

Prahald, C. K. and G. Hamel (1990). The Core Competence of the Corporation. *Harvard Business Review*. May–June, pp. 79–91.

Vepsalainen, A. P. J. and G. L. Lauro (1988). Analysis of R & D Portfolio Strategies for Contract Competition. *IEEE Transactions on Engineering Management*. **35**(3), August, 181–186.

____20
PROBABILITY ESTIMATES

Some of the project selection techniques presented in Part I require estimates of probability of success of a project, either technical success or marketing success. Other techniques require estimates of probabilities in conjunction with outcomes, costs, time to completion, market size, and other factors. That is, instead of estimating a single value for a criterion (e.g., cost), the analyst is required to obtain estimates of several values and the probability of each.

In some respects obtaining probability estimates is easier than getting the "right" point estimate, in that the analyst can exercise the entire range of possible values. However, estimation of probabilities brings in another set of difficulties. Kahneman et al. [1982] identified several biases that affect estimates probabilities. These are

1. **DESIRABLE / UNDESIRABLE EVENTS**. People tend to overestimate the likelihood of desirable events and underestimate the likelihood of undesirable events.
2. **AVAILABILITY**. People tend to underestimate the probability of events for which they have no previous experience with analogous events, and especially tend to underestimate the probability of events that have never occurred.
3. **LOW / HIGH PROBABILITY EVENTS**. People tend to overestimate the probability of events that are very unlikely but have occurred, in part because they have little experience with them.
4. **ANCHORING**. When given new information, people tend to make changes in their probability estimates that are too small. That is, they underestimate the degree of change justified by new information.

185

Souder [1969] reports several projects in which R & D managers were asked to make estimates of probability of success for their projects. In each case, he notes that the managers were tutored in subjective probability before supplying the estimates. This is important, since many R & D managers will have only vague notions of probability and how to estimate it.

Methods for eliciting probability estimates from people have been developed, which are intended to help overcome the biases described by Kahneman et al. [1982], and to provide the tutoring found necessary by Souder [1969]. In addition, methods have been developed for reestimating probabilities when new information is obtained. Methods for each are presented in this chapter.

20.1   ESTIMATING PROBABILITIES

There is usually no disagreement when one speaks of the probability of the roll of a die. It is taken for granted that the probability of getting any number of spots, from one to six, on the roll of a fair die, is one-sixth.* Where people may balk, however, is in assigning a probability to an event that is unique—which can happen only once if it happens at all. The kind of probability represented by rolling a die is referred to as "frequentist" probability. One can roll a die many times and count the frequency with which each face comes up. However, by definition, one cannot repeat a unique event. What, then, does it mean to assign a probability to the possible occurrence of a unique event?

Tribus [1969] has shown that assigning a probability to such an event amounts to encoding in numerical form whatever information one has about that event. This operation is perfectly legitimate, even though the result is often referred to as a "subjective probability." Thus a statement of the probability of success of an R & D project should be looked upon, not as the frequency with which this project would succeed if repeated many times, but as a numerical expression of the information that the person making the estimate has about the project. This information may include prior experience with similar projects, knowledge of the goals of the project and the tasks to be accomplished to meet those goals, knowledge of the uncertainties that must be resolved in meeting the goals, and knowledge of the capabilities of the people carrying out the project.

Eliciting a subjective probability from the project director can be done in much the same way as ratings on a 0–10 scale can be obtained for other factors about a project. One must use an anchored scale that helps the probability estimator place the project correctly on the scale.

---

*However, note the circularity in definition. A "fair" die is one for which the probability of getting each face is one-sixth.

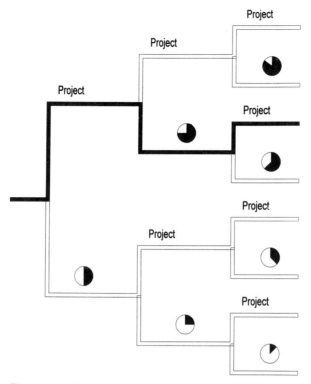

Figure 20.1. Example of choices between bets and the project.

One way of providing such an anchored scale is shown in Figure 20.1. Here the person making the estimate is given a sequence of choices between betting on the project and betting on a "roulette wheel." To illustrate the use of this procedure, a hypothetical sequence of choices is mapped in black. The estimator is first asked whether they would prefer to bet on the project or on a 50–50 roulette wheel. In this example, the estimator has selected the project as their preferred bet, indicating their subjective view that the odds on the project are better than even. Next, however, the estimator has preferred a 75–25 roulette wheel to the project, indicating their subjective estimate that the odds on the project's success are less than 3 : 1. On their third choice, they have preferred the project to a 62.5–37.5 roulette wheel, indicating that the odds on the project are better than 5 : 3. At this point, the estimated probability of success of the project is bracketed between 62.5 and 75%. It may not be worth trying to refine the estimate any more closely. The result could simply be rounded to 70%. Had the estimator preferred the 50–50 roulette wheel to the project, the next choice would have been between the project and a 25–75 roulette wheel, as shown in the lower one-half of the figure. This would have been refined further by additional choices.

As this example indicates, within three choices, the project director's estimate of the project's probability of success can be narrowed to a range of 12.5 percentage points. This range is probably as narrow as can reasonably be expected. However, a fourth choice can bring the range down to 6.25%, if the project director feels comfortable in making such a choice.

A project director can produce a subjective estimate of the project's probability of success by using the equivalent of an anchored scale. This estimate may not correlate well with the final outcome if it is made at the outset of the project, but it does provide a starting point for evaluating the project.

20.2 UPDATING PROBABILITY ESTIMATES

As reported by Souder [1969], project directors can improve the quality of their probability estimates as the project progresses, and further information is obtained. However, they may still be subject to the "anchoring" bias reported by Kahneman et al. [1982]. One means for overcoming this bias is the use of Bayes' rule for combining probabilities.

Consider two events A and B, which *need not be* independent (and for our purposes should not be). The probability of both events occurring is given by

$$P(AB) = P(A|B)P(B) \tag{20.1}$$

In words, this states that the probability of both A and B occurring is equal to the conditional probability of A occurring when it is known that B has occurred, multiplied by the probability of B occurring regardless of whether or not A occurs. (The first term on the right is read "probability of A given B." If A and B are independent, this is simply $P(A)$, and the equation is still valid.) This equation amounts to a definition of conditional probability, and is tautologically true. However, the definition is completely symmetrical, and we can equally well write

$$P(AB) = P(B|A)P(A) \tag{20.2}$$

Equating the right-hand sides of the two equations and solving for one of the conditional probabilities, we obtain Bayes' rule:

$$P(A|B) = \frac{P(B|A)P(A)}{P(B)} = \frac{P(B|A)P(A)}{P(B|A) + P(B|\overline{A})} \tag{20.3}$$

where $\overline{A}$ is read "not A" and means A fails to occur. The second form on the right is useful primarily when there are more than the two possibilities A and B. However, this form is valid even when there are only two possibilities.

How is Bayes' rule utilized? One important use is to "update" a probability estimate when "new" information is obtained. Suppose we are concerned about an event A. Suppose there is a related event B, such that B, if it occurs at all, will occur before A. Suppose we have initial estimates of $P(A)$, $P(B)$, and the probability $P(B|A)$ that if A occurs, B will already have occurred. Now suppose that we watch for B, and find that it does occur. We can then update our estimate of the probability of A by using Eq. 20.3, substituting the initial values on the right-hand side. This update is free of the "anchoring" bias noted by Kahneman et al. [1982].

Let us make this more concrete with an example. An R & D project has been proposed to develop a new product. An improved component for the product is to be developed as part of the project. If the component development fails, a lower performance but currently available component will be substituted. The project director estimates that the probability of success for the improved component is 85%. The project director estimates that the overall probability of success for the entire project is 75%, taking into account other considerations as well as the new component. Finally, the project director estimates that if the project is to be successful, the probability that the improved component will be required is 90%.

Suppose the improved component is successfully developed. What can we then say about the probability of success for the entire project? Using Bayes' rule, we have

$$P(\text{project}|\text{component}) = \frac{P(\text{component}|\text{project})P(\text{project})}{P(\text{component})}$$

$$= \frac{0.9*0.75}{0.85} = 0.794$$

Using Bayes rule, we find that once the component development has proven successful, the overall probability of success of the project has been raised to slightly over 79%. This computation is of course only as good as the estimates that went into it. Nevertheless, the use of Bayes rule to combine new information with old overcomes the anchoring bias that Kahneman et al. [1982] identified as a significant problem in subjective probability estimates.

20.3   SUMMARY

Many project selection techniques require use of probability estimates to compute expected values for project payoffs and costs. These probability values must be obtained subjectively, from those who are informed about the circumstances surrounding the project. The numerical value of the estimate represents an encoding of the estimator's information about the project. An estimating procedure, similar to the anchored scales used in obtaining other estimates, can be helpful in eliciting probability estimates from project personnel. Bayes rule can be used to update probability estimates when new information is obtained, such as successful completion of some task that is part of the project.

20.4 QUESTIONS FOR CLASS DISCUSSION

1. Measure the length of a toothpick. Draw a series of equally spaced lines on a sheet of paper, where the spacing between the lines is greater than the length of the toothpick. Suppose you threw the toothpick on the paper, into the area within the two outermost lines. What is the probability that it will intersect one of the lines? Generate your estimate using the method of Figure 20.1. Carry out the experiment, throwing the toothpick on the paper 100 times. How good was your estimate? (*Note:* The correct formula for computing the probability is given in Appendix 3.)

20.5 FURTHER READINGS

Kahneman, D., P. Slovic, and A. Tversky (1982). *Judgment Under Uncertainty: Heuristics and Biases*, Cambridge: Cambridge University Press.

Press, S. James (1989). *Bayesian Statistics*. New York: Wiley.

Souder, W. E. (1969). The Validity of Subjective Probability of Success Forecasts by R & D Project Managers. *IEEE Transactions on Engineering Management*. **16**(1), February, 35–49.

Tribus, M. (1969). *Rational Descriptions Decisions and Designs*. New York: Pergamon Press.

____21
SUMMARY

Previous chapters have presented a wide range of project selection techniques, and a wide range of factors that can be taken into account or included in project selection decisions. The analyst or decision maker needs to select from among the several techniques the one or ones that most closely fit the decision situation in which a selection must be made.

Table 21.1 lists the project selection techniques presented in the earlier chapters. Table 21.2 lists the factors that have been discussed as affecting selection of projects, or suitability of project selection methods. Figure 21.1 presents a comparison of methods (columns) according to those factors that they can include, or that they must include, and any special considerations that affect the methods' suitability for particular applications. This table summarizes the information presented in detail in the earlier chapters. It can be used as a quick guide to the selection of the appropriate techniques for a particular situation, with more refined selection based on the chapters describing the techniques.

TABLE 21.1   Project Selection Techniques

RANKING METHODS

1. Pairwise comparison
2. Scoring models
3. Analytic hierarchy procedure

ECONOMIC METHODS

4. Net present value
5. Internal rate of return
6. Cash flow payback
7. Expected value

PORTFOLIO OPTIMIZATION METHODS

8. Mathematical programming
9. Cluster analysis
10. Simulation
11. Sensitivity analysis

AD HOC METHODS

12. Profiles
13. Interactive methods
15. Cognitive modeling

MULTI-STAGE DECISIONS

16. Decision theory

TABLE 21.2 Comparison Factors for Evaluating R & D Projects

FACTORS THAT CAN BE INCLUDED

1. Cost
2. Payoff
3. Probability of technical success
4. Probability of market success
5. Market size
6. Market share
7. Availability of required staff
8. Degree of organizational commitment
9. Strategic positioning from project
10. Degree of competition
11. Favorability of regulatory environment

SPECIAL INPUT REQUIREMENTS

12. Requires precise cash flow information
13. Requires precise life cycle information
14. Requires probability of technical success
15. Requires probability of market success

SPECIAL FEATURES

16. Considers resource dependencies
17. Considers budget constraints
18. Considers technical interactions
19. Considers market interactions
20. Incorporates program considerations
21. Can be used for large numbers of projects
22. Allows comparison with other investments
23. Suited for research stage
24. Suited for development stage

Project Selection Technique

Factors	1	2	3	4	5	6	7	8	9	10	11	12	13	14	15
Cost	•	•	•	•	•	•	•	•		•	•	•	•	•	•
Payoff	•	•	•	•	•	•	•	•		•	•	•	•	•	•
Prob. Tech. Success	•	•	•			•				•	•				•
Prob. Mkt. Success	•	•	•			•				•	•				•
Market Size	•	•	•	•	•	•	•	•		•	•	•	•	•	•
Market Share	•	•	•	•	•	•	•	•		•	•	•	•	•	•
Avail. Req'd. Staff	•	•	•				•			•		•	•		
Degree of Org. Commit.	•	•	•						•			•	•		
Strategic Positioning	•		•					•	•			•	•	•	
Degree of Competition	•	•	•					•	•			•	•	•	•
Favorable Regulatory Environ.	•	•	•					•	•			•	•	•	•
Requires Cash Flow				•	•	•	•	•							•
Requires Life Cycle Data				•	•	•	•	•							•
Requires Prob. Tech. Success						•									•
Requires Prob. Mkt. Success						•									•
Considers Resource Depend.							•		•			•			
Considers Budget Constraints							•		•			•			
Considers Technical Interact.							•		•			•			
Considers Mkt. Interact.							•		•			•			
Incorp. Program Considerations							•	•				•	•	•	
Suitable for Large Nos. Proj.		•		•	•	•		•	•	•		•	•	•	•
Compar. w/Other Investments				•	•	•		•							•
Suited for Rsch. Stage	•	•	•					•	•	•	•	•	•	•	•
Suited for Devel. Stage	•	•	•	•	•	•	•	•	•	•	•	•	•	•	•

Figure 21.1. Comparison of project selection techniques according to the factors they take into account.

21.1 FURTHER READINGS

Souder, W. E. (1978). Analytical Effectiveness of Mathematical Models for R & D project Selection. *Management Science*. **19**(8), April, 907–923.

Souder, W. E. and T. Mandakovic (1986). R & D Project Selection Models. *Research Management*. **29**(4), July–August, 36–42.

APPENDIX 1

ANNOTATED BIBLIOGRAPHY

This bibliography contains short summaries of the contents of articles that present R & D project selection methods. In general, survey articles have not been included.

Aaker, D. A. and T. T. Tyerbjee (1978). A model for the Selection of Interdependent R & D Projects. *IEEE Transactions on Engineering Management*. **25**, May, 30–36.

This paper discusses a means for selecting a portfolio of projects in which some interdependencies may exist. Each project is assumed to add to the profitability of existing or new products. It is further assumed that the incremental net present value (NPV) of this addition can be determined for each project and each product (existing or new). It is also assumed that the probability of success of each project is known. In the absence of interdependencies, a portfolio of projects would be selected that maximized the expected increment in NPV. Two types of interdependence are considered. Effect dependence exists when success of one project increases or decreases the NPV of another project (enhancing sales or cannibalizing sales). Technical interdependence exists when success or failure of one project alters the probability of success or failure of another project. Resource overlap exists when one project can take advantage of work done in another project, so that the total cost of both is less than the sum of their individual costs. (This article does not consider cases of resource competition.) Given the overlaps and dependencies, the model then selects the portfolio that stays within the total budget and that maximizes the EXPECTED increment to NPV.

Albala, A. (1975), Stage Approach for the Evaluation and Selection of R & D Projects. *IEEE Transactions on Engineering Management*. **22**(4), November, 153–164.

The author argues that at different stages in the R & D process, different selection techniques are appropriate. For instance, techniques requiring much detailed numerical data are inappropriate for early stages of the R & D process. This approach is compatible with the idea of R & D as a sequential decision-making process. The stages considered in the article are (1) exploratory (paper studies, literature search, patent search, preliminary laboratory research); (2) applied research in the laboratory; (3) pilot plant; (4) commercial investment. Other categorizations may be appropriate for other cases. The important point is that the stages should have clear boundaries determined by the objectives and scope of the work, and that uncertainty should be significantly reduced by each subsequent stage. Screening at stage 1 should focus on commercial and technical issues. At stage 2 a scoring model or profile chart should be used. At stage 3 profitability criteria, discounted by probabilities of success, are appropriate. At stage 4 conventional investment models are appropriate, incorporating investment required, manufacturing costs, market forecasts, and discounted cash flow.

Baker, N. and J. Freeland (1975), Recent Advances in R & D Benefit Measurement and Project Selection Methods. *Management Science*. **21**(10), June, 1164–1175.

This paper presents a survey of the literature on methods for measuring the benefit from R & D projects, and for allocating resources to the projects. No new results are reported.

Bard, J. F., R. Balanchandra, and P. E. Kaufmann (1988). An Interactive Approach to R & D Project Selection and Termination. *IEEE Transactions on Engineering Management*. **35**(3), August, 139–146.

This paper discusses a method for monitoring the progress of individual projects. First, four critical factors are evaluated. These factors are

1. Government regulations.
2. Raw material availability.
3. Market conditions.
4. Probability of technical success.

Failure on any one may justify termination. A scoring technique, involving a set of key variables, is then used to determine which of the remaining projects may be a candidate for termination. The key variables are

1. Positive chance event (external).
2. Product life cycle stage.
3. Pressure on project leader.
4. R & D manager is project champion.
5. Probability of commercial success.
6. Support of top management.

7. Project worker commitment.

8. Smoothness of technological route.

9. End user market.

10. Projection champion appearing near end.

11. Company profitability.

12. Anticipated competition.

13. Presence of internal competition for resources.

14. Number of projects in R & D portfolio.

The score is the number of variables that have not deteriorated since the last review. A score of nine or more indicates high likelihood of success; scores of six to eight indicate marginal projects; scores lower than six indicate high probability of failure. Of those projects that survive the scoring, a portfolio optimization model is then used to allocate resources among surviving projects and new starts. As a result of the allocation, some projects may drop below a threshold for probability of success. These are then terminated.

Brockhoff, K. and A. Pearson (1992). Technical and Marketing Aggressiveness and the Effectiveness of Research and Development. *IEEE Transactions on Engineering Management*. **39**(4), November, 318–324.

This paper examines the interactions between technical and marketing aggressiveness, and the relationship between these interactions and R & D effectiveness. Technical aggressiveness for an R & D lab is measured by relative emphases on such things as defensive versus offensive R & D, imitative versus innovative R & D, radical versus innovative process change, and general versus specialized R & D. Marketing aggressiveness of the firm is measured by relative emphases on such things as low-versus high-quality products, low versus high prices, penetration versus skimming pricing dynamics, and market penetration versus opening up new markets. Those firms that were high on both R & D and marketing aggressiveness were characterized as "risk takers," those low on both R & D and marketing aggressiveness were characterized as "risk avoiders," and those high on one and low on the other were characterized as "risk balancers." The findings were that risk takers and risk avoiders both had moderate sales growth. Within the risk balancers, however, there were major differences. Those high on aggressive marketing but low on aggressive R & D had the highest sales growth; those high on aggressive R & D but low on aggressive marketing had the lowest sales growth. In terms of harmony between R & D and marketing, firms low on both R & D and marketing aggressiveness had the highest degree of harmony, those high on both had an intermediate level of harmony, and those high on R & D aggressiveness but low on marketing aggressiveness had the lowest degree of harmony. The authors draw the conclusion that harmony between R & D and marketing is not necessarily a good indicator of market success. If neither is trying very hard, relations will be harmonious, but sales growth will be low. If R & D is aggressive but marketing is not, both sales growth and harmony will be low. If marketing is aggressive but R & D is not, harmony will be moderate, but sales growth will be big.

Clarke, T. E (1974), Decision-Making in Technologically Based Organizations: A Literature Survey of Present Practice. *IEEE Transactions on Engineering Management*. **21**(1), February, 9–23.

This paper presents a survey of R & D project selection techniques found in the literature. The author first surveys literature on idea generation. He reports that many studies find that ideas that are based on perceived customer need are more successful than ideas that are based on technical capability. He also finds that while many authors urge that the marketing department should be brought into the process of project selection, there is no agreement on the timing, that is, whether this should be done while the innovation is still in the concept stage, or as late as when it is ready for production. The author also lists criteria that various researchers have found as being used in the selection process. He reports that some authors find decision criteria not only becomes better defined at later stages of a project's life, but the criteria change from the time of initial decision to later decisions in the final stages of the project. Market-oriented criteria are more appropriate at later stages in the development process, while technical and scientific criteria are more appropriate at early stages. However, marketing criteria must be applied to some extent, even at the earliest stages. The author finds that very few formal selection models have actually been employed. He lists the findings of several researchers as to why this is the case.

Cochran, M. A., E. B. Pyle III, L. C. Greene, H. A. Clymer, and A. D. Bender (1971). Investment Model for R & D Project Evaluation and Selection. *IEEE Transactions on Engineering Management*. **18**(3), August, 89–100.

This paper describes a method for selecting a portfolio of projects that maximizes expected net present value (ENPV). For each candidate project, the anticipated cash flow profile is determined. This profile is discounted at the cost of capital. Expectations are then taken into account in two ways. Anticipated income is multiplied by the estimated probability of technical success. Estimated expenditures are multiplied by the estimated probability that the project will actually be carried to the point that technical success or failure will be determined. That is, the possibility that the project might be dropped before completion is included. The program then selects the set of projects that maximizes ENPV subject to the constraint that a budget level is not exceeded. The program also conducts a sensitivity analysis, to determine the effect on the decision of changing probability of success, project cost, and anticipated income. The program employs an integer programming routine to make the selection.

Cooper, M. J. (1978). An Evaluation System for Project Selection. *Research Management*. **21**, July, 29–33.

The author presents a scoring model for project selection. The primary contribution of the paper is a systematic taxonomy of criteria that should be included in the model. Three main types of criteria are proposed: impact, feasibility, and research merit. Impact involves the extent to which the project is relevant to organizational goals, is supported by higher authority or customers, and the extent to which the customer is involved in the project. Feasibility involves technological risk, the technical competence of the organization, and the effectiveness of management. Research merit involves the extent to which the project presents an opportunity for good research, and the extent to which it enhances the research talents of the staff. A multiplicative scoring model is proposed. A project high on all three major criteria would be selected ahead of a project that falls short on one or more of the three criteria.

Czajkowski, A. F. and S. Jones (1986). Selecting Interrelated R & D Projects in Space Technology Planning. *IEEE Transactions on Engineering Management*. **33**(1), February.

This paper discusses the problem of selecting a portfolio of R & D projects that have interactions. Three categories of interaction are considered:

1. Cost or resource utilization.
2. Outcome or technical interaction (enabling/enhancing projects).
3. Benefit or payoff interaction (benefits depend on completion of other projects).

Enabling projects are required if a program is to be completed; enhancing projects increase the value of an already enabled program. A programming model is described that maximizes the value of the set of programs, subject to constraints on budget, on inclusion of all enabling projects required for each program, and possible inclusion of enhancing projects for some programs. Technological risk may be incorporated into the model through use of chance constraints [i.e., a constraint may be violated only with probability $(1 - \beta)$ for suitably chosen β]. The solution provides sets of projects that are optimal at a given budget level, for each of several budget levels. The procedure is illustrated on a set of NASA earth resources programs and projects.

Dias, O. Pereira, Jr. (1988). The R & D Project Selection Problem With Fuzzy Coefficients. *Fuzzy Sets and Systems*. **26**(3), June 299–316.

This paper presents an alternative to the zero-one integer or nonlinear programming problem involved in selecting a portfolio of projects that maximizes returns under multiple objectives. The initial goal is to find all the portfolios that are members of the fuzzy set of nondominated solutions. Because this goal may result in a large number of solutions that are not readily distinguished, an alternative goal is proposed, in which a set of candidate portfolios is evaluated. This approach does not provide an "optimal" solution, but does provide a rapid means of evaluating alternative portfolios.

Dodson, E. N. (1985). Measurement of State of the Art and Technological Advance. *Technological Forecasting & Social Change*. **27**(2/3), May, 129–146.

This paper describes several measures of the state of the art (SOA), and discusses means to estimate the degree of advance of a particular development project from the prior SOA. The motivation for developing these measures of SOA advance is to estimate the cost to achieve the required degree of advance. The author presents several historical examples of SOA measures and claims good correlation with development costs.

Fiksel, J., L. A. Cox, D. L. Richardson, and A. G. Adamantiades (1983). Selection of Nuclear Safety Research and Development Projects Through Value-Impact Analysis, *Nuclear Safety*. **24**(1), January–February, 12–25.

This paper proposes a technique for ranking R & D projects by assigning an index number to each project. The index number is derived by dividing each alternative into components, which are small, mutually exclusive sets of attributes. The net value contribution of each component is then determined (value of contribution minus costs). The net values for the components are then summed for each project. The index number is intended to include both monetary and nonmonetary considerations. The authors argue that decomposing the assignment of an index number to a project in this fashion has three advantages. (1) It makes complicated problems manageable. (2) It documents the decision for the public record (especially important for projects, such as nuclear power plants). (3) It provides a framework for collective decision making, since different persons may evaluate different components. A shortcoming of the procedure is that the value of the components must be measured in dollar terms, to be compatible with costs in dollar terms. That is, a nonmonetary payoff must be given a dollar value. This must be done subjectively, in the absence of a market for the payoff. This method is called value impact analysis (VIA).

Fox, E. G. and Norman R. Baker (1985). Project Selection Decision Making Linked to a Dynamic Environment. *Management Science*. **31**(10), October, 1272–1285

The authors describe a simulation model that attempts to capture some of the reality of portfolio selection. The simulation model includes a project generation model, a decision model, and a profitability model. The project generation model randomly generates possible projects, each with completion time, a cost, a probability of success, and an impact. Projects are randomly drawn from three types: product improvement, which increases market share; process improvement, which decreases variable costs; and projects that increase production capacity. The decision model selects projects based on an objective of maximizing discounted increase in profitability, taking into account project interactions, and subject to a budget constraint. The profitability model computes profitability on the basis of price, cost, total market size, production capacity, total fixed cost, and cost of projects selected. A total of 18 different sets of market conditions was investigated, including all possible combinations of total market size, price, and potential market share. There were 30 replications of each market condition. The data collected were the numbers of each type of project selected. Main, two-way and three-way interactions were computed. The main conclusion is that market conditions will alter the types of projects selected. The authors note that the particular project selection model they used was myopic in its emphasis on profitability. Such a decision-making process would fail to satisfy the long-term need to anticipate and exploit technological breakthroughs. Through comparison with the literature, the authors conclude that their simulation was successful in capturing the behavior of certain types of decision makers faced with particular environmental conditions.

Gear, A. E. (1974). Review of Some Recent Developments in Portfolio Modeling in Applied Research and Development. *IEEE Transactions on Engineering Management*. **21**(4), November, 119–125.

This article describes the use of linear (or integer) programming to select a portfolio of R & D projects that provides maximum return to the organization while satisfying constraints such as limits on the availability of critical resources (skills, unique equipment, etc.). Each candidate project may enter the selection process in several forms (different funding levels, different starting dates). The program assures that no more than one version of a project is selected, and that the portfolio of projects does not demand more of some resource than is available. The conventional linear programming approach can be modified to include uncertainty about project payoff, and to include multiple objectives for projects (i.e., payoff cannot be expressed in a single number).

Gear, T. E., A. Geoffrey Lockett, and A. Paul Muhlemann (1982). A Unified Approach to the Acquisition of Subjective Data in R & D. *IEEE Transactions on Engineering Management*. **29**(1), February, 11–19.

This paper describes a method for obtaining scores for individual projects when the input data are ratios derived from pair comparisons. Participants are asked to make pairwise comparisons among the members of a set of projects, where the projects are compared on specific criteria. For example, compare projects A and B on short-term profits, on technical certainty, and on staff enthusiasm, resulting in three ratios. The ratios for all pairs of projects are determined on each of the criteria to be scored. For each criterion, a square matrix is obtained where the rows and columns are the projects and the cell entries are the ratios on the particular criterion. The largest eigenvalue for each matrix is computed; the eigenvalues are normalized to sum to 1, and the normalized eigenvalues become the weights associated with each criterion. The weights are then used in a scoring model, where the scores for each project are derived from the eigenvectors of the criterion matrices. The Delphi procedure was used to obtain the criteria on which the projects were to be rated.

Graves, S. B. and J. L. Ringguest (1991). Evaluating Competing R & D Investments. *Research-Technology Management*. July–August, 32–36.

This paper addresses the present value computations applied to cash flows from R & D activities. It shows that use of present value computations requires some rigid assumptions about the decision maker, which may not be valid in the R & D context. In particular, a discount rate that is constant over time may not be valid. In addition, there may be cash flow circumstances under which discounting does not make sense (e.g., if the firm goes bankrupt in the near term, a long-term large positive cash flow becomes purely hypothetical, even though the computation shows a large positive present value). This paper applies a method known as generalized present value to the analysis of cash flows from R & D projects. Generalized present value does not require a constant discount rate, and permits the decision maker to take discontinuities, such as bankruptcy, into account in comparing alternative cash flow profiles. The paper then presents a technique for dealing with uncertainty in project outcomes (i.e., alternative cash flow profiles), once the generalized present value of each profile is obtained. For each project, this involves determining a certainty equivalent such that the decision maker is indifferent between it and the gamble represented by the project with uncertain outcome. The conjunction of the two methods overcomes the undesirable compounding of risk present when risk-adjusted discount rates are utilized. This compounding automatically introduces an undesirable bias against projects with long-term payoffs.

Hall, D. L. and A. Nauda (1990). An Interactive Approach for Selecting IR & D Projects. *IEEE Transactions on Engineering Management*. **37**(2), May, 126–133

This paper presents a method for selecting IR & D projects in an organization doing business with the Department of Defense (DoD). The purpose of IR & D is to put the firm in a better position to compete effectively for future DoD contracts. The process begins with an assessment of requirements, using inputs from the business units themselves, from customers, from executive management, and from the engineering staff. These requirements are then distributed to business units, marketing, and engineering, in the form of a request for proposal (RFP). The units respond to the RFP with proposals for projects. These proposals describe a DoD problem, define a research objective for the project, and present an approach to achieving the research objective. They also include a competition analysis, a market assessment, and an assessment of the technology. These proposals are collated, and redundancies are resolved. A package of refined proposals is then sent to several evaluators in engineering and in business units. Each proposal is to be rated on a 0–10 scale, according to how well it meets a set of technical evaluation criteria and a set of business evaluation criteria. Ratings for each project are then averaged, and the average technical score is plotted against the average business score. Those with high technical and business scores are considered for funding. Those that are high only on one of the two categories are considered for revision, to improve their overall rating. Those scoring low on both technical and business categories are dropped from consideration. The high-scoring projects are then refined into detailed proposals that are forwarded to top management for approval. This method depends heavily on judgment throughout. The key feature is that by using a systematic process, both technical and business judgment are focused on meeting anticipated customer needs.

Hazelrigg, G. A., Jr., and F. L. Huband (1985). RADSIM—A Methodology for Large-Scale R & D Program Assessment. *IEEE Transactions on Engineering Management*. **32**(3), August.

This paper presents a Monte Carlo simulation model for large-scale R & D projects. Each alternative approach to the goal is divided into alternative projects, each consisting of a sequence of phases. Within each phase, subprojects are identified that are discrete entities with specific outcomes. For each subproject, the technical outcome required for success of the overall project is specified (power, weight, temperature, etc.). The likelihood of achieving the specified threshold level of performance in each subproject is estimated. The entire program, including all alternatives, is "forward simulated" using Monte Carlo methods, with each subproject succeeding or not as given by the probability estimates. A few hundred simulation runs are assumed to provide a reasonable sampling of the space of possible outcomes. Interactions among the subprojects can be taken into account. Other constraints, such as limiting the number of projects within each alternative, or limiting the number of alternatives after particular phases, can be included. Output includes probability of achieving commercialization of each alternative, probability distribution of the date for achieving commercialization, probability distributions for start dates of phases and subprojects, and probability distributions of end dates for phases and subprojects.

Helm, J. (1992). The Viability of Using Cocomo in the Special Application Software Bidding and Estimating Process. *IEEE Transactions on Engineering Management*. **39**(1), February, 42–58.

This paper examines the accuracy of the Cocomo estimating tool for estimating software development costs. It provides an overview of software cost estimating techniques, comparing them as to input information required, and the originators' assertions about conditions under which they can be used. The author then collected data from several past software development projects in his firm. The conclusions of the study were that a properly calibrated version of Cocomo would give accurate predictions, but that people must be trained to provide accurate, uniform, and consistent data for calibrating the model.

Islei, G. G. Lockett, B. Cox, and M. Stratford (1991). A Decision Support System Using Judgmental Modeling: A Case of R & D in the Pharmaceutical Industry. *IEEE Transactions on Engineering Management*. **38**(3), August, 202–209.

This paper describes the use of the analytic hierarchy procedure (AHP) to evaluate R & D projects in a pharmaceutical company. The article describes in detail the procedure by which word scales (anchor points) were developed to assist managers in rating the various characteristics of the projects. The resulting model has been used both for portfolio balance and individual project monitoring.

Khorramshagol, R., H. Azani, and Y. Gousty (1988). An Integrated Approach to Project Evaluation and Selection. *IEEE Transactions on Engineering Management*. **35**(4), November, 265–270.

This technical note describes an application of linear goal programming (LGP) to R & D resource allocation. Two major problems encountered in use of LGP are (1) identification of the goals and target levels for each: and (2) the trade-offs among the goals, so deviations can be weighted properly. The authors propose to deal with these problems by using Delphi to obtain agreement on goals and target levels and to suggest possible alternative projects, and the analytical hierarchy procedure (AHP) to set priorities among the objectives. The LGP model is then used to select the project(s) that will be supported.

Khorramshahgol, R. and Y. Gousty (1986). Delphic Goal Programming (DGP): A Multi-Objective Cost/Benefit Approach to R & D Portfolio Analysis, *IEEE Transactions on Engineering Management*. **33**(3), August, 172–175.

This technical note proposes the use of Linear Goal Programming (LGP) for allocating resources to a portfolio of R & D projects. Goal programming (GP) is a variant of linear programming in which a desired value is established for each of several objectives. The allocation of resources is then chosen to minimize the sum of deviations from the desired values. The authors propose the use of the Delphi procedure for obtaining group consensus on objectives and their desired values.

Liberatore, M. J. (1987). An Extension of the Analytic Hierarchy Process for Industrial R & D Project Selection and Resource Allocation. *IEEE Transactions on Engineering Management*. **34**(4), February, 12–18.

This paper discusses the use of the analytic hierarchy process (AHP) for ranking R & D projects. Use of AHP requires that a problem be decomposed into a hierarchy of elements or alternatives. At each level, the elements are subjected to pairwise comparisons to estimate their relative importance to elements at the next higher level. The resulting importance numbers are arrayed as a matrix. The first eigenvalue of the matrix is computed, and the corresponding eigenvector contains the priority scores for alternatives at that level. The priority vectors are then combined to obtain the rating of each element at the bottom of the hierarchy to the goal or objective at the top.

Liberatore, M. J. (1988). A Decision Support System Linking Research and Development Project Selection With Business Strategy. *Project Management Journal*. **19**(5), November, 14–21.

This article describes how R & D projects can be linked with business strategy. Several business objectives are developed to support the mission of the firm. Strategies are developed for each business objective. The AHP is used to rate the importance of each objective to the mission, and of each strategy to each objective. Finally, project evaluation criteria are developed for each strategy. Analytic hierarchy procedure is again used to rate each project according to how it contributes to the overall mission of the firm. The results can be used simply to rank the projects, or if multiple funding levels for the projects can be evaluated as to their contributions to the strategies, a portfolio model can be developed that maximizes the total priority over all funded projects.

Liberatore, M. J. and G. J. Titus (1983). The Practice of Management Science in R & D Project Management. *Management Science*. **29**(8), August, 962–974.

This article reports the results of a survey of budget directors and R & D staff officials in firms in a wide range of industries, regarding the R & D resource allocation methods used in their firm. Of the financial methods used, cost/benefit analysis, payback period, and net present value/internal rate of return were the most commonly used, with one-half to three-quarters of the respondents familiar with each actually using them. Checklists and scoring models were also used, but to a lesser extent than other selection methods, with about one-half of those familiar with them actually using them. Decision analysis and decision trees were less widely used, with only about one-third of those familiar with them actually using them. Mathematical programming models were not used at all, despite the familiarity of the respondents with them. For project scheduling, Gantt charts, project network diagrams, and project network analysis were widely used.

Lockett, A. G. and A. E. Gear (1973). Representation and Analysis of Multi-Stage Problems in R & D. *Management Science*. **19**(8), April, 947–960.

This article addresses the issue of multi-stage decision making in R & D projects. For each possible project, a "project tree" is prepared. The project is divided into periods or phases, which need not be of the same length. The key issue is that at the end of each period, either a decision is made or a chance outcome occurs. Within each period, the project may be pursued at any of several resource levels, where multiple resources may be included (i.e., a vector of resources, such as personnel, funding, or specialized test equipment). Each such alternative level of effort is treated as a distinct alternative choice for a decision node. The project tree is extended to the desired time horizon, and the value of each path through the tree evaluated at the time horizon. Alternative branches in the tree may reflect uncertainty about resource levels needed or time to complete a particular phase. Folding back the tree may eliminate some branches as being inferior to alternative branches. That is, the value at the end of the path is smaller than the value at the end of other paths that could be chosen instead. The reduced tree is then taken as a representation of the possible courses of the project. The question is then, given a set of such reduced project trees, "to which subset of activities should resources be applied in period 1, in order to be on an optimal path in terms of maximizing the sum of the values derived from eventual project completions?" The authors use Net Present Value (NPV) as the optimization criterion, but note they chose it for expository purposes only. They do not recommend it as being superior to alternatives. If the number of alternatives (branches at the right end of all the trees) is small enough, a linear or integer program can be used to evaluate the entire set of paths, subject to the constraints on resources in each period, and subject to the constraint that only one version of each project may be selected. The result is the set of projects with the highest expected value that satisfies the constraints. If the number of possible paths is too large for complete enumeration, the authors illustrate by example simulation of the set of projects, obtaining estimates of the probability of each possible path. These estimated probabilities can then be used to compute expected values for each path. These expected values are then used as the programming solution. The entire procedure can be rerun at the beginning of each period, deleting projects whose value has dropped too low, and adding projects that seem to have promise of giving better value than those in the previous period's portfolio. The authors note that the solution is not robust, since different simulation runs will give different portfolios in the first period. They then recommend a heuristic procedure based on the mean value of each possible path (derived from the simulation), adding projects to the portfolio until a resource constraint is exceeded.

Lockett, G., B. Hetherington, and P. Yallup (1984). Modeling a Research Portfolio Using AHP: A Group Decision Process. *R & D Management*. **16**(2), April, 151–160.

This paper describes the use of the analytical hierarchy procedure (AHP) to rank a set of projects in a pharmaceutical firm. Criteria used were therapeutic need, competitive position of the firm, technical feasibility (itself subdivided into biological, chemical, and clinical feasibility), degree of general support for the project, existence of a project champion, ancillary uses for the research, competence of the existing staff, and the extent to which the project has long-term potential as a research topic. A primary conclusion of the research was that the AHP leads to team building in the organization.

Lootsma, F. A., T. C. A. Mensch, and F. A. Vos (1990). Multi-criteria analysis and budget reallocation in long-term research planning, *European Journal of Operational Research*. **47**, 293–305.

This paper describes the application of a two-stage analysis technique to a set of nonnuclear energy projects. The first stage involved weighting a set of criteria. A set of criteria was developed, and decision makers were asked to make paired comparisons among the criteria, rating them on a scale of indifference, weak preference, strong preference, or dominance. These comparisons were used to compute weights for the criteria, using a method related to fuzzy set theory (analytic hierarchy procedure could also be used). The projects were then subjected to pairwise comparisons under each criterion, using the same scale as before. This gave weights for each project under each criterion. The final weighted score for each project was derived from the weights of the criteria, and the weights of the projects under the criterial. Given the project scores, a portfolio problem was solved next, to reallocate funding among the projects on the assumption that increased funding would increase the benefit from the project, and decreasing funding would decrease the benefit. Using several possible funding–benefit relationships, funding was reallocated to maximize total benefit. It was found that for the range of variation of funding levels considered, the resulting allocations were not particularly sensitive to the precise funding–benefit relationship chosen.

Mandakovic, T. and W. E. Souder (1985). An Interactive Decomposable Heuristic for Project Selection. *Management Science*. **31**(10), October, 1257–1271.

This paper describes an interactive and iterative technique for selecting an optimal portfolio of projects, when the candidate projects may include several versions of the same project, only one of which may be chosen. Formally, the task is to select that set of projects that maximizes some measure of return to the organization, subject to resource constraints (and perhaps other policy constraints). The authors point out that in principle, a pricing scheme for resources required by project managers can lead to an optimum portfolio, if the allocation is made by linear programming. However, in many cases nonlinear programming is required. In this case, a pricing scheme may break down. Instead, the authors offer a heuristic solution that involves multiple stages, with one project selected at each stage. As each project is selected, the available resources are reduced. Given the remaining resources, each project manager is asked to nominate the one project that has the highest payoff per unit of remaining resources. From this set, the single project with highest payoff per unit of resources is selected, and the project managers advised of the amount of resources remaining. They repeat the nomination, and again a selection is made. This process continues until all resources are used, or no remaining candidate project can be conducted within the remaining resources. The authors argue that this heuristic will achieve a portfolio within a few percent of optimum. (Essentially the same paper appears as A Flexible Hierarchical Model for Project Selection and Budget Allocation. *R & D Management*. **15**(1), 1985, 23–29.)

Madey, G. R. and B. V. Dean (1985). Strategic Planning for Investment in R & D Using Decision Analysis and Mathematical Programming. *IEEE Transactions on Engineering Management*, v EM-32, n 2, May.

This paper describes use of goal programming to choose a portfolio of projects that minimizes simultaneous deviation from the goals of the firm. Firm goals may include not only future profit but sales growth and return on investment (ROI). Each project is characterized as to its effect on the goals over a time horizon. The portfolio is then selected to minimize deviations from the desired values, subject to constraints, such as budget, availability of specialized test equipment, and other resource constraints. The mixed-integer nonlinear programming problem implicit in selecting the portfolio can be solved but only with enormous consumption of computer time for realistic problems. This paper presents results of several approximations to the exact solution, and shows that some of these are of acceptable accuracy.

Matthews, W. H. (1991). Kissing Technological Frogs: Managing Technology as a Strategic Resource. *European Management Journal*. **9**(2), June, 145–148.

This paper points out that there is a gap between long-term research, which is usually treated as overhead, and short-term development, which is treated as investment. Projects that fall in this gap are too expensive to be treated as overhead, but too uncertain to be treated as an investment. It is proposed that such projects be treated as "options," Long-term research answers the technical question "Is it possible?" and leads to the managerial question, "Is it attractive?" If the project is attractive, then the technical question comes, "Is it practical?" If that question is answered affirmatively, the managerial question becomes, "Is it desirable?" If it is desirable from a marketing standpoint, the next technical question becomes, "How do we do it?" which is a development question. The question of practicality is the one to be answered by "options" projects. These are funded at a necessarily high level, but only until the practicality question is answered. At the first indication that a bright idea from research is not practical, the project is terminated. The key to success in treating these projects as options is to identify at the outset what technical and commercial uncertainties exist, and focus on answering them as quickly and inexpensively as possible.

Mathieu, R. G. and J. E. Gibson (1993). A Methodology for Large-Scale R & D Planning Based on Cluster Analysis. *IEEE Transactions on Engineering Management*. **40**(3), August, 283–292.

This paper describes a technique for identifying clusters of "similar" R & D projects in a laboratory. The method relies on a distinction between "system-level" technologies and "element-level" technologies. A system-level technology is one that requires the integration of two or more element-level technologies. The procedure starts with generation of an interaction matrix, where entries of 1 or 0 indicate whether an element-level technology (columns) interacts with or supports a system-level technology (rows). Once the matrix is filled out, a dissimilarity measure can be computed between each pair of element-level technologies. The article demonstrates two dissimilarity measures: Euclidean distance and Jaccard coefficient, both commonly used in cluster analysis. The dissimilarity measures form a lower triangular matrix with 1s on the diagonal. The dissimilarity matrix is then subjected to cluster analysis, to identify clusters or groups of element-level technologies that are "similar" in their support for system-level technologies. The authors recommend three clustering methods: average linkage method, centroid method, and Ward's minimum variance method. Once technology clusters have been determined by cluster analysis, each cluster is placed in a two-by-two matrix of average sales growth and market share (similar to the Boston Consulting Group strategic planning matrix). The clusters are further coded to show market size and cluster cohesiveness (measured by average separation of cluster members). Support priority should then be given to clusters with high-market share, high-average growth rate, large market, and high-group synergy (small average distance within the cluster). The authors further point out that a decision maker wishing to minimize risk of program failure might prefer to support a larger number of clusters, while a decision maker seeking high payoff and willing to take high risks might prefer to support only a small number of clusters. The methodology does not force either decision. The article provides an illustration of the technique based on space technologies.

Meadows, D. L. (1968). Estimate Accuracy and Project Selection Models in Industrial Research. *Industrial Management Review*. **9**, Spring, 105–119.

This paper suggests that a major reason that existing formal project selection models are unused is that they require estimates as inputs, and the accuracy of the estimates is so low that the model outputs are meaningless. The author presents results from four laboratories, comparing initial estimates of cost and likelihood of success with final cost and degree of technical or commercial success. It was found that the initial cost estimates explain only about 25% of the variance in final actual costs. Likewise, initial estimates of the likelihood of both technical and commercial success are very inaccurate. The article concludes with a sensitivity analysis of a simple scoring model for project selection. The finding is that typical error magnitudes lead to significant errors in ranking and selecting projects.

Mehrez, A. (1988). Selecting R & D Projects: A Case Study of the Expected Utility Approach. *Technovation*. **8**, 299–311.

This paper describes an experimental use of expected utility to evaluate a project. All possible alternatives for a project are identified (e.g., alternative solutions to each technological problem). The probability of each possible outcome was estimated subjectively. The net cash flow for each subsequent period (out to some time horizon) was estimated. The expected present worth of the project was them computed, summing over all possible outcomes. Instead an alternative computation utilized the expected utility, where the utility of the cash flow in each period was used instead of the cash flow itself. The author reports extreme difficulty in obtaining some of the data required.

Mehrez, A., S. Mossery, and Z. Sinuany-Stern (1982), Project Selection in a Small University R & D Laboratory. *R & D Management*. **12**(4), 169–174.

This paper presents a case study of selecting interrelated R & D projects under conditions of constrained resources. The projects are identified as contributing to certain attributes important to the laboratory (in this case, profitability, technological advancement, and suitability to the laboratory). Each possible subset of projects is rated as to its utility (0–1 scale) to each attribute (i.e., for each attribute, only those subsets are considered for which each project contributes to that attribute). The attributes themselves are then rated as to their utility to the laboratory. The solution is then to maximize the function:

$$U = \sum_{i=1}^{n} k_i \sum_{j=1}^{m} u(a_{ij}) y(a_{ij})$$

where there are n attributes and m projects, a_{ij} is a subset of projects, $y(a_{ij})$ is 1 if a_{ij} is the subset of projects chosen and zero otherwise, $u(a_{ij})$ is the utility of subset a_{ij}, and k_i is the utility of attribute i, where the maximization is subject to the condition that all constraints on resources are met (lab budget, availability of personnel, etc.). This is done using Keeney's approach to multiattribute utility functions.

Melachrinoudis, E. and K. Rice (1991). The Prioritization of Technologies in a Research Laboratory. *IEEE Transactions on Engineering Management*. **38**(3), August, 269–278.

This paper describes the successful use of a scoring model to prioritize technologies in an Army laboratory. The model incorporates both objective and subjective data. A normalization scheme was used to convert the ranges of the objective variables to the same as the range for the subjective variables. Weights for the criteria were developed using the analytic hierarchy procedure.

Miles, R. F., Jr. (1980). The SIMRAND Methodology: Simulation of Research and Development Projects. *Large Scale Systems*. **7**(1), August, 59–67.

This paper describes a technique for alternatives where each alternative is itself a network involving alternative paths. A given alternative is analyzed as follows. It is laid out as a network, showing each step or phase, and all the alternatives at each step or phase. A common measure of preference is required for all steps, such as total cost. For each step, a cumulative distribution for the probability of different values of the measure of preference is required (e.g., probability that the cost will be a particular value). The network is then expanded such that each possible path through it is represented as an alternative. A Monte Carlo analysis is then conducted to develop a cumulative probability distribution of the measure of preference for the entire network. This cumulative probability distribution may be used to compute an expected value of the measure of preference (e.g., expected cost). However, if a utility function on the measure of preference is available, an equivalent certainty utility may be computed instead. The project selection process then involves picking those networks with the best certainty equivalent utility.

Moore, J. R. Jr., and N. R. Baker (1969). An Analytical Approach to Scoring Model Design—Application to Research and Development Project Selection. *IEEE Transactions on Engineering Management*. **16**(3), August, 90–98.

This paper describes a means of designing scoring models to be used in the early stages of research, when little information is available without a project. A major problem in scoring model design is assigning scores to factors that already have numerical values (e.g., dollar cost, number of scientists required, or hours of use of specialized equipment). The authors recommend obtaining past data on projects, and computing the mean and standard deviation of each factor to be considered. The range of values is divided into intervals each of which is one-half of the standard deviation (σ)

wide, with one interval centered on the mean (μ). These intervals are then assigned values from 1 (less than $\mu - 1.75\sigma$) to 9 (greater than $\mu + 1.75\sigma$). The virtues of this approach are that all factors in the model are put on the same scale, and that particular factors do not "pile up" at one end of the scale or the other, but are distributed through the entire range of scale values.

Morris, P. A., E. O. Teisberg, and A. L. Kolbe (1991). When Choosing R & D Projects, Go With Long Shots. *Research-Technology Management*. **34**(1) January–February, 35–40.

The authors argue that R & D projects should be considered in the light of the firm's long-term strategy rather than as isolated projects. The authors define "risk" as the expected loss if a project is *not* successful. The authors argue that under a wide range of circumstances, greater downside risk is associated with greater upside payoff if the project *is* successful. That is, there is a wider range of possible outcomes in a high-risk project than in a low-risk project. The argument is based on the concept of a two-stage decision process. The first decision is whether to fund an R & D project. The second decision is whether to implement the results of the project. Clearly, if the project fails, it will not be implemented. The critical point is that given success of the R & D project, the expected payoff from implementing a high-risk project will be greater than the payoff from implementing a low-risk project. Put another way, if the implementation stage is reached, the project that was riskier at the outset will turn out to have the higher expected payoff for implementation. The authors argue that selecting riskier individual projects need not result in an overall riskier portfolio (greater risk of no payoff from any project) if the projects are chosen to be independent, or better yet, if they are negatively correlated (one does well in circumstances in which another does poorly, and vice versa).

Oral, M., O. Keitani, and P. Lang (1991). A Methodology for Collective Evaluation and Selection of Industrial R & D Projects. *Management Science*. **37**(7), July, 871–885.

This paper presents a procedure for selecting a set of R & D projects to be funded, from among a set of candidate projects whose total cost exceeds the available budget. The procedure begins with the selection of a set of criteria by which projects are to be judged. This may require a consensus among the stakeholders involved in the evaluation. However, no consensus is required for the weights to be assigned to each criterion. Next, for each candidate project, a set of weights is derived, which presents that project in its most favorable light. For instance, if a project has high-market potential but also low probability of success, market potential would be given a large weight and probability of success would be given a small weight. Each candidate project is then evaluated using the same weights as those obtained for the first project. This process is repeated for each candidate project. That is, for each candidate project, a set of weights is derived, which presents that project as favorably as possible. These weights are then applied to all the other candidate projects. The result is that each candidate project receives as many scores as there are projects. A *concordance* score is then computed for each candidate Project i relative to each other candidate j. The concordance is simply the number of scores for Project i that exceed the scores for Project j. If, by all the possible sets of weights, Project i outscores Project j, then it is assumed that Project i is superior to Project j even though no consensus has been reached on weights. This absolute dominance is unlikely in most cases. Hence, the concordance score for most projects will be less than n, the total number of candidate projects. Once the concordance scores are obtained, a threshold is set, such that below that threshold, differences in concordance scores are not considered to be significant. The final step is to identify a set of projects that fit within the budget, and that satisfy certain consistency criteria (e.g., no project should be excluded whose concordance outranks at least one project included in the set). The authors point out that this method achieves consensus on *choice* of projects rather than consensus on *values* attributed to the criteria. By using this procedure, the various stakeholders can reach consensus on a set of projects to be funded, even though each stakeholder may weight the criteria differently.

Poensgen, O. H. and H. Hort (1983). R & D Management and Financial Performance. *IEEE Transactions on Engineering Management*. **30**(4), November, 212–222

This paper describes research on the relationship between R & D organization and overall firm performance. R & D organization is characterized in terms of the degree of centralization of the R & D activity in the firm. Performance of the firm is characterized by return on capital. Only firms spending more than 1.5% of revenues on R & D were included in the analysis. The results were that in large companies, the influence of marketing on R & D is beneficial up to a certain point, but too great an influence on marketing on R & D reduces return on capital. In small companies, the greater the influence of marketing, the lower the return on capital. The authors conclude that in a small company, the R & D activity is too small to effectively make its influence felt if marketing has too much control. In a large company, R & D is large enough that if it is not subject to some marketing influence, it becomes isolated and loses touch with the market. In general, the authors found that organizing R & D by scientific discipline leads to greater return on capital than does organization by project, regardless of firms size.

Ringuest, J. L. and S. B. Graves (1990). The Linear R & D Project Selection Problem: an Alternative to Net Present Value. *IEEE Transactions on Engineering Management*. **37**(2), May.

This paper addresses the problem of selecting a portfolio of R & D projects subject to budget and other constraints. The authors point out that using net present value (NPV) as the optimization criterion makes some very restrictive assumptions about the decision maker's time preferences for income. The decision maker may face constraints, such as net cash flow in a particular period, which would cause him/her to choose a lower NPV portfolio, thus reducing the cash flow problem. The proposed solution is to formulate the problem as a multiple objective linear program with annual cash flows as the objectives. The solution maximizes the annual cash flows individually, rather than maximizing their discounted sum. The result is a set of nondominated alternatives, from which the decision maker may choose. Filtering or clustering may be used to reduce the number of "similar" choices if the set of nondominated solutions is still too large.

Saaty, T. L. (1983). Priority Setting in Complex Problems. *IEEE Transactions on Engineering Management*. **30**(2), August, 140–155.

This paper presents the analytic hierarchy method, with several everyday examples to illustrate the features of the method.

Schmidt, R. L. (1993). A Model for R & D Project Selection with Combined Benefit, Outcome and Resource Interactions. *IEEE Transactions on Engineering Management*. **40**(4), November, 403–410.

This paper describes a model for selecting a portfolio of projects to maximize measure of payoff (e.g., net present value) when there are several different kinds of simultaneous interactions among the projects. Types of interactions considered in the paper include resource constraints, cost, or other resource overlaps between projects resulting in reduced costs (e.g., common experiments or measurements or common test item fabrication), and altered payoffs (e.g., complementary products resulting in increased sales if both are offered; cannibalization of sales). Solution of the model involves integer nonlinear programming. The author presents an algorithm by which the integer nonlinear problem can be converted to an integer problem with quadratic objective functions and quadratic constraints. Solutions to problems of practical size (10 projects) can be carried out on a PC within a few seconds.

Schwartz, S. L. and I. Vertinsky (1977). Multi-Attribute Investment Decisions: A Study of R & D Project Selection, *Management Science*. **24**, November 285–301.

This paper reports a study in which executives of Canadian firms were given information about six attributes of 60 hypothetical projects, and asked to rate the probability that they would fund each project. A decision model was prepared for each responding executive, by using stepwise linear regression of probability of funding on attribute values. An alternative analysis used discriminant analysis to identify those attributes that seemed to be relevant in the funding decision. As might be expected, high probability of funding was associated with short payback period, high impact on market share, and high likelihood of receiving government funding for the R & D. Project cost was not a significant discriminator among projects. The regression coefficients showed that decision makers were willing to make trade-offs, that is, funding a longer payback project if probability of success was high or impact on market share was high. Executives in small companies took high risks for high rates of return only if project cost was low.

Simmons, D. B. (1992). A Win–Win Metric Based Software Management Approach. *IEEE Transactions on Engineering Management*. **39**(1), February 32–41.

This paper presents an approach to planning and staffing software development projects based on metrics for programmer performance. Programmer productivity is measured directly by a software package that automatically collects data on programmer activity. Patterns of programmer activity can be used to identify problems, and to determine progress toward completion of the project. Several models of programmer productivity are discussed as tools for staffing.

Smith, L. A. and T. Mandakovic (1985). Estimating: The Input into Good Project Planning. *IEEE Transactions on Engineering Management*. **32**(4), November, 181–185.

This paper presents a summary of the literature on estimating various quantities, particularly time to carry out a project, but also cost and risk. The paper concludes that the following measures can be taken to improve the quality of estimates.

1. Develop more levels in the work breakdown structure.
2. Use relevant historical data.
3. Estimate in phases of the project.
4. Use several estimating techniques.
5. Use professional estimators.
6. Use a two-stage iterative procedure.
7. Introduce greater accountability of persons making estimates.

Souder, W. E. (1978). Analytical Effectiveness of Mathematical Models for R & D project Selection. *Management Science*. **19**(8), April, 907–923.

This paper presents the results of applying 4 different mathematical project selection models *ex post* to 30 projects for which data, management decision, and actual outcome were known. The allocations were simulated for each of four successive 6-month periods, using actual data from the projects at the same stage of completion. Estimated probability of success was collected from the project manager each 6 months during the actual course of the project. The author notes that probability of success estimates made after 18 months and after 24 months correlated well with actual project outcome (success or failure). Probability estimates made earlier in the course of the project correlated very poorly with the eventual outcome. An *ex post* "optimum" portfolio was selected, that is, funding only those projects that actually succeeded, to identify the best that could have been achieved. A "benchmark" portfolio was obtained by funding each project at the same percentage of its requested budget. For each model, the payoff was compared with the "benchmark" portfolio and with the actual portfolio selected by the project managers. Not surprisingly, it was found that the models uniformly gave better results than the "benchmark" portfolio. That is, using any of the models would give better results than "equalizing the pain" among the projects. What was surprising was that each of the models did better than the actual portfolios as selected by the project managers. What was even more surprising was that the benchmark portfolio, which simply equalized the pain, also did better than the actual portfolios selected by the project managers. A calculation was also made of "regret expenditures," that is, expenditures made on projects that were ultimately failures. During the first three periods, the actual portfolios had lower regret expenditures than did any of the model portfolios. In the last two periods, however, most model portfolios, as well as the benchmark portfolio, had lower regret expenditures than did the actual portfolios. This implies that project managers effectively reduced the budgets of ultimate failures early in their development, but did not reduce them sufficiently during later phases. The research also uncovered a tendency of managers to reduce the funding of projects whose success had become almost certain, and redeploy the resources to those projects where additional funding could increase the probability of success. None of the models tested included this possibility. The author concludes that early in the life cycle of a project, a "benchmark" allocation is probably the most effective (i.e., equalizing the pain among projects at the same life cycle stage). Later in the life cycle, a 0–1 model, which defunds low-probability-of-success projects and fully funds high-probability-of-success projects, does better than either a benchmark or expected value model. The author also notes that his analysis did not include either scoring models or risk analysis models. Hence his analysis cannot draw any conclusions about the relative merits of these types of model.

Souder, W. E. (1969). The Validity of Subjective Probability of Success Forecasts by R & D Project Managers. *IEEE Transactions on Engineering Management*. **16**(1), February, 35–49.

This paper presents the results of research on 11 projects in the research laboratory of a chemical company. Periodically during the course of the projects, the responsible project leader was asked to estimate the probability that the project would meet its technical objectives within time horizons of 3, 12, and 24 months. Final determination of success or failure of the project was made by higher management. Those probability estimates made later in the course of the project had much higher correlation with the final outcome than did those at the outset.

Souder, W. E. and T. Mandakovic (1986). R & D Project Selection Models. *Research Management*. **29**(4), July–August, 36–42.

In this paper the authors trace the disappointing history of R & D project selection models. They conclude that a major reason for failure of these models is that they fail to take into account the human interactions that are critical in making decisions within organizations. They recommend that allocation models be used, not as a means for making decisions, but as a means for internal communication about the factors that must be taken into account in making decisions about R & D project selection and resource allocation. Once the models help achieve consensus, decisions about allocation can be made more easily.

Stahl, M. J. and A. M. Harrell (1983). Identifying Operative Goals by Modeling Project Selection Decisions in Research and Development. *IEEE Transactions on Engineering Management*. **30**(4), November, 223–228.

This paper describes how the goals actually used by decision makers in a laboratory were identified and made explicit. Project selection in the laboratory was customarily done by a board of senior laboratory officials. Board members were supposed to be using six criteria in evaluating projects. In practice, it was found that there was considerable disagreement among board members regarding projects to be approved for funding. It was decided to run an experiment to identify the actual goals utilized by the board members and their advisors. A set of hypothetical projects was devised. The set was designed to be a half-replicate of a full factorial design. In the full design, there would be one project for each possible combination of "excellent" and "acceptable" ratings on each of the six criteria. The half-replicate design omitted one-half of the possible combinations. These projects were then rated as "approve" or "disapprove" by each of the individuals taking part. Multiple regression analysis was used to determine the actual weights the participants were applying to each of the six factors. The results showed that four of the criteria were being given too little weight by most of the participants. However, differences in the weights assigned to the two criteria actually being used were responsible to the disputes. The outcome of the effort was to develop a scoring model that incorporated the weights that the selection board members agreed should be applied to each of the six criteria. The use of this model allowed the board members to focus on those projects near the cutoff point, while the model identified those projects whose scores were so high or low that the funding decision about them was obvious.

Stahl, M. J., T. W. Zimmerer, and Z. Gulati (1984). Measuring Innovation, Productivity, and Job Performance of Professionals: A Decision Modeling Approach. *IEEE Transactions on Engineering Management*. **31**(1), February, 25–29.

This paper describes an experiment in which managers and professionals were asked to rate a set of profiles describing hypothetical professional researchers on job performance, productivity, and innovation. Each profile included six characteristics. The design was a half replicate of a full factorial design, in which each respondent evaluated 32 profiles. The findings were that there were no interactions among the six factors, and the ratings among the participants were highly consistent. The average R^2 for job performance was 0.75, that for productivity was 0.73, and that for innovation was 0.76. However, the ratings of managers and of professionals were different, and the difference was statistically significant. The professionals tended to give more weight to input factors, such as "works hard" and "works well with peers;" the managers tended to give more weight to "long-term effectiveness." The author concludes that the decision modeling approach is an effective means of identifying the factors that managers and professionals use to rate R & D workers.

Taylor, B. W., L. J. Moore, and E. R. Clayton (1982). R & D Project Selection and Manpower Allocation with Integer Nonlinear Goal Programming. *Management Science.* **28**(10), October, 1149–1158.

This paper describes an integer goal programming approach to the problem of selection which projects to pursue, and the number of researchers to be allocated to each project, given constraints on the number of researchers available and the maximum number that can be used on each project. Goal programming is intended to minimize either underachievement or over-achievement of each goal. A nonlinear relationship was assumed between staffing level and probability of success for each project. A nonlinear relation-ship between staffing level and time to completion was also developed. Both sets of relationships were based on estimates from persons involved with the projects. An overall budget represents a constraint on the number of pro-jects. Each project has an estimated return if successful. The first goal was to achieve a probability of success of 0.6 for each project selected. A second goal was to remain within the budget. A third goal was to minimize negative deviations from the desired expected return from selected projects. A fourth goal was to assure that the probability of no failures among the selected projects was at least 0.25 (i.e., no project was to be staffed at such a low level that the probability of at least one failure exceeded 0.25). A fifth goal was to minimize positive deviations in time to completion. A sixth goal was to minimize total time consumed by all selected projects. This in effect limits the number of projects selected, since reducing staffing on a project extends the length of the project. Another constraint was to minimize the overcapac-ity utilization of the computer (up to 100% capacity, the existing computer could be used at marginal cost of zero; overcapacity use could be leased at additional expense).

A seventh goal was to assure that the set of selected projects did not include mutually exclusive projects (those that required the same scarce resources). The final constraint was that a minimum of two out of four "preferred" projects must be selected. The set of projects was small enough that goal programming could be accomplished by complete enumeration. All solutions that satisfied the first priority goal were selected. Those that satisfied a second priority goal were selected from this group. This process continued until total goal achievement is no longer possible, at which point solutions are selected on the basis of minimum deviation from goals. The authors conclude that the problems previously encountered in attempting to use a linear zero-one goal programming model can be overcome by using an integer nonlinear goal programming model. Such a model retains the benefits of multi-criteria goal consideration inherent in goal programming, while incorporating nonlinear relationships between resource allocation and project outcome.

Thomas, H. (1985). Decision Analysis and Strategic Management of Research and Development. *R & D Management*. **15**(1), January, 3–22.

This paper describes the use of decision trees, net present value (NPV), and internal rate of return (IRR) as a means of selecting projects in the electronics and pharmaceutical industries. It was found that the electronics industry is faced with short product life cycles. In this situation, Monte Carlo simulation is an effective means of estimating the probability distribution for NPV, IRR, and payback period, given subjective estimates of the probabilities of sales, prices, and costs. The pharmaceutical industry, by contrast, faces long development times, followed by a moderate period of patent protection. Net present value calculations typically militate against such long-term projects. A particular problem with NPV calculations is the use of risk-adjusted discount rates. The risk profile may not be constant with time, hence a discount rate adjusted for the highest risk level may give an incorrectly low NPV. In such a case, decision trees, with probabilistic nodes and nonrisk-adjusted NPVs at the ends of the branches, give a more realistic picture of the situation, and are more valid as tools for guiding decisions.

Vepsalainen, A. P. J. and G. L. Lauro (1988). Analysis of R & D Portfolio Strategies for Contract Competition. *IEEE Transactions on Engineering Management*. **35**(3), August, 181–186.

This technical note discusses use of portfolio methods for selecting among candidate projects that will increase the likelihood of winning a competitive contract. The method takes into account preferences of customers for product characteristics, the degree of influence of each customer over the selection of the winner, and the capabilities of the competing bidders. Individual projects can then be evaluated in terms of how much they increase various product characteristics, the preferences of the customers, and the degree of influence of the customers. The portfolio chosen is that which appears to enhance the overall chance of winning by the greatest amount. The analysis can be extended to take into account the strategic response of the other competitors, and adjustments made in the portfolio.

PROJECT MENUS

PROJECT MENU 1

Project	Cost ($1000)	Market Share (Pct.)	Market Size ($Mill.)	Prob. Tech. Success (Pct.)	Prob. Market Success (Pct.)	Stage of Innov.	Mfg. Improv. Rating	Skills Avail.	Degree of Product Regulation	Fab. Shop Hours	Project Source	Computer Hours	Product Champion	Strategic Position
1	48	11	430	32	25	Bas. Rsch.	3	TRAIN	NONE	60	R & D Lab	29	NO	LOW
2	38	12	340	36	49	Bas. Rsch.	10	YES	EXTENSIVE	189	Production	48	YES	HIGH
3	40	10	180	79	75	Com'l Dev.	3	HIRE	NONE	105	Customer	51	YES	HIGH
4	43	13	290	60	70	Com'l Dev.	9	YES	EXTENSIVE	174	Marketing	23	NO	LOW
5	35	28	1220	48	42	Com'l Dev.	4	TRAIN	EXTENSIVE	191	R & D Lab	20	YES	HIGH
6	25	28	1340	27	35	Com'l Dev.	9	YES	NONE	55	Production	51	NO	LOW
7	26	20	610	79	57	Bas. Rsch.	2	HIRE	EXTENSIVE	196	Customer	47	NO	LOW
8	41	15	1010	93	70	Bas. Rsch.	10	YES	NONE	120	Marketing	34	YES	HIGH
9	53	10	810	40	73	App. Rsch.	3	YES	NONE	208	R & D Lab	51	NO	HIGH
10	81	12	560	31	75	App. Rsch.	7	TRAIN	EXTENSIVE	59	Production	33	YES	LOW
11	97	10	710	96	34	Prototype	3	YES	NONE	224	Customer	28	YES	LOW
12	51	13	1180	63	34	Prototype	9	HIRE	EXTENSIVE	82	Marketing	40	NO	HIGH
13	89	16	460	43	56	Prototype	1	YES	EXTENSIVE	66	R & D Lab	52	YES	LOW
14	78	16	180	45	62	Prototype	7	TRAIN	NONE	176	Production	24	NO	HIGH
15	97	23	270	62	30	App. Rsch.	5	YES	EXTENSIVE	109	Customer	28	NO	HIGH
16	90	21	430	57	48	App. Rsch.	6	HIRE	NONE	235	Marketing	50	YES	LOW

PROJECT MENU 2

Project	Cost ($1000)	Market Share (Pct.)	Market Size ($Mill.)	Prob. Tech. Success (Pct.)	Prob. Market Success	Stage of Innov.	Mfg. Improv. Rating	Skills Avail.	Degree of Product Regulation	Fab. Shop Hours	Project Source	Computer Hours	Product Champion	Strategic Position
1	57	76	1234	72	79	Com'l Dev.	1	YES	EXTENSIVE	179	Production	55	YES	HIGH
2	75	73	1234	69	68	Com'l Dev.	7	TRAIN	NONE	71	R & D Lab	28	NO	LOW
3	62	50	1518	48	28	Bas. Rsch.	5	YES	EXTENSIVE	223	Marketing	28	NO	LOW
4	67	72	1271	41	35	Bas. Rsch.	10	HIRE	NONE	111	Customer	49	YES	HIGH
5	66	35	438	56	50	Bas. Rsch.	2	YES	NONE	124	Production	54	NO	LOW
6	57	44	885	56	51	Bas. Rsch.	7	TRAIN	EXTENSIVE	164	R & D Lab	26	YES	HIGH
7	76	47	941	46	45	Com'l Dev.	5	YES	NONE	133	Marketing	24	YES	HIGH
8	66	37	927	34	31	Com'l Dev.	8	HIRE	EXTENSIVE	157	Customer	56	NO	LOW
9	32	67	490	51	30	Prototype	5	TRAIN	EXTENSIVE	108	Production	34	YES	LOW
10	44	55	852	64	31	Prototype	8	YES	NONE	150	R & D Lab	49	NO	HIGH
11	30	56	888	24	56	App. Rsch.	5	HIRE	EXTENSIVE	55	Marketing	57	NO	HIGH
12	47	64	444	41	62	App. Rsch.	6	YES	NONE	183	Customer	24	YES	LOW
13	39	20	1305	53	44	App. Rsch.	4	TRAIN	NONE	181	Production	25	NO	HIGH
14	25	37	1538	54	29	App. Rsch.	7	YES	EXTENSIVE	148	R & D Lab	55	YES	LOW
15	22	26	1501	48	65	Prototype	3	HIRE	NONE	150	Marketing	40	YES	LOW
16	26	49	1349	48	54	Prototype	6	YES	EXTENSIVE	126	Customer	31	NO	HIGH

PROJECT MENU 3

Project 1

Year	R & D Cost	Capital	Advert.	Profit	Cash Flow	Cumulative
1	35				−35	−35
2	74				−74	−109
3	162				−162	−271
4	97				−97	−368
5	58	91			−149	−517
6		114			−114	−631
7		131	73	106	−98	−729
8			128	262	134	−595
9			105	462	357	−238
10			102	538	436	198
11			100	520	420	618
12			91	373	282	900
13			103	331	228	1128
14			97	312	215	1343
15			90	243	153	1496

Project 2

Year	R & D Cost	Capital	Advert.	Profit	Cash Flow	Cumulative
1	30				−30	−30
2	76				−76	−106
3	169				−169	−275
4	98				−98	−373
5	52	93			−145	−518
6		119			−119	−637
7		139	74	208	−5	−642
8			135	404	269	−373
9			90	657	567	194
10			109	771	662	856
11			106	749	643	1499
12			108	609	501	2000
13			105	464	359	2359
14			93	364	271	2630
15			104	314	210	2840

PROJECT MENU 3 (*Continued*)

Project 3

Year	R & D Cost	Capital	Advert.	Profit	Cash Flow	Cumulative
1	30				−30	−30
2	77				−77	−107
3	160				−160	−267
4	98				−98	−365
5	52	88			−140	−505
6		114			−114	−619
7		136	95	156	−75	−694
8			158	252	94	−600
9			114	456	342	−258
10			124	528	404	146
11			126	542	416	562
12			124	387	263	825
13			125	341	216	1041
14			128	288	160	1201
15			127	226	99	1300

Project 4

Year	R & D Cost	Capital	Advert.	Profit	Cash Flow	Cumulative
1	31				−31	−31
2	77				−77	−108
3	164				−164	−272
4	93				−93	−365
5	56	80			−136	−501
6		113			−113	−614
7		133	101	235	1	−613
8			156	379	223	−390
9			120	629	509	119
10			110	720	610	729
11			110	750	640	1369
12			115	556	441	1810
13			110	437	327	2137
14			116	375	259	2396
15			113	359	246	2642

PROJECT MENU 3 (*Continued*)

Project 5

Year	R & D Cost	Capital	Advert.	Profit	Cash Flow	Cumulative
1	35				−35	−35
2	78				−78	−113
3	162				−162	−275
4	95				−95	−370
5	52	130			−182	−552
6		167			−167	−719
7		171	83	138	−116	−835
8			132	303	171	−664
9			98	453	355	−309
10			94	518	424	115
11			90	501	411	526
12			101	390	289	815
13			106	347	241	1056
14			90	252	162	1218
15			106	272	166	1384

Project 6

Year	R & D Cost	Capital	Advert.	Profit	Cash Flow	Cumulative
1	32				−32	−32
2	75				−75	−107
3	168				−168	−275
4	97				−97	−372
5	51	125			−176	−548
6		163			−163	−711
7		177	73	191	−59	−770
8			129	391	262	−508
9			99	635	536	28
10			103	729	626	654
11			109	747	638	1292
12			99	584	485	1777
13			96	483	387	2164
14			103	424	321	2485
15			107	342	235	2720

PROJECT MENU 3 (*Continued*)

Project 7

Year	R & D Cost	Capital	Advert.	Profit	Cash Flow	Cumulative
1	38				−38	−38
2	70				−70	−108
3	160				−160	−268
4	98				−98	−366
5	58	124			−182	−548
6		169			−169	−717
7		171	99	133	−137	−854
8			144	257	113	−741
9			119	472	353	−388
10			110	532	422	34
11			128	565	437	471
12			123	419	296	767
13			119	326	207	974
14			120	271	151	1125
15			120	250	130	1255

Project 8

Year	R & D Cost	Capital	Advert.	Profit	Cash Flow	Cumulative
1	36				−36	−36
2	75				−75	−111
3	166				−166	−277
4	99				−99	−376
5	50	136			−186	−562
6		166			−166	−728
7		183	106	205	−84	−812
8			154	354	200	−612
9			128	621	493	−119
10			112	763	651	532
11			111	717	606	1138
12			117	583	466	1604
13			114	436	322	1926
14			113	353	240	2166
15			119	301	182	2348

PROJECT MENU 3 (*Continued*)

Project 9

Year	R & D Cost	Capital	Advert.	Profit	Cash Flow	Cumulative
1	26				−26	−26
2	77				−77	−103
3	164				−164	−267
4	193				−193	−460
5	161				−161	−621
6	88				−88	−709
7	38	97			−135	−844
8		118			−118	−962
9		132	87	129	−90	−1052
10			125	295	170	−882
11			92	453	361	−521
12			108	518	410	−111
13			90	518	428	317
14			93	392	299	616
15			106	329	223	839

Project 10

Year	R & D Cost	Capital	Advert.	Profit	Cash Flow	Cumulative
1	31				−31	−31
2	80				−80	−111
3	159				−159	−270
4	197				−197	−467
5	166				−166	−633
6	88				−88	−721
7	34	98			−132	−853
8		119			−119	−972
9		121	74	206	11	−961
10			138	409	271	−690
11			95	649	554	−136
12			90	702	612	476
13			99	760	661	1137
14			95	577	482	1619
15			96	449	353	1972

PROJECT MENU 3 (*Continued*)

Project 11

Year	R & D Cost	Capital	Advert.	Profit	Cash Flow	Cumulative
1	26				−26	−26
2	81				−81	−107
3	160				−160	−267
4	198				−198	−465
5	165				−165	−630
6	88				−88	−718
7	35	85			−120	−838
8		104			−104	−942
9		130	95	132	−93	−1035
10			140	252	112	−923
11			115	462	347	−576
12			111	547	436	−140
13			116	502	386	246
14			112	373	261	507
15			123	361	238	745

Project 12

Year	R & D Cost	Capital	Advert.	Profit	Cash Flow	Cumulative
1	34				−34	−34
2	79				−79	−113
3	163				−163	−276
4	192				−192	−468
5	163				−163	−631
6	88				−88	−719
7	32	83			−115	−834
8		106			−106	−940
9		124	108	210	−22	−962
10			141	353	212	−750
11			112	609	497	−253
12			111	737	626	373
13			120	761	641	1014
14			125	570	445	1459
15			120	477	357	1816

PROJECT MENU 3 (*Continued*)

Project 13

Year	R & D Cost	Capital	Advert.	Profit	Cash Flow	Cumulative
1	26				−26	−26
2	77				−77	−103
3	164				−164	−267
4	199				−199	−466
5	160				−160	−626
6	84				−84	−710
7	38	122			−160	−870
8		153			−153	−1023
9		172	85	108	−149	−1172
10			131	278	147	−1025
11			105	452	347	−678
12			105	500	395	−283
13			106	570	464	181
14			90	354	264	445
15			92	309	217	662

Project 14

Year	R & D Cost	Capital	Advert.	Profit	Cash Flow	Cumulative
1	31				−31	−31
2	81				−81	−112
3	160				−160	−272
4	192				−192	−464
5	162				−162	−626
6	87				−87	−713
7	38	130			−168	−881
8		157			−157	−1038
9		171	84	221	−34	−1072
10			127	391	264	−808
11			105	601	496	−312
12			105	756	651	339
13			101	705	604	943
14			90	584	494	1437
15			90	494	404	1841

PROJECT MENU 3 (*Continued*)

Project 15

Year	R & D Cost	Capital	Advert.	Profit	Cash Flow	Cumulative
1	30				− 30	− 30
2	76				− 76	− 106
3	155				− 155	− 261
4	195				− 195	− 456
5	160				− 160	− 616
6	83				− 83	− 699
7	31	124			− 155	− 854
8		165			− 165	− 1019
9		181	107	138	− 150	− 1169
10			144	268	124	− 1045
11			129	409	280	− 765
12			120	560	440	− 325
13			119	559	440	115
14			127	406	279	394
15			124	347	223	617

Project 16

Year	R & D Cost	Capital	Advert.	Profit	Cash Flow	Cumulative
1	29				− 29	− 29
2	83				− 83	− 112
3	160				− 160	− 272
4	195				− 195	− 467
5	168				− 168	− 635
6	80				− 80	− 715
7	37	138			− 175	− 890
8		153			− 153	− 1043
9		186	100	198	− 88	− 1131
10			156	395	239	− 892
11			121	636	515	− 377
12			121	723	602	225
13			129	745	616	841
14			125	562	437	1278
15			126	470	344	1622

PROJECT MENU 4

Project 1

Year	R & D Cost	Capital	Advert.	Profit	Cash Flow	Cumulative
1	37				−37	−37
2	79				−79	−116
3	163				−163	−279
4	99				−99	−378
5	58	96			−154	−532
6		100			−100	−632
7		120	72	163	−29	−661
8			133	301	168	−493
9			93	455	362	−131
10			98	523	425	294
11			95	555	460	754
12			107	401	294	1048
13			102	322	220	1268
14			108	308	200	1468
15			102	272	170	1638

Project 2

Year	R & D Cost	Capital	Advert.	Profit	Cash Flow	Cumulative
1	32				−32	−32
2	70				−70	−102
3	161				−161	−263
4	92				−92	−355
5	56	90			−146	−501
6		101			−101	−602
7		138	86	229	5	−597
8			120	384	264	−333
9			100	660	560	227
10			107	771	664	891
11			100	747	647	1538
12			92	598	506	2044
13			99	490	391	2435
14			104	361	257	2692
15			107	328	221	2913

PROJECT MENU 4 (*Continued*)

Project 3

Year	R & D Cost	Capital	Advert.	Profit	Cash Flow	Cumulative
1	33				−33	−33
2	73				−73	−106
3	160				−160	−266
4	97				−97	−363
5	58	91			−149	−512
6		112			−112	−624
7		128	106	148	−86	−710
8			153	257	104	−606
9			123	470	347	−259
10			128	568	440	181
11			121	538	417	598
12			121	360	239	837
13			128	356	228	1065
14			118	260	142	1207
15			112	235	123	1330

Project 4

Year	R & D Cost	Capital	Advert.	Profit	Cash Flow	Cumulative
1	38				−38	−38
2	79				−79	−117
3	166				−166	−283
4	92				−92	−375
5	57	91			−148	−523
6		118			−118	−641
7		137	105	218	−24	−665
8			151	403	252	−413
9			123	619	496	83
10			119	717	598	681
11			119	706	587	1268
12			127	623	496	1764
13			116	476	360	2124
14			115	368	253	2377
15			127	330	203	2580

PROJECT MENU 4 (*Continued*)

Project 5

Year	R & D Cost	Capital	Advert.	Profit	Cash Flow	Cumulative
1	37				−37	−37
2	79				−79	−116
3	164				−164	−280
4	99				−99	−379
5	57	134			−191	−570
6		154			−154	−724
7		184	88	129	−143	−867
8			131	276	145	−722
9			93	473	380	−342
10			105	546	441	99
11			106	504	398	497
12			99	351	252	749
13			101	319	218	967
14			108	302	194	1161
15			100	217	117	1278

Project 6

Year	R & D Cost	Capital	Advert.	Profit	Cash Flow	Cumulative
1	38				−38	−38
2	71				−71	−109
3	166				−166	−275
4	96				−96	−371
5	54	135			−189	−560
6		157			−157	−717
7		184	80	245	−19	−736
8			137	365	228	−508
9			108	666	558	50
10			98	732	634	684
11			108	704	596	1280
12			91	574	483	1763
13			104	474	370	2133
14			91	400	309	2442
15			106	333	227	2669

PROJECT MENU 4 (*Continued*)

Project 7

Year	R & D Cost	Capital	Advert.	Profit	Cash Flow	Cumulative
1	35				−35	−35
2	73				−73	−108
3	161				−161	−269
4	90				−90	−359
5	57	135			−192	−551
6		163			−163	−714
7		177	104	156	−125	−839
8			146	264	118	−721
9			116	420	304	−417
10			121	554	433	16
11			124	566	442	458
12			118	400	282	740
13			116	350	234	974
14			115	314	199	1173
15			113	245	132	1305

Project 8

Year	R & D Cost	Capital	Advert.	Profit	Cash Flow	Cumulative
1	38				−38	−38
2	70				−70	−108
3	165				−165	−273
4	90				−90	−363
5	57	138			−195	−558
6		158			−158	−716
7		180	107	234	−53	−769
8			150	358	208	−561
9			112	621	509	−52
10			127	700	573	521
11			122	723	601	1122
12			110	564	454	1576
13			112	448	336	1912
14			123	378	255	2167
15			112	344	232	2399

PROJECT MENU 4 (*Continued*)

Project 9

Year	R & D Cost	Capital	Advert.	Profit	Cash Flow	Cumulative
1	28				−28	−28
2	83				−83	−111
3	156				−156	−267
4	193				−193	−460
5	167				−167	−627
6	87				−87	−714
7	34	94			−128	−842
8		105			−105	−947
9		120	77	149	−48	−995
10			132	281	149	−846
11			95	461	366	−480
12			94	521	427	−53
13			99	564	465	412
14			90	412	322	734
15			94	338	244	978

Project 10

Year	R & D Cost	Capital	Advert.	Profit	Cash Flow	Cumulative
1	30				−30	−30
2	83				−83	−113
3	163				−163	−276
4	194				−194	−470
5	166				−166	−636
6	89				−89	−725
7	38	80			−118	−843
8		102			−102	−945
9		123	79	237	35	−910
10			139	412	273	−637
11			95	630	535	−102
12			92	766	674	572
13			106	723	617	1189
14			103	613	510	1699
15			108	478	370	2069

PROJECT MENU 4 (*Continued*)

Project 11

Year	R & D Cost	Capital	Advert.	Profit	Cash Flow	Cumulative
1	34				− 34	− 34
2	84				− 84	− 118
3	160				− 160	− 278
4	195				− 195	− 473
5	164				− 164	− 637
6	85				− 85	− 722
7	32	85			− 117	− 839
8		104			− 104	− 943
9		131	96	103	− 124	− 1067
10			144	304	160	− 907
11			110	473	363	− 544
12			112	574	462	− 82
13			111	506	395	313
14			121	423	302	615
15			120	369	249	864

Project 12

Year	R & D Cost	Capital	Advert.	Profit	Cash Flow	Cumulative
1	34				− 34	− 34
2	84				− 84	− 118
3	157				− 157	− 275
4	196				− 196	− 471
5	163				− 163	− 634
6	80				− 80	− 714
7	30	99			− 129	− 843
8		110			− 110	− 953
9		127	113	193	− 47	− 1000
10			155	370	215	− 785
11			118	671	553	− 232
12			114	719	605	373
13			115	746	631	1004
14			125	569	444	1448
15			115	461	346	1794
			112	402		
			110	369		

PROJECT MENU 4 (*Continued*)

Project 13

Year	R & D Cost	Capital	Advert.	Profit	Cash Flow	Cumulative
1	33				− 33	− 33
2	77				− 77	− 110
3	160				− 160	− 270
4	195				− 195	− 465
5	162				− 162	− 627
6	82				− 82	− 709
7	34	123			− 157	− 866
8		162			− 162	− 1028
9		171	79	161	− 89	− 1117
10			136	263	127	− 990
11			105	416	311	− 679
12			105	574	469	− 210
13			99	539	440	230
14			91	375	284	514
15			97	302	205	719

Project 14

Year	R & D Cost	Capital	Advert.	Profit	Cash Flow	Cumulative
1	32				− 32	− 32
2	78				− 78	− 110
3	156				− 156	− 266
4	194				− 194	− 460
5	165				− 165	− 625
6	88				− 88	− 713
7	37	126			− 163	− 876
8		164			− 164	− 1040
9		188	87	178	− 97	− 1137
10			122	401	279	− 858
11			99	634	535	− 323
12			106	746	640	317
13			105	722	617	934
14			105	572	467	1401
15			100	425	325	1726

PROJECT MENU 4 (*Continued*)

Project 15

Year	R & D Cost	Capital	Advert.	Profit	Cash Flow	Cumulative
1	29				−29	−29
2	76				−76	−105
3	160				−160	−265
4	192				−192	−457
5	168				−168	−625
6	82				−82	−707
7	38	131			−169	−876
8		156			−156	−1032
9		179	111	150	−140	−1172
10			143	306	163	−1009
11			115	458	343	−666
12			129	544	415	−251
13			122	523	401	150
14			128	393	265	415
15			119	370	251	666

Project 16

Year	R & D Cost	Capital	Advert.	Profit	Cash Flow	Cumulative
1	33				−33	−33
2	78				−78	−111
3	164				−164	−275
4	194				−194	−469
5	166				−166	−635
6	89				−89	−724
7	35	120			−155	−879
8		161			−161	−1040
9		180	99	212	−67	−1107
10			147	353	206	−901
11			123	644	521	−380
12			124	715	591	211
13			122	732	610	821
14			116	582	466	1287
15			124	490	366	1653

PROJECT MENU 5

Project 1 Year	R & D Cost	Capital	Advert.	Profit Low	Medium	High
1	30					
2	70					
3	164					
4	95					
5	52	91				
6		119				
7		121	81	70	109	141
8			123	168	278	335
9			95	290	423	550
10			96	381	547	703
11			101	345	527	678
12			100	259	410	523
13			103	254	372	480
14			92	157	260	326
15			99	147	240	304
Probability				0.23	0.46	0.31

Project 2 Year	R & D Cost	Capital	Advert.	Profit Low	Medium	High
1	32					
2	70					
3	164					
4	97					
5	59	89				
6		101				
7		133	76	143	237	299
8			129	254	418	511
9			92	429	663	837
10			91	488	713	876
11			95	467	716	880
12			105	364	580	725
13			101	315	471	599
14			108	227	351	448
15			109	243	358	464
Probability				0.18	0.30	0.52

PROJECT MENU 5 (*Continued*)

Project 3 Year	R & D Cost	Capital	Advert.	Profit Low	Profit Medium	Profit High
1	37					
2	79					
3	160					
4	96					
5	52	89				
6		100				
7		139	98	82	127	161
8			152	190	298	364
9			113	315	460	584
10			123	329	520	664
11			112	355	552	694
12			118	243	355	444
13			127	240	349	429
14			127	213	309	390
15			111	179	257	334
Probability				0.11	0.52	0.37

Project 4 Year	R & D Cost	Capital	Advert.	Profit Low	Profit Medium	Profit High
1	36					
2	75					
3	164					
4	96					
5	59	93				
6		110				
7		121	106	124	193	248
8			142	220	365	448
9			126	457	655	812
10			110	457	737	891
11			112	466	739	897
12			123	394	584	722
13			116	307	446	568
14			118	247	375	481
15			126	210	337	417
Probability				0.21	0.32	0.47

PROJECT MENU 5 (*Continued*)

Project 5 Year	R & D Cost	Capital	Advert.	Profit Low	Medium	High
1	34					
2	78					
3	165					
4	98					
5	56	124				
6		169				
7		180	89	76	114	146
8			127	208	322	386
9			106	281	467	567
10			108	353	554	715
11			99	345	514	619
12			94	272	395	480
13			105	195	315	385
14			104	199	306	373
15			92	154	224	289
Probability				0.22	0.33	0.45

Project 6 Year	R & D Cost	Capital	Advert.	Profit Low	Medium	High
1	38					
2	72					
3	164					
4	92					
5	59	121				
6		167				
7		179	79	160	232	297
8			128	275	418	528
9			107	369	614	795
10			98	451	751	927
11			98	460	717	887
12			98	368	580	752
13			91	294	453	550
14			100	247	367	448
15			107	220	361	444
Probability				0.12	0.54	0.34

PROJECT MENU 5 (*Continued*)

Project 7 Year	R & D Cost	Capital	Advert.	Profit Low	Medium	High
1	32					
2	70					
3	167					
4	98					
5	51	127				
6		160				
7		173	98	104	163	202
8			147	212	311	394
9			126	280	422	513
10			114	378	553	710
11			118	312	501	604
12			128	273	404	488
13			118	195	315	398
14			122	175	263	328
15			128	162	249	314
Probability				0.16	0.47	0.37

Project 8 Year	R & D Cost	Capital	Advert.	Profit Low	Medium	High
1	39					
2	73					
3	160					
4	91					
5	50	128				
6		166				
7		184	109	148	217	277
8			145	213	353	428
9			113	426	647	808
10			121	456	707	906
11			112	470	705	916
12			115	427	613	754
13			111	280	439	569
14			115	238	380	462
15			129	256	370	449
Probability				0.16	0.37	0.46

PROJECT MENU 5 (*Continued*)

Project 9 Year	R & D Cost	Capital	Advert.	Profit Low	Medium	High
1	26					
2	79					
3	157					
4	199					
5	166					
6	84					
7	30	82				
8		116				
9		133	82	78	112	139
10			137	181	282	346
11			96	292	472	584
12			97	339	543	699
13			99	380	558	702
14			94	244	384	487
15			93	220	361	458
Probability				0.23	0.33	0.44

Project 10 Year	R & D Cost	Capital	Advert.	Profit Low	Medium	High
1	33					
2	83					
3	159					
4	197					
5	162					
6	85					
7	39	93				
8		100				
9		127	85	145	236	288
10			123	267	411	508
11			90	416	610	736
12			90	448	709	884
13			108	450	744	917
14			91	384	605	734
15			92	273	449	557
Probability				0.12	0.51	0.37

PROJECT MENU 5 (*Continued*)

Project 11 Year	R & D Cost	Capital	Advert.	Profit Low	Medium	High
1	33					
2	79					
3	164					
4	192					
5	160					
6	88					
7	37	92				
8		111				
9		137	96	111	168	212
10			153	203	312	380
11			116	253	422	524
12			126	348	521	662
13			113	305	508	654
14			117	273	394	505
15			115	207	339	431
Probability				0.25	0.48	0.27

Project 12 Year	R & D Cost	Capital	Advert.	Profit Low	Medium	High
1	25					
2	77					
3	159					
4	196					
5	166					
6	86					
7	31	97				
8		107				
9		131	101	136	226	287
10			151	252	408	514
11			116	433	643	832
12			121	511	749	934
13			119	425	704	854
14			128	372	605	737
15			121	310	489	616
Probability				0.18	0.46	0.36

PROJECT MENU 5 (*Continued*)

Project 13 Year	R & D Cost	Capital	Advert.	Profit Low	Medium	High
1	25					
2	83					
3	155					
4	196					
5	168					
6	89					
7	34	124				
8		160				
9		171	78	107	160	193
10			120	172	252	325
11			95	289	456	591
12			95	349	506	631
13			95	351	532	664
14			99	261	416	534
15			90	219	356	461
Probability				0.10	0.42	0.47

Project 14 Year	R & D Cost	Capital	Advert.	Profit Low	Medium	High
1	31					
2	79					
3	158					
4	192					
5	167					
6	88					
7	35	132				
8		158				
9		173	83	145	217	269
10			139	230	356	445
11			104	387	623	774
12			96	523	747	909
13			95	468	757	919
14			99	354	580	753
15			109	296	474	589
Probability				0.13	0.33	0.54

PROJECT MENU 5 (*Continued*)

Project 15 Year	R & D Cost	Capital	Advert.	Profit Low	Profit Medium	Profit High
1	31					
2	83					
3	163					
4	194					
5	166					
6	80					
7	36	131				
8		166				
9		180	98	95	142	176
10			152	205	323	407
11			116	293	434	560
12			122	356	551	671
13			113	360	525	647
14			122	240	394	497
15			117	235	359	450
Probability				0.20	0.46	0.34

Project 16 Year	R & D Cost	Capital	Advert.	Profit Low	Profit Medium	Profit High
1	30					
2	81					
3	160					
4	190					
5	161					
6	83					
7	32	120				
8		163				
9		173	100	123	183	227
10			141	283	420	528
11			117	423	625	777
12			110	479	774	941
13			124	465	753	916
14			111	356	583	713
15			110	302	458	552
Probability				0.16	0.52	0.32

PROJECT MENU 6

Project 1 Year	R & D Cost	Capital	Advert.	Profit Low	Profit Medium	Profit High
1	39					
2	70					
3	167					
4	95					
5	57	91				
6		101				
7		132	71	85	142	183
8			135	166	274	333
9			100	284	447	548
10			96	380	548	695
11			93	373	544	695
12			93	269	385	490
13			99	211	311	380
14			100	176	281	342
15			109	153	220	272
Probability				0.16	0.42	0.41

Project 2 Year	R & D Cost	Capital	Advert.	Profit Low	Profit Medium	Profit High
1	32					
2	79					
3	163					
4	98					
5	58	95				
6		102				
7		138	84	150	217	268
8			124	253	394	500
9			106	426	674	846
10			103	486	763	941
11			109	470	737	926
12			100	423	609	785
13			107	272	449	550
14			105	222	368	470
15			108	219	352	445
Probability				0.22	0.46	0.32

PROJECT MENU 6 (*Continued*)

Project 3 Year	R & D Cost	Capital	Advert.	Profit		
				Low	Medium	High
1	33					
2	73					
3	162					
4	92					
5	55	97				
6		102				
7		131	98	103	149	192
8			156	176	275	344
9			119	291	429	527
10			114	352	538	664
11			117	307	506	634
12			127	249	381	495
13			118	217	343	419
14			114	197	300	376
15			123	160	247	314
Probability				0.21	0.36	0.43

Project 4 Year	R & D Cost	Capital	Advert.	Profit		
				Low	Medium	High
1	32					
2	76					
3	163					
4	96					
5	52	81				
6		104				
7		139	96	134	209	251
8			152	268	405	515
9			114	396	655	834
10			116	507	760	917
11			127	459	731	944
12			117	400	607	738
13			124	305	491	625
14			123	244	398	495
15			129	201	309	374
Probability				0.22	0.41	0.37

PROJECT MENU 6 (*Continued*)

Project 5 Year	R & D Cost	Capital	Advert.	Profit Low	Medium	High
1	39					
2	70					
3	167					
4	97					
5	56	123				
6		158				
7		182	82	74	112	139
8			123	194	295	356
9			103	293	421	529
10			101	345	505	646
11			95	360	573	695
12			95	271	414	497
13			96	192	300	368
14			90	195	321	405
15			102	156	241	290
Probability				0.12	0.31	0.57

Project 6 Year	R & D Cost	Capital	Advert.	Profit Low	Medium	High
1	31					
2	73					
3	162					
4	90					
5	58	128				
6		158				
7		174	79	122	190	230
8			139	255	386	485
9			95	430	615	768
10			90	471	716	878
11			106	473	759	952
12			109	377	609	790
13			92	302	462	565
14			99	259	399	506
15			109	217	348	422
Probability				0.13	0.37	0.50

PROJECT MENU 6 (*Continued*)

Project 7 Year	R & D Cost	Capital	Advert.	Profit		
				Low	Medium	High
1	36					
2	77					
3	164					
4	92					
5	58	122				
6		165				
7		188	100	67	104	132
8			151	188	273	340
9			119	304	458	590
10			111	328	534	655
11			124	340	552	675
12			116	274	398	515
13			124	222	370	471
14			117	199	287	353
15			118	136	214	258
Probability				0.20	0.53	0.27

Project 8 Year	R & D Cost	Capital	Advert.	Profit		
				Low	Medium	High
1	35					
2	70					
3	169					
4	97					
5	53	136				
6		167				
7		180	112	150	236	307
8			142	238	361	468
9			116	430	615	765
10			113	476	721	880
11			121	439	716	894
12			122	422	614	777
13			129	301	481	617
14			110	216	350	446
15			119	227	352	430
Probability				0.16	0.50	0.34

PROJECT MENU 6 (*Continued*)

Project 9 Year	R & D Cost	Capital	Advert.	Profit Low	Medium	High
1	34					
2	78					
3	155					
4	193					
5	169					
6	83					
7	39	91				
8		103				
9		137	89	73	116	146
10			129	190	287	357
11			91	303	459	581
12			105	319	502	619
13			109	359	531	664
14			99	249	414	533
15			105	252	363	465
Probability				0.18	0.51	0.32

Project 10 Year	R & D Cost	Capital	Advert.	Profit Low	Medium	High
1	30					
2	84					
3	158					
4	197					
5	160					
6	87					
7	37	86				
8		100				
9		126	81	160	230	288
10			137	240	367	448
11			94	427	634	803
12			104	506	743	927
13			105	441	731	904
14			107	362	602	757
15			92	287	478	579
Probability				0.16	0.49	0.34

PROJECT MENU 6 (*Continued*)

Project 11 Year	R & D Cost	Capital	Advert.	Profit Low	Medium	High
1	30					
2	80					
3	161					
4	193					
5	165					
6	86					
7	30	81				
8		116				
9		138	95	79	117	152
10			151	169	257	309
11			114	293	421	509
12			121	320	531	682
13			119	339	563	712
14			113	274	414	508
15			123	237	373	480
Probability				0.21	0.42	0.37

Project 12 Year	R & D Cost	Capital	Advert.	Profit Low	Medium	High
1	29					
2	82					
3	156					
4	198					
5	162					
6	86					
7	37	84				
8		104				
9		133	114	120	188	243
10			143	274	403	501
11			122	434	658	816
12			118	491	718	893
13			116	503	760	921
14			113	385	568	718
15			117	296	472	593
Probability				0.13	0.41	0.46

PROJECT MENU 6 (*Continued*)

Project 13 Year	R & D Cost	Capital	Advert.	Profit Low	Medium	High
1	31					
2	75					
3	160					
4	193					
5	165					
6	83					
7	38	124				
8		156				
9		177	80	74	123	155
10			122	211	319	395
11			95	296	450	548
12			94	336	506	639
13			97	340	529	665
14			105	261	400	512
15			98	235	357	438
Probability				0.19	0.41	0.40

Project 14 Year	R & D Cost	Capital	Advert.	Profit Low	Medium	High
1	32					
2	77					
3	160					
4	196					
5	167					
6	88					
7	34	137				
8		159				
9		182	86	163	247	307
10			122	255	379	475
11			99	392	630	804
12			108	530	760	983
13			108	481	761	937
14			104	398	609	735
15			106	315	491	634
Probability				0.21	0.32	0.48

PROJECT MENU 6 (*Continued*)

Project 15 Year	R & D Cost	Capital	Advert.	Profit Low	Medium	High
1	31					
2	75					
3	160					
4	192					
5	168					
6	80					
7	31	124				
8		156				
9		175	97	98	147	177
10			151	196	288	348
11			112	277	449	554
12			122	313	517	623
13			127	304	504	622
14			124	245	359	458
15			112	211	350	448
Probability				0.15	0.51	0.34

Project 16 Year	R & D Cost	Capital	Advert.	Profit Low	Medium	High
1	26					
2	80					
3	161					
4	191					
5	164					
6	83					
7	33	131				
8		162				
9		180	95	125	200	244
10			144	274	419	530
11			121	428	656	850
12			127	450	725	933
13			122	480	723	915
14			129	343	569	718
15			129	282	441	532
Probability				0.19	0.38	0.43

PROJECT MENU 7

Completed Project	Source Lines of Code (K)	No. of Modules	Security Requirements	Actual Cost ($K)
1	129	2,088	5	5,776.9
2	73	791	5	4,454.0
3	112	1,266	9	5,696.6
4	49	415	9	2,782.4
5	196	2,803	1	10,043.3
6	117	735	5	5,223.2
7	63	504	9	4,026.4
8	44	944	7	2,632.0
9	661	7,770	2	28,237.0
10	471	7,598	4	22,703.8
11	217	3,361	9	9,095.5
12	886	7,405	7	33,525.5
13	686	16,682	4	27,133.4
14	490	9,505	3	23,738.6
15	1,306	17,695	7	49,571.6
16	352	6,008	9	15,770.8

PROJECT MENU 8

Completed Project	Source Lines of Code (K)	No. of Modules	Security Requirements	Actual Cost ($K)
1	44	312	1	2,521.1
2	65	1,296	2	3,749.6
3	149	2,591	6	7,279.1
4	5	78	7	1,277.8
5	87	1,861	5	5,187.7
6	193	992	2	8,839.2
7	97	821	9	4,546.9
8	43	709	8	2,583.8
9	762	10,782	3	35,847.0
10	870	9,518	5	33,121.6
11	333	2,737	10	14,693.7
12	862	12,375	6	36,777.5
13	580	12,241	2	22,899.7
14	1,444	20,495	2	54,746.6
15	203	2,272	8	10,369.9
16	1,440	7,971	7	59,467.1

APPENDIX 3
NUMERICAL TABLES

TABLE A3.1 Efficiency of Illumination Sources

Year	Source	Efficiency (lumens/W)
1850	Paraffin candle	0.1
1879	Edison's first lamp	1.6
1892	Acetylene lamp	0.7
1894	Cellulose filament	2.6
1901	Mercury arc	12.7
1907	Tungsten filament	10.0
1913	Inert gas filled	19.8
1928	Sodium lamp	20.0
1935	Mercury lamp	40.0
1942	Fluorescent lamp	55.0

Source:–Encyclopedia Britannica, 1964.

TABLE A3.2 Official Aircraft Speed Records (1920 – 1947)

Year	Speed (miles/h)
February 7, 1920	171.04
October 9, 1920	181.86
October 10, 1920	184.36
October 20, 1920	187.98
November 4, 1920	192.01
December 12, 1920	194.52
September 26, 1921	205.22
September 21, 1922	211.90
October 13, 1922	222.97
February 15, 1923	233.01
R 29, 1923	236.59
March 29, 1923	236.59
November 2, 1923	236.59
November 4, 1923	266.58
December 11, 1924	278.48
September 5, 1932	294.38
September 4, 1933	304.98
December 25, 1934	314.32
September 13, 1935	352.39
November 11, 1937	379.63
March 30, 1939	463.92
April 26, 1939	469.22
November 7, 1945 (jet)	606.26
September 7, 1946	615.78
June 19, 1947	623.74

TABLE A3.3   Critical Values for the Student-*t* Distribution

Degrees of Freedom	Confidence Interval Width (%)			
	20	50	90	99
1	0.325	1.000	6.314	63.657
2	0.289	0.816	2.290	9.925
3	0.277	0.765	2.253	5.841
4	0.271	0.741	2.132	4.604
5	0.267	0.727	2.015	4.032
6	0.265	0.718	1.943	3.707
7	0.263	0.711	1.895	3.499
8	0.262	0.076	1.860	3.355
9	0.261	0.703	1.833	3.250
10	0.260	0.700	1.812	3.169
11	0.2y0	0.697	1.796	3.106
12	0.259	0.695	1.682	3.055
13	0.259	0.694	1.771	3.012
14	0.258	0.692	1.761	2.977
15	0.258	0.691	1.753	2.947
16	0.258	0.690	1.746	2.921
17	0.257	0.689	1.740	2.898
18	0.257	0.688	1.734	2.878
19	0.257	0.688	1.729	2.861
20	0.257	0.687	1.725	2.845
21	0.257	0.686	1.721	2.831
22	0.256	0.686	1.717	2.819
23	0.256	0.685	1.714	2.807
24	0.256	0.685	1.711	2.797
25	0.256	0.684	1.708	2.787
26	0.256	0.684	1.706	2.779
27	0.256	0.684	1.703	2.771
28	0.256	0.683	1.701	2.763
29	0.256	0.683	1.699	2.756
30	0.256	0.683	1.697	2.750
> 30	0.256	0.674	1.645	2.576

Note: To get the probability in the tails of the distribution, subtract the value at the column head from 1.0. Since the tails are symmetrical, one-half the tail probability will lie on either side of the confidence interval. For instance, if there are 7 degrees of freedom, and a 25% lower tail is desired, the critical point will be 0.711 standard deviations *below* the mean.

TABLE A3.4   Jet Engine Data

Year	Thrust/Weight	Fuel Economy	Maximum Thrust (lb)
1943	1.88	0.813	1,600
1944	1.94	0.781	1,600
1944	2.82	1.000	3,400
1944	2.08	0.971	5,200
1944	2.20	0.840	4,000
1944	2.40	1.111	6,000
1944	3.12	1.587	2,925
1946	2.23	1.515	5,700
1948	2.38	1.250	9,700
1948	1.95	1.587	5,850
1948	2.90	0.893	5,000
1949	2.69	1.163	17,500
1949	2.50	1.111	9,000
1949	2.53	0.893	4,600
1949	3.31	1.000	6,350
1949	2.77	1.099	7,200
1950	2.37	1.250	9,700
1952	3.20	0.526	9,500
1952	3.28	0.926	883
1953	3.17	1.075	8,000
1953	3.45	0.917	920
1954	3.58	1.163	10,000
1955	3.10	0.323	16,000
1956	2.89	1.290	11,200
1957	2.59	1.290	11,200
1958	4.17	0.465	24,500
1960	4.35	1.923	17,000
1960	6.52	1.042	3,000
1962	4.15	1.869	18,000
1962	4.60	0.509	17,000
1962	4.20	1.869	18,000
1963	4.20	1.869	18,000
1963	4.20	1.869	18,000
1963	4.50	1.786	21,000
1963	6.80	0.450	4,080
1966	7.20	1.010	2,850
1967	4.50	1.709	14,500
1967	4.67	0.509	17,820
1967	4.56	0.400	18,500
1968	4.57	1.546	14,500
1968	4.82	0.383	20,840
1969	4.94	0.332	20,350
1969	5.70	3.175	40,805
1971	6.31	0.408	25,100
1972	7.50	0.469	5,000
1972	6.30	2.506	51,711

TABLE A3.4 **(Continued)**

Year	Thrust/Weight	Fuel Economy	Maximum Thrust (lb)
1973	7.80	0.461	23,830
1974	4.40	1.786	21,000
1974	6.38	2.703	9,065
1981	4.80	2.755	21,634
1981	5.80	2.857	10,000
1983	7.10	0.407	30,780
1985	1.40	0.481	28,620
1985	7.40	0.444	23,770
1987	5.80	3.030	41,700
1989	6.50	0.455	3,850
1989	8.00	0.488	29,000

Note: Formula for computing the probability that a needle will intersect one of a series of equally spaced parallel lines:

$$P = 2L/\pi d$$

where L is the length of the needle and d is the separation between the lines.

INDEX